The Heart of the Game

The Heart of the Game

JIMMY GREAVES

TIME WARNER
BOOKS

TIME WARNER BOOKS

First published in Great Britain in October 2005
by Time Warner Books

A CIP catalogue record for this book
is available from the British Library.

ISBN 0 316 73076 9

Typeset in Imprint by M Rules
Printed and bound in Great Britain
by Clays Ltd, St Ives plc

Time Warner Books
An imprint of
Time Warner Book Group UK
Brettenham House
Lancaster Place
London WC2E 7EN

www.twbg.co.uk

This book is dedicated to Lynn, Mitzi, Danny and Andrew –
our children who are also very good friends.

Apart from everything else, Irene and I want to keep on the
right side of our offspring; in the future they'll be the ones
who decide which home we're going into.

Contents

Acknowledgements

A big thank you to the following for their valued expertise and assistance in the creation of this book: Julian Alexander and all at Lucas Alexander Whitley; Barclays Bank plc, in particular Julian Wilshaw; Ken and Jean Bolam; Tom Bromley and all at Time Warner Books UK; Phill Dann; Don Mackay; Arthur Montford; Manchester United plc, in particular Mike Maxfield; Rob Raby; and Steve and Deb Waterall.

I would like to express my sincere thanks to Les Scott whose collaboration has been invaluable to me in the writing of this book. To my mind Les is one of the best football writers of our time. In addition to his prowess as a football writer he has written extensively for television, radio, the stage and penned the screenplay for the movie *The Rose of Tralee*. Thanks Les: 'What would you say to a cold beer?' – 'Don't get comfortable in that glass.'

For Lauren, Ruby, Jane, Toni and Charley.

Jimmy Greaves, 2005

CHAPTER ONE

In order to make a prawn sandwich from scratch, you must first create the universe

It was a Friday night in a Leicester hotel. Spurs were playing Leicester City the following day and manager Bill Nicholson gathered the players around him for a pre-match chat. The conversation moved from the following day's game to that of football in general. We players were airing our views and putting the football world to rights; not that any of our talk ever accomplished that. Conversation turned to the lasting, addictive allure of football. Spurs' cerebral and erudite skipper, Danny Blanchflower, held the floor.

'Whether you're a player, manager, trainer, director, supporter, reporter, kit man or tea lady, football possesses the power to make the week ahead sparkle with a sense of joyous well-being, or black with the unpalatability of unrealised hope and expectation,' said Danny with typical lyricism and poignancy:

> No play, movie or TV programme, work of literature or music induces such a polarisation of emotion on a weekly basis. We curse football for having this power. Conversely, it is football's power to so readily and regularly corrupt emotions and senses that is the addictive and enduring appeal of the game. It's an intangible power. It exists somewhere out in the ethers. It is the heart of the game.

Over forty years have passed since Danny made that profound

statement about football. That I can quote him so precisely is because he later put his words down in a letter. Over the years I have often found myself thinking about what Danny said. His words have remained with me in much the same way a great song or hilarious joke can have such an impact that you only have to hear it once for it to remain with you for ever.

That it is over forty years since Danny said those words, to my mind, doesn't make them any less relevant today. On the contrary, I feel the point he was making has even more relevance today than it did all those years ago. At the time Danny talked of 'the heart of the game', football was still a working-class leisure pursuit. For a good many people, however, football was and always will be more than a leisure pursuit, more than simply a game. Football is not a sport you take up, like golf or squash. It is passed on from generation to generation, so that it is almost a part of one's genetic make-up. As in a relationship with a loved one, our attachment to football makes us emotionally vulnerable. Hence Danny's reference to football having the power to polarise emotion. It doesn't matter how successful a career one may have, how happy and content one is with life, the fact that come Saturday tea-time football can energise or depress is testimony to the power it has over us. The game has altered unbelievably over the years but this power, 'the heart of the game', has remained as changeless as heaven.

A childhood pal of mine was once given a knife as a birthday present by his dad. Throughout childhood and into his adult life my pal loved and treasured that knife. His dad gave him the knife as a present on his thirteenth birthday, which my pal took as a sign that his dad now considered him to be leaving his childhood behind and developing into an adult. A couple of years later, much to his chagrin, my pal broke the handle of the knife. Once over his initial sadness at having broken the treasured knife, he bought a replacement handle. Some years after that, the blade broke. He bought a replacement blade and the knife was as good as new again. The strange thing was, in the years that followed whenever he talked of that knife, my pal always referred to it as 'the knife my dad gave me on my thirteenth birthday'. In reality it was anything but. The knife was totally different. Both the handle and blade had been replaced. No part of the original knife remained. Yet my pal still loved the knife, believing it to be the one his dad had given him as a birthday present all those years ago.

I mention that story because I believe the way we think and feel about football is similar to the way my pal loved and treasured that knife. Like my pal's knife, football has changed beyond recognition. Football today is different from how it was fifteen years ago, and totally different from how it was in the sixties. Yet the emotional attachment we feel for the game remains unchanged. Football's basic function, symbolism and, more importantly, power to dictate feelings and affect our sensibilities, remains unaltered. As the emotion and feelings of my pal for the knife his father gave him never changed, though the knife did, so too does our emotional attachment to football remain constant, albeit the game is almost unrecognisable now from how it was forty years ago.

For some years I had it in mind to write a book about what Danny called 'the heart of the game'. To offer a personal view as to how football has changed in the fifty years since I first entered the game as a callow teenager at Chelsea. To examine the various roles of those involved, either directly or indirectly, with football. The sport is no better or worse now than the day in 1955 when I first walked into Stamford Bridge to begin my career as a player-cum-office boy. It is, however, so very, very different. I would like to explore the many changes that have taken place in football over the years; how the roles of manager, player, director, supporter and that of the media have changed as football underwent a metamorphosis from the working-class game I knew as a player to the multi-million-pound cult-celebrity-led industry it is today.

There is a lot to be said for the modern game, but it is not all roses. For example football academies are fine in theory, but in practice they are not working. I want to address that issue, explaining how academies have fallen far short of their original aim of producing home-grown talent for clubs. Television's saturation coverage has spawned a new audience for football. These people do not attend matches but watch football solely on television. They are consumers rather than supporters. In pandering to the needs of this new breed, who like to see their football devoid of what former Spurs assistant manager Eddie Baily called 'a level of aggression necessary to ensure we don't end up playing Cinderella football, where we don't quite make it to the ball', television is attempting to sanitise the game. In so doing, it is turning football into something it never was and was never intended to be.

The game is faster now than in my day as a player. But the often-cited notion that today's players are fitter and stronger than those of the sixties and seventies simply doesn't ring true. One aspect of the modern game that is better is the quality of the pitches. Those that today's footballers play on are superb, week in and week out. These 'billiard table' surfaces are the main reason why the game is faster than in my day as a player. But there is a downside to this. Pristine pitches have resulted in many of the skills and techniques of yesteryear being lost to the game for ever.

The game is now beset by people who have little or no empathy with football: image managers, chief executives, agents, and commercial and marketing directors who see football simply as a career move, and whose experience and knowledge of the game are scant. As football strives to be a more competitive business such people have acquired positions of influence and authority within the game. It is a matter of great concern for all genuine lovers of football, for whom the culture and traditions of the sport in this country mean something, that there are decision-makers in the game whose influence is in inverse proportion to their knowledge and feelings for football. Yet there are still many of us who understand the game as true fans should: through our nerve ends. The way genuine lovers of the sport feel about football is no different now from how it was fifty years ago, even though little of the game that was then now remains. Football compels us to faith and optimism. While a manager or player is only as good as his last game, the sustenance of the supporter is jam tomorrow. The fan of Rochdale or Halifax Town lives in hope. Hope that one day their club will be successful and they will experience personally what the permanently elaborate structures of common living deny us – glory. The pursuit of which is at the very heart of the game.

Many people involved in the running of football today have little time to give even a cursory glance over their shoulder to what has happened in the past. Yet it is the events of yesteryear that have created the game we know today. My aim in this book is to look back, assess the present and also to look forward. In so doing to try and highlight what football has lost and gained. Football's past is not a chronicle of wasted time. On the contrary, it is the key to understanding all that is happening in football today and will happen in the future. Should chief executives, many of whom refer to genuine lovers of the game not as supporters or fans but as 'customers', possess a sound knowledge of football and its past, the game would be the better for it. I doubt whether many do.

This new breed of football administrator, while equipped with business nous, appears to have little knowledge of the history and traditions of the game. As such they display little empathy with, and fail to meet the real needs of, supporters. These fans are being sold everything from club credit cards and insurance to replica shirts and underwear, under the auspices of being loyal to their club. In encouraging the purchase of such, supporters are regaled by fatuous marketing straplines such as 'Feel the pride and the passion'.

Genuine supporters feel pride and passion in the course of a game of football, not by owning a club credit card. Equally, when players display real passion such as in recent encounters between Arsenal and Manchester United, television companies regularly take the moral high ground. They frown upon robust and fractious play, frightened it will be an affront to the sensibilities of their consumers who will tune out of football for ever.

For the consumer who follows the game solely on a screen, football appeals to the eye. For true fans, however, football also engages the heart and mind. That it does can be put down to genuine lovers of football having been touched by the heart of the game.

CHAPTER TWO

The manager – A doormat in a world of muddy boots

The role of the player has changed little since organised football began in the Victorian age. Put simply, he plays the game with the aim of scoring goals at one end while preventing them at the other. By contrast, the role of the manager has changed much over the years. When I started out in football the remit of a manager was not only to manage the team, but also the club itself. Regarding the former, many managers did little more than pay lip service to that task. When I joined Chelsea as a fifteen-year-old in the summer of 1955, the manager was the former Arsenal, Chelsea and England centre forward Ted Drake. As a youth-team player Ted appeared to me as some sort of Howard Hughes figure. I often heard his name being bandied about, I was aware of his power and influence but rarely, if ever, did I see Ted in the course of a week. Training was supervised by the club's trainers and, with the exception of the first team, the respective managers of Chelsea's other principal teams (the reserves, youth team and colts).

After consultation with his subordinate managers, Ted would emerge from his office on a Friday morning to pin up the teams for Saturday's games. When a player was promoted or demoted from one team to another, I cannot recall Ted ever taking that player aside and explaining the reasons behind the decision. I made my first-team debut on the opening day of the season of 1957–8 against Tottenham Hotspur. I discovered I was playing in the first team simply by seeing my name on the team sheet after training on Friday morning. At no point during the day did Ted tell me the reason for my selection or give me any words of advice or guidance. In fact Ted didn't say anything to me at White Hart Lane prior to the game itself except for 'All the best'. So often did Ted confine himself to those three words prior to a match, the Chelsea players referred to themselves as the 'all the best team'.

The majority of managers in the late fifties were figureheads. Perhaps it was because managers ran a club in every sense of the word that they didn't have time to supervise training or turn their minds to tactical ploys. Many managers also doubled up as the club secretary, a throwback to the pre-war years. Their main responsibility was to the team, but their duties could also involve arranging match-day catering which, though it amounted to little more than ordering tea, Bovril and pies, ate into their time (pardon the pun). Jack Barker was manager of Derby County from 1953 to 1955. One Monday morning Jack found himself on the telephone to a local baker's who supplied Derby County with pies on match days. 'The meat in your pies is really something else,' Jack informed his supplier. 'God knows what it is, but it isn't meat that's for sure,' came the reply.

The idea that part of the remit of a contemporary manager could involve being responsible for match-day pies is absurd. But fifty years ago the brief of the manager was broad. In the early fifties the Arsenal manager was Tom Whittaker, whose official title was that of 'Secretary-Manager'. That is how Whittaker's job title appeared in the Arsenal match-day programme. Some clue as to which role was given priority can be obtained from the job title itself, whereby 'secretary' precedes 'manager'. Aston Villa's manager at the time was George Martin, whose job title was 'Manager/Assistant Secretary'.

That some clubs placed little emphasis on the manager, his role and effect on the team is evidenced by the Newcastle

United match programmes of the early fifties. Under the heading 'Club Officials', the Newcastle programme of the day lists the names of the club's directors, the treasurer, secretary and assistant secretary. Significantly there is no mention of the manager who, incidentally, was Stan Seymour. Stan was manager of Newcastle United from 1939 to 1947 and again from 1950 to 1954. During his latter spell Newcastle won the FA Cup twice (1951 and 1952), but seemingly that still wasn't good enough for him to merit a mention in the list of club officials in the match-day programmes. It is an omission indicative of the importance, or the lack of it, placed upon the role of a manager by club directors. In the fifties many managers, to use a modern phrase, were multi-tasking. But even though they were fulfilling a variety of roles, it did not mean they were handsomely paid. A manager's salary was not much more than that of his players. Footballers supplemented their income by taking jobs outside the game in the close season. Managers couldn't do this, so some reverted to more devious means of earning extra income.

The Blackpool manager Joe Smith was a wily bird. Joe, like many other managers, claimed expenses for such matters as travel when running the rule over players who had been recommended to him or entertaining his scouts. At one stage Joe submitted a weekly expenses claim for having had lunch with a Jim McFadden, a freelance scout based north of the border who kept Joe informed of emerging players in the Scottish League.

One morning Joe arrived in his office to find a curt memo from the Blackpool secretary. The tenet of which was that the secretary and treasurer had been reviewing Joe's lunch expenses, had checked up on the name Jim McFadden and could find no scout of that name working in Scottish football. The secretary concluded by asking Joe for 'an immediate explanation'. Straight away Joe sent a memo back to the club secretary that read, 'I've been had. The man is clearly an imposter, I shall cease entertaining him immediately.' As I say, Joe Smith was a wily bird.

For all his limitations both tactically and verbally, Ted Drake guided Chelsea to the League Championship in 1954. But not all managers were like Ted and Joe Smith. Some, like Manchester United's Matt Busby, were an exception when it came to training methods.

In 1948 Manchester United faced Blackpool in the FA Cup final. Blackpool had the upper hand in the first half and led 2-1 at half-time thanks, in the main, to the efforts of the two Stans, Matthews and Mortensen. Stan Matthews told me that during the half-time interval the Blackpool manager Joe Smith said very little other than to encourage his players to 'keep it going'. He added, 'Try to get another goal in this half, lads, so I can enjoy my cigar. It being the Cup final, I've treated myself to a reet good 'un.' In the other dressing room, however, United's Matt Busby was plotting Blackpool's downfall.

To counteract the threat of Matthews and Mortensen, Matt Busby told United's Stan Pearson and Henry Cockburn to get tighter and close down Blackpool skipper Harry Johnston and Hughie Kelly in the middle of the pitch. Busby also instructed the United outside left, Charlie Mitten, to drop deeper and help his full back Johnny Aston deal with Stan Matthews.

The effect of this tactical manoeuvre was to change the course of the Cup final. With Harry Johnston and Hughie Kelly hassled and hustled whenever they received the ball, the service to Stan Matthews on the wing all but dried up. When Johnston or Kelly did manage to pass the ball to Matthews, Stan found himself with two opponents to cope with in Aston and Mitten. With Stan Matthews more or less out of the picture the service to Blackpool's free-scoring centre forward Stan Mortensen withered on the vine. United took the game to Blackpool in the second half, with Busby urging his defenders to 'push on'. Having bossed the game in the first half,

Blackpool were not so much outfought in the second half as outwitted and, as a consequence of that, outplayed. United scored three times without reply to beat Blackpool 4-2.

As Stan Matthews also told me, 'At the time it was very unusual to encounter a manager who paid so much attention to tactics as Matt Busby did during that final. It completely flummoxed Blackpool. I knew Matt from his days as a player at Manchester City in the thirties. He was a gifted wing half, but he never struck me then as a cerebral player. After that Cup final, however, my attitude to him changed. I was of the mind Matt was going to be some manager.' Truer words have rarely been spoken.

In many respects Joe Smith embodied the past and Matt Busby the future of football management. In five seasons, from 1947 to 1951, Manchester United were runners-up in Division One on four occasions, before finally clinching the title in 1951–2. While United players were as free to express themselves as Matthews was at Blackpool, Matt Busby also introduced tactical awareness to the team, though never to the extent where it was counterproductive to individual flair. The tactics deployed by Matt were simple, because he knew that football is a simple game.

By the late 1950s, the role of the manager was shifting. There were two principal changes. Managers had become more aware of the value of tactics and were deploying simple game plans in almost every match, though not to the detriment of individual flair. The second change affected the tenure of a manager at a club – it was becoming shorter!

The resounding defeats inflicted on England by Hungary in 1953 and the failure of Walter Winterbottom's team to make any impression in the 1954 World Cup in Switzerland emphasised to all what some had known for years: England were no longer the masters of world football. Following the 1954 World Cup there was a discernible switch towards Continental and

South American training methods, together with a greater awareness of the importance of tactics. Though the tactics deployed were never at the expense of individual skills, throughout the English game there was a growing awareness of the importance of the role of a manager in team affairs. It was generally believed that the time had come for a full-scale over-haul of our methods. The national press led the way, demanding answers while offering some solutions of their own, such as the methods of training that had been adopted on the Continent, in particular Austria.

Prior to joining West Ham United, Malcolm Allison had been a full back with Charlton Athletic. In the mid-fifties Malcolm found himself in Austria while doing his national service and spent much of his free time watching top Austrian clubs in training. What he saw impressed him and made him realise that the training he had been subjected to at Charlton was of little benefit to him as a player and to the team in general. Big Mal made a study of Austrian training methods and tactics. When his national service was over, Mal returned to the Valley and tried to persuade the Charlton manager, Jimmy Seed, to adopt some of the innovative methods he had seen. Seed dismissed Big Mal's ideas outright. As Mal said, 'Jimmy Seed was happy continuing with the traditional methods of training, which amounted to little more than the players doing a few laps of the cinder track, a few exercises, then in to the dressing room for a shower and a "Woodbine". At Charlton, as with most clubs, we rarely used a ball in training because there was this ridiculous theory that to deny a player the ball in train-ing would make him more hungry for it during a game.' Big Mal continued to argue with Seed about training methods until the Charlton boss had had enough of Mal's protestations and placed him on the transfer list. West Ham United came in for him and on the day Big Mal left the Valley, characteristically he let Jimmy Seed know what he thought of his training and him as a manager.

'What makes you think you know so much about football?' asked Seed as Mal prepared to leave his office for the last time.

'Talking to you,' replied Mal.

Malcolm Allison was not alone in his belief that English football would have to endure radical change if it was to catch up with the standard of football then being played on the Continent. Respected club managers such as Matt Busby, Stan Cullis (Wolves), Joe Mercer (Sheffield United) and Arthur Rowe (Spurs) met with the England manager, Walter Winterbottom, to find an answer to what was considered the ailing English game. What emerged was a forceful appeal to clubs to cooperate in the creation of a strong national team by releasing players more freely and for longer periods, so that Winterbottom could organise more meaningful and productive training sessions. In addition to which the top managers, such as Busby, Cullis, Mercer and Rowe, all agreed that a key element in the development of the game in England was greater tactical awareness. The Hungarian experience in 1953 had been a harrowing one for English football, but to quote the then motto of Wolverhampton Wanderers, 'out of darkness cometh light'.

As tactics became more important to the fortunes of a team so too did the manager. The kudos and stature of the manager improved as a result of this new responsibility, but there was a downside to this as far as managers were concerned. If a manager could be responsible for the success of a team, he was also to be responsible for its failure. When things did not go to plan, the price managers paid for having assumed greater responsibility of team affairs and an elevated status within a club was the sack. Before the late fifties it was rare for a club to change its manager every two or three years, as most do now. Throughout the history of the game, once a manager had been appointed he could expect a lengthy period of employment in that role. In 1957 Sunderland's manager was Bill Murray. He was only the club's fourth manager since 1905, a period of fifty-two years. At the same time Vic Buckingham was only West Bromwich Albion's fifth manager since 1896. Stan Cullis, who had been manager of Wolves since 1948, was the Molineux club's third manager in thirty years. These long periods of management were not confined to the top clubs. Sides in the lower reaches of the Football League were also happy to run with the same manager for a considerable number of years. In 1957 Swindon Town were enjoying the services of what was only their fifth manager in fifty years; and Andy Smailes was Rotherham United's fifth manager since the club was originally formed in 1870, a period of eighty-seven years! Contrast that statistic to the spell in the 1980s when Rotherham had six managers in just eight years. Between 1910 and 1956–7, a period of forty-six years, Scunthorpe United used the services of five managers. In the space of four years, from 1956 to 1960, Scunthorpe United saw the same number come and go.

If the 'Hungarian watershed' woke up English football to the importance of tactics, then it was the reaction to the 1960 European Cup final that was to create the origins of the 'tracksuit manager' and usher in the golden age of the British manager. The term 'tracksuit manager' simply meant a manager who had forsaken the traditional administrative role and taken it upon himself to organise the team's daily training as well as tactics. He couldn't appear on the training ground wearing a suit, hence the term 'tracksuit manager'. Tommy Docherty, who took over from Ted Drake in 1961, was Chelsea's first tracksuit manager.

    I was on tour with England on the occasion of Real Madrid's 7-3 European Cup final victory over what was a very good Frankfurt side. The England team were in Hungary, which refused to broadcast the match as Real included in their ranks the great Ferenc Puskas, who had fled the country following the Russian invasion of 1956. However, the manager of the hotel in which the England party was staying was a big football fan, and he'd managed to set the television so that it picked up Swiss television. I remember sitting with my England team-mates and being mesmerised by the football produced by Real Madrid. It was as if I had been transported to football heaven. Real produced a fantastic display of fluid, purist, attacking football, high on technique and consummate skill. I had never seen a team play such brilliant football. I can only liken it to having discovered Shakespeare, Picasso and the Beatles all on the same night. A truly formative experience from which there was no going back. To place Real's performance in perspective from a British point of view, Eintracht Frankfurt had scored twelve against Glasgow Rangers in the two-legged semi-final. Rangers were widely considered to be one of the best teams in Great Britain. For the team who enjoyed such a convincing margin of victory over one of our best sides then to be beaten 7-3 by Real Madrid made many realise that the standard of British football was a long way behind that of the Continent. While England at the time did not boast the genius of Di Stefano and Puskas, generally speaking our game possessed players of equal calibre to those of the rest of the Real team and certainly that of the Germans. The difference was that these two sides had shown us that individual skill is best employed when harnessed as collective talent. The hub around which every move of Real's evolved was Di Stefano and Puskas, but those two football geniuses orchestrated play to suit the players around them. The rest of the Real team played up to them as a Proms orchestra would Sir Malcolm Sargent.

Almost overnight the seeds of revolution in English foot-ball were sown. These, such as they were, came in the form of former players who, having seen Real Madrid's superlative performance, signed up in 1960 for what was Walter Winterbottom's first major FA coaching school at Lilleshall. Winterbottom wanted to modernise the English game, to make teams more effective as a unit in a framework that allowed for individual flair. Another of his aims was to improve the technique of players, which, in general terms, he felt was not as good as that of the top Continental and South American players.

Among the recruits to Winterbottom's first major coaching course were Bob Paisley, Tommy Docherty, Malcolm Allison, Don Revie, Dave Sexton, Peter Taylor (of Clough–Taylor fame), Bert Johnson (Leicester City) and Frank O'Farrell (later to manage both Leicester City and Manchester United). As players and coaches, these former players would play an intrinsic role in the development of English football throughout the sixties and seventies. When these first recruits to the FA coaching school returned to their clubs, they combined what they had learned from Walter Winterbottom with their own ideas to exert a hitherto unknown influence on English football. In so doing they spawned the 'cult of the manager'.

As the fifties drew to a close, English football rid itself of the long-serving, largely administrative manager who rarely saw his players from one Saturday to the next. The likes of Matt Busby, Stan Cullis, Bill Nicholson and Joe Mercer survived because they recognised the game was changing and by way of their own innovative ideas on how football should be played, together with their 'hands on' style of management, played a key role in effecting change. Come the early sixties the graduates of Winterbottom's coaching school began to wield their influence at clubs and on the English game in general. Tommy Docherty and Don Revie were established as managers at Chelsea and Leeds United respectively, while Bert Johnson (Leicester City), Dave Sexton (Chelsea), Bob Paisley (Liverpool) and Jimmy Adamson (Burnley) were just some of Walter Winterbottom's other 'students' to hold key coaching positions.

The interval from the late sixties to the late eighties was a 'golden period' for managers. Though the threat of dismissal was more of a possibility than it had been at any other time in the twentieth century, while in situ most managers ruled the roost. Free from the diversions their predecessors had had to contend with, managers concentrated totally on team affairs. Which meant supervising training and selecting the team, negotiating contracts, and signing and selling players. Never had the position of the manager in the English game been so strong. Managers held sway, both in the media and at their respective clubs. This situation endured until the late eighties when agents and that new breed of football administrator, the chief executive, began their rise, in so doing eroding the power of the manager.

Following the formation of the Premiership, the television money that flooded into football was further added to by commercial revenue generated by blue-chip companies, which saw television's saturation coverage of the game as the perfect vehicle for self-promotion. In keeping with its new image as a multi-million-pound industry, football engaged non-football people in key positions. In order that they be run like a 'proper' business, many clubs appointed chief executives, the majority of whom came into the game for the first time, having honed their skills in other areas of business. The creation of chief executives and the ever-increasing power and influence of players' agents, keen to make their pile under the auspices of solely representing the interests of their clients, ate away at the position of managers. Come the nineties the golden period of the manager was over. He was still responsible for selecting the team and exerted a considerable influence over who should and should not be signed, but in many respects was beholden to agents and chief executives.

The role and influence of the manager has been further diminished, in some cases even marginalised, with the emergence in recent years of the 'director of football'. This position was once the sole domain of Continental clubs, where teams were run by a director of football and coach as opposed to a manager. However, with more and more foreign players, coaches and, in some cases, club chairmen entering English football, many clubs have also adopted the Continental idea of having a director of football as well as a manager. This has eroded still further the traditional role of a manager, and has also led to some celebrated cases of managers leaving clubs because they have felt their position within them to have been compromised. Harry Redknapp's exit from Portsmouth in 2004 is a case in point.

Chief executives, players' agents, directors of football and the ever-growing remit of coaches have all contributed to a redefinition of the role of the football manager. Of course there are some managers who by way of longevity of tenure have redefined their own roles within a club. Arsène Wenger, Sir Alex Ferguson and Dario Gradi at Crewe Alexandra have, through success real and relative, cemented their positions at their respective clubs. Ferguson and Gradi have both, in their own ways, created a seat of power at their clubs not unlike those created by Don Revie at Leeds United, Bob Paisley at Liverpool and Brian Clough at Nottingham Forest. In creating their own dynasty at their respective clubs, Ferguson and Gradi are a hark back to the golden age of football management when managers dictated what went on at a club and how the club was run. But these days Ferguson, Wenger and Gradi are exceptions to the rule. What we are seeing is a return to the days when I began as a player in the fifties, a time when the role and influence of the football manager was not omnipresent within a club.

The former Sunderland manager Bob Stokoe once said 'It's easy to be a good manager, all you have to do is sign good players'. That was true forty years ago and it is still true now. The difference being that today you need huge amounts of money to sign the good players. Harry Catterick was the first manager who achieved real success for a club by way of spending an unprecedented amount in the transfer market. In 1961 Harry left his post as manager of Sheffield Wednesday to take over as manager of Everton. Harry was a studious man, quietly spoken, who was so calm and collected he handled a crisis with all the confidence of a man dialling his own telephone number. When confronted with a problem at the club he dealt with it in a firm but fair and diplomatic manner. What's more he always dealt with problems 'behind closed doors' and was at pains to play down matters when questioned by the press. As Harry once said, 'In dealing with problems at a football club, when in public it is better to say nothing. Remember, you never see a fish on a wall with its mouth shut.'

In 1962–3 Harry Catterick led Everton to the League title with a team that cost a huge amount money. Having spent £180,000 on five players in 1961–2, the following season Catterick hit the headlines when he signed Tony Kay from Sheffield Wednesday for £60,000 and winger Alex Scott from Rangers for a fee of £40,000. Though Matt Busby at Manchester United had created a British transfer fee record when paying Torino £115,000 for Denis Law in July 1962, for Catterick to have spent £280,000 on seven players in a period of six months was unheard of in English football. The press were saying the game had gone 'money mad' and dubbed Everton the 'Cheque Book Champions'.

Everton's Championship success of 1962–3, and moreover the fact that Harry Catterick had spent £280,000 on players, was a watershed for English football. From that moment on it was widely believed that money was a key ingredient to success. Catterick was not a great manager in the sense that Shankly, Paisley, Ramsey, Busby, Stein, Clough and Nicholson were great. He was a good manager who, because he had been given an enormous amount of money to spend and had spent that money wisely on new signings that helped Everton win the Championship, was widely considered to be a 'very good manager', a status he secured by guiding Everton to the FA Cup in 1966.

In the contemporary game it is no longer sufficient for a

manager to have considerable funds at his disposal in order for him to bring top players to a club. He must also be perceived as a 'big name' in management. Players and in particular their agents are primarily motivated by money when signing for a club. Rare are the instances today of a player signing for a new club for less money when his career is on the upward curve, though it did happen in the past. My old Spurs team-mate Alan Gilzean joined the club from Dundee in 1965. At the time Sunderland were also keen to sign Gilly. They matched the £65,000 Spurs had offered Dundee for his services, and offered Gilly a lot more money than Spurs were willing to pay him. Gilly, however, opted for Spurs. As he said, 'Spurs and Sunderland were both First Division clubs who enjoyed large attendances. Sunderland offered me more in the way of wages, but I opted for Spurs simply because I thought I would enjoy my football more at White Hart Lane than Roker Park.' I wonder how many current Premiership players would have similar priorities to Gilly?

In the late eighties, the perception emerged that a manager had to be a 'name' in order for him to attract star players. With all due respect, Harry Catterick was not a big name in management, unlike Matt Busby, Bill Nicholson, Stan Cullis and Alf Ramsey. Catterick, however, had been able to fend off competition from Bill Nicholson for Hearts centre forward Alex Young, and from Matt Busby for Blackburn's Roy Vernon, simply because he outbid them in the transfer market. Players had little say in the matter of which club they would join. Once their existing club had agreed a fee, the player was on his way to the highest bidder, whether he liked it or not. I had personal experience of this at Chelsea. I didn't want to sign for AC Milan, but once the deal had been done between the two clubs the Chelsea secretary, John Battersby, though sympathetic to my plight, told me, 'No ifs or buts about it, Jimmy, son. You gotta go.'

Don Mackay was manager of Blackburn Rovers from 1987

to 1991, in which time Rovers were beaten in the play-offs for
a place in what was then the First Division on two occasions.
Under Mackay, Rovers also won the Full Members Cup at
Wembley in 1987; not the most important of trophies but
Rovers' first of any note since 1928. Having previously been
bereft of funds, in what would prove to be his last season as
Rovers manager, Mackay began to benefit from the finance
made available to him by Blackburn's new owner, Jack Walker.
The money in question was nowhere near the generous
amounts Walker would soon put into the club, but Mackay
used what money was now at his disposal to sign some quality
players, such as Ossie Ardiles and Frank Stapleton. It could be
said that in both cases their best days as players were behind
them; however both Ardiles and Stapleton were still eminently
capable of doing a fine job at Blackburn – and did.

Mackay's signing of these two players was a statement of
intent. Buoyed by Jack Walker's money, Blackburn were on
the up. With a considerable amount of money to spend in the
transfer market it appeared that Mackay was on course to
realise the dreams of the club and its supporters, and guide
Rovers to promotion to the top flight. Mackay's downfall,
however, came when he attempted to a sign a top-flight player
who was still in his prime.

Knowing that Gary Lineker wanted to return to English
football from Barcelona, Mackay made a bid for the England
striker. The favourites for Lineker's signature were Spurs,
managed by Terry Venables, and there, from Mackay's point of
view, lay the rub. Don Mackay told Gary Lineker and his agent
John Holmes that penny for penny he could match the fee
being asked by Barcelona and the deal offered to Lineker by
Spurs. He added that if push came to shove Blackburn were in
a position to top Spurs' offer. Don Mackay did a great job of
selling Blackburn Rovers, outlining the ambitions Jack Walker
had for the club – how Walker was willing to invest millions of
pounds of his own money to ensure the club would, in the

near future, be in a position to compete with Arsenal and Manchester United and have a stadium befitting of such a club.

When clubs were rich they sent for Ron Atkinson; when they were skint they sent for Don Mackay and he never let them down. But Mackay, for all the respect shown him by his fellow managers, was not a big-name manager as far as top players were concerned. Gary Lineker signed for Spurs, one of the reasons behind his choice being Terry Venables. Though Jack Walker respected Don Mackay as a manager, Walker knew his money was in itself not enough to attract the really big-name players to Ewood Park. The club also needed a big-name manager. In 1991 Mackay was replaced by Kenny Dalglish, one of the greatest players ever to have graced the British game and someone who, as player-manager, had won the League and Cup double with Liverpool. With Dalglish as manager and a substantial sum of money available, Blackburn Rovers were an eminently more attractive proposition to star players: Alan Shearer joined from Southampton and Chris Sutton from Norwich City as Dalglish created a team that was to bring the Premiership title to Blackburn in 1995.

One of the marks of a good manager is how he copes with pressure. It is all relative. Sir Alex Ferguson and Arsène Wenger are subjected to pressure, as are the managers of teams struggling at the foot of League Two. Though no doubt Gary Peters at Shrewsbury Town and Graham Barrow at Bury would willingly swap the pressure they feel for that endured by Wenger and Ferguson. Pressure gets to some managers and their reaction to it isn't always positive. In 1995 Leyton Orient allowed a documentary camera inside their dressing room. (Why, oh why, do people agree to it? They never come across favourably.) The camera caught the Orient manager, John Sitton, reacting to the fact that his team were trailing 3-0 at half-time.

'You, you fucking little shit, and you, you fucking big shit, when I tell you to do something, you fucking well do it!' ranted Sitton. 'And if you want to come back at me we'll have a right sort out. Pair up if you like and pick some one to help you, and you can bring your dinner – because by the time I'm finished with you, you're going to need it.'

A manager has to show his players who is boss. He must never be intimidated by them and without doubt Sitton wasn't. But his manic raving will have had no positive effect. He wasn't providing answers to the problems that had resulted in his team being three goals down at half-time. The Orient players would have known their manager would be far from happy with their performance and would have expected a rollicking. Sitton's response to the situation and the pressure he was feeling, however, would not have engendered respect for him among his players, especially as the verbal fusillade was captured on camera for the nation and consequently the players' families to see. And no player wants his family to see him being belittled.

In the culture of the dressing room it is accepted that a manager must 'name names', that is, point a finger at those who are letting the side down. Sitton's reaction went beyond personal admonishment. Not only was there nothing constructive for the players in what he said, but the timbre and tone of his speech were so over the top it bordered on the comic. Sitton's reaction was akin to the manic rantings of John Cleese's Basil Fawlty. The phrase 'and you can bring your dinner' is pure Fawlty. It is so surreal and irrational as to be comic, and when a manager cuts a comic figure in front of his team, the players' respect for him goes out of the window. Passion and pressure got the better of John Sitton on that particular occasion and, to be fair to John, most managers will have had similar outbursts at some point in their career. Ted Drake was an amiable, level-headed manager. Ted was a gentlemen of the old school, and there is a lot to be said for that old school. He was dignified and for the most part calm and collected in his dealings with players.

But on occasions even Ted would lose it and have it in for players. I know, because I was once on the receiving end of a post-match burst of anger from Ted and I hadn't even played in the game! I was seventeen and scoring a lot of goals in the Chelsea first team. Ted, aware that I was still developing physically, didn't want to play me in every game and for me to suffer burn out. So he rested me. The rest was much longer than Ted had orginally indicated it would be. Six weeks, in fact. Even at the time I didn't think such a prolonged period of inactivity was doing me any good. I was itching to play football again and when I was restored to the first team, I was lacking in match fitness and as such a bit rusty.

I came back to play against Darlington in an FA Cup tie at Stamford Bridge. Darlington were in the Fourth Division (so nothing new there, then). It was a game Chelsea were expected to win easily but Darlington went away with a 2-2 draw. Ted Drake had not been enamoured with my performance and dropped me for the replay at Feethams. I was named as a travelling reserve and watched the match from the stands. The game was a disaster for Chelsea. The score was 1-1 at the end of normal time but Darlington ran Chelsea ragged in extratime and won 4-1. In the dressing room after the game Ted Drake was livid. He laid into my team-mates while I stood up in a corner thanking my lucky stars that I hadn't been a part of the debacle. I thought I was safe, but not a bit of it. When Ted finished his rant he stormed out of the changing room, only to return immediately and point a finger at me.

'And as for you, Mr bloody Under 23 starlet,' roared Ted, 'some bloody player you are! You can't even get in this fackin' side!'

Brian Clough belongs to that select band of true managerial greats. The best manager England never had. Clough didn't suffer fools gladly. He was forever being quoted in the press, because just about everything he said was so eminently quotable. He was a man of great contrasts. He was impatient, dogmatic, arrogant and confrontational, but also sympathetic to the needs of those around him. He was brash and belligerent, but also understanding. At times he could be crude, but he was generally impeccably well-mannered. He could be hard-faced yet also compassionate, complicated yet a believer in simple homespun philosophies. Many saw him as conceited; he was but he also displayed considerable humanity. He often assumed the role of the antagonist, just as equally that of a peacemaker. He aroused contradictory reactions in everyone because he was a man of wild contradictions. An enigma in football management.

I have often heard it said that Brian Clough bullied his players, but I have never heard this from anyone who played under Clough. As an ex-pro myself, I know a manager will never get players to go out on to the park and give him 100 per cent effort and commitment as the result of him bullying them into doing it. John McGovern played for Clough at Hartlepool United, Derby County, Leeds and Nottingham Forest. John O'Hare was a team-mate of Clough's at Sunderland and later played under him at both Derby and Forest. McGovern and O'Hare were consummate pros, reasonable and rational lads not lacking in grey matter. I ask you, would either of those players have followed Cloughie about if they had known him to bully players?

When Clough had to make a point to a player, he didn't go ballistic. In his early days at Forest, Cloughie introduced two young wingers, Terry Curran and John Robertson, to the first team. Wingers are notoriously inconsistent; they can be brilliant one game and virtually anonymous the next. Of the two you would have plumped for Curran to make a big name for himself in the game. He seemed to have it all whereas Robertson's strength seemed confined to an ability to take a man on and make a telling cross. It was Robertson, however, who was to go on and make a big name for himself. His mental attitude was right while that of Curran was thought by Clough to be suspect. John Robertson didn't display the all-round skills and technique of Curran but what he had going for him was consistency. As Clough once said of him, 'He's a little fat lad. When you come down to it, that's a good description. He's a little fat lad but he is one of the best deliverers of the ball in the game today. He does that consistently well, and by virtue of that is a lad who can do great things on a football field.'

Terry Curran frustrated Clough. This was basically because Clough thought Terry could be a great player should he only get his mental attitude right and show some consistency in his play. Clough once told me that following one game in which Curran had been largely anonymous, he asked the winger to accompany him to the touchline. Clough and Curran stood at the side of the pitch as the Forest groundsman replaced divots, the winger unsure what he was supposed to be looking at.

'Well, go on then,' ventured Clough. 'It's got me beat, so show me where it is.'

Curran was perplexed. He didn't have a clue what Clough was talking about or getting at.

'Show you what, boss?' he asked.

'It's obviously out there somewhere, but I can't see it. You'll have to point it out to me,' said Clough, his voice very relaxed.

'Point what out, boss?'

'The hole.'

'What hole, boss?'

'The hole you got down into and hid in for ninety minutes this afternoon,' said Clough in characteristically laconic fashion. Clough then offered Curran a knowing look and walked away.

Brian Clough and Peter Taylor took over at Hartlepool United in 1965. I remember Hartlepool United prior to them taking over, but such was the perilous state of the club and so poor had been the team for some years I doubt many 'Pool fans like to remember such times. Having enjoyed an illustrious playing career, too many former players nowadays who seek to take up management want to walk into a top job. Few seem to want to start at the bottom, learn and graduate. When Brian Clough took over as manager of Hartlepool his first press conference was conducted in a fashion that was to be characteristic of him. 'Regarding management, Peter and I knew we would have to start at the bottom and work our way up. But having assessed the situation here it quickly became apparent to us things are so bad, our first job will be to elevate this club to the bottom.'

Clough wasn't exaggerating. Finances at Hartlepool were so dire the club couldn't afford the cost of a coach to take them to away games. For their first away match at Southport, Peter Taylor managed to borrow an old coach from a pal. Taylor drove the bus to Southport and Clough drove them back. A few weeks later Peter Taylor was unable to get hold of the old coach, so Hartlepool travelled to Barnsley in cars. Clough insti-gated the club's first proper youth policy (which produced John McGovern) while Taylor set about signing new players. Taylor went back to his old club, Burton Albion of the Northern Premier League, and signed goalkeeper Les Green (who would later play for them at Derby County), Stan Aston and Tony Parry. All three were more than capable of playing League football and, along with other new recruits, Clough and Taylor created a team that revolutionised Hartlepool's for-tunes. Hartlepool had been perennial applicants for re-election. The club had been scrubbing about at the foot of Division Four since 1960 and home attendances had fallen to little over 2000. In Clough's first season in charge Hartlepool reached the dizzy heights of mid-table and the following season just failed to make the promotion places. Attendances at Victoria Park more than doubled and Clough's standing as a manager of some promise was in the ascendancy. Clough applied for the vacant manager's job at Derby County, following a recommen-dation from the great Raich Carter, and the rest, as they say, is history. Or as Peter Taylor once said of the situation, 'Brian applied for the vacant job at Derby, and the rest . . . is some-thing snooker players use when they can't reach their balls.'

Brian Clough's humanity and generosity of spirit were not a matter of public knowledge. During his time at the Baseball Ground one of the Derby players encountered money problems. The player in question was not a regular in the Derby first team but a good club man who when called upon by Clough did a good job for him in midfield. The player had gone through an acrimonious and expensive divorce and word got round the Derby dressing room that the player had received legal correspondence demanding he pay debts totalling £600 or the bailiffs would be sent in. Far from having £600 the player had next to nothing as nigh on all his wages were gobbled in maintenance payments and his existing mortgage. One morning after training he was getting dressed when he was suddenly aware of something bulging in one of the pockets of his jacket. On placing a hand inside he was stunned to find an envelope containing £600 in notes. No one ever owned up to putting the money there. The player in question never did find out who his mystery benefactor was. But ask him, or any Derby player of the time, and they have no doubt whatsoever as to who put the money there.

In my time as player, broadcaster and journalist I have got to know many managers. Three of them I got to know very well indeed: Walter Winterbottom and Alf Ramsey, during my time as an England player, and Bill Nicholson, with whom I had eight very happy and one unhappy year at Spurs.

I shall always have a special place in my heart for Walter Winterbottom as he was the man who gave me my debut for England Under 23s and the full national side, being as he was manager of both. Walter was also in charge of the England Youth side, the Football League Representative team and was also the Football Association's National Head Coach. Talk about multi-tasking. I don't know how much the FA paid Walter, but whatever it was it wasn't enough.

Winterbottom was the first man ever to be appointed

England team manager. He took up the role in 1946, though 'manager' was somewhat of a misnomer as the England team were picked by the FA's selection committee. Needless to say, this frustrated Walter who was forever battling – he would say negotiating – with the FA in an attempt to wrest England team selection from a blazer brigade committee that instinctively admired any player who had but a modicum of talent and was modest about it. Walter advised the committee as to who they might choose, but from what I gather it was an onerous and frustrating task that often left him riddled with angst. Walter was a scholarly man not given to fits of temper. A man with a slow, pleasant and refreshing voice, like the first cup of tea of the day made audible. He was studious where football was concerned, and technically minded, though his methods were nowhere near as complicated as those of coaches today. He set a good example to his players, whom he respected, and we returned that respect.

Walter's first eye-opening experience of the FA selection committee took place at the Victoria Hotel, Sheffield, a matter of weeks after his appointment as England manager. Walter joined the chairman of the selection committee and eight other members of the FA, one of whom was representing Eton College, another Oxbridge Universities. As I once told him, 'The signs were there for you right from the start'. They all sat round a table, each putting their nominations forward for every position in the team. Walter recalled there were five names put forward for the first position of goalkeeper. The list was reduced by voting with a show of hands until it came down to two names for the goalkeeper's jersey, which was to be decided by a first-past-the-post vote.

When that was done Walter asked his fellow committee members how many of them had actually seen the five goalkeepers in action that season, or in fact any of the other players in contention for an England place. The reply astonished him. Not one member of the selection committee had seen any of the players in action that particular season. Walter quickly realised that selection for the England team, far from being based on ability, was based on a number of other factors. Committee members were putting forward the names of players from clubs they were attached to, often for no other reason than the fact that international status for a player afforded the club greater kudos, to say nothing of increasing that player's value in the transfer market. Others were considered for a place in the England team as a reward for long service. As Walter said, 'Leslie Compton's club loyalty to Arsenal prompted one committee member to say, "He really is a decent chap, why not give him a chance?"'

Walter realised straight away that the system needed a major overhaul. It helped his cause when he was put in charge of the Football League Representative side as he would occasionally use selection of that team as a vehicle for rewarding players who were 'decent chaps'. As he admitted, 'Not an ideal situation but at least such players were no longer getting into the England team.'

Walter persuaded members of the selection committee to go out and watch players, and some were even allocated specific matches to watch individual players. Little by little Walter made his presence felt in the England set-up, but the FA took a giant step back after he put forward his ideas for how England should prepare for World Cups. In 1959 England were due to play an international match – there was no such thing as a friendly in those days, every England game was considered to have great importance – against Sweden at Wembley. Walter had the idea of developing a young England team over a cycle of four years with a view to it peaking for the finals of the World Cup.

For the Sweden game he persuaded the FA to allow him to select the team he wanted. The FA selection committee was compliant with this request and Walter selected what was the youngest team ever to have represented England. I was a member of that team, along with other young players such as Trevor Smith (Birmingham City), John Connelly (Burnley), Ron Flowers (Wolves), Bobby Charlton (Manchester United), Tony Allen (Stoke City) and the Middlesbrough pair, Brian Clough and Eddie Holliday. The last three were players with Second Division clubs.

England lost 3-2. It was only our second defeat on home soil against foreign opposition (the other being the watershed mauling meted out by Hungary in 1953). The FA was so incensed selection of the England team immediately reverted back to the committee. Brian Clough was never selected for England again, and Walter Winterbottom's idea of developing an England team within a four-year cycle for the World Cup was ditched.

An indication of how Walter Winterbottom's forward thinking was on the right lines is the fact that four of the team which faced Sweden in 1959 – Bobby Charlton, John Connelly, Ron Flowers and myself – were all members of Alf Ramsey's 1966 World Cup squad, as were two of Walter's reserves, George Eastham and Ron Springett.

When Alf Ramsey took over as England manager in 1963 – it is worth remembering Ramsey was second choice, Burnley skipper Jimmy Adamson having turned down the FA's offer of the England job – Alf accepted the role on certain conditions: that he and he alone should be responsible for picking the England team, and that he should be allowed to reinstate Walter Winterbottom's plan of developing teams in three- to four-year cycles with a view to preparing for World Cups!

I have often heard it said that Alf Ramsey and I didn't get on. We did. I have also heard it said and read it often that Alf dropped me from the England team during the 1966 World Cup. He didn't. I played in the first three matches of England's group. In the final game, against France, I picked up an injury that required fourteen stitches. The format of the World Cup

finals in 1966 was very demanding. As I lay in my bed following the game against France I knew should England reach the
World Cup final I wouldn't be playing. England played France
on a Wednesday night and were due to play Argentina on the
Saturday. If England beat Argentina they would play in the
semi-finals the following Wednesday night. I was not going to
be fit for either of those matches. Should England get through
the semi-finals, the World Cup final was to take place three
days later on a Saturday. In the event of England reaching the
final I knew that even if I declared myself fit Alf wouldn't
change a winning team. I was devastated, of course, but I knew
immediately after the game against France that my World Cup
was over. I must admit, come the final, I harboured a slight
hope that Alf might include me, but that was my heart talking.
My head told me I was going to be a spectator as there were no
substitutes.

Alf and I didn't always see eye to eye, but I liked him both as
a man and a manager. He was always fair in his dealings with
players, always scrupulously honest, a man of unyielding
integrity and absolute loyalty. He bore no grudges and he had
no favourites. Oh, and one more thing about Alf: he remains to
this day the best manager England have ever had. Winning the
World Cup was, of course, Alf's greatest achievement. He did,
however, achieve much even before England played their first
game under his charge – by telling the FA's blazer brigade that
he was only going to accept the job of England manager on his
terms. Believe me, persuading that lot to accept such a condition was some achievement on the part of Alf.

Despite guiding England to the World Cup Alf enjoyed at
best an uneasy relationship with his employers at the FA. I
remember going on a tour with England in the summer of
1964. At the end of the tour Alf gave a little speech. He
thanked the players for their efforts and good conduct. He
thanked his backroom staff, Harold Shepherdson and Les
Cocker (all two of them!), and concluded by saying, 'I would

particularly like to thank all the FA officials who have travelled with us on this tour, for having the good sense to keep out of our way.'

That went down with the FA like a parachute with a hole in it. It took a long time, but they finally found Alf vulnerable when England failed to qualify for the finals of the 1974 World Cup. Ted Phillips played for Alf in the Ipswich Town side that won the First Division Championship in 1961. In 1974 Ted had been in London on business and caught a train back to Ipswich. On boarding the train he saw Alf and took a seat next to him. Alf was delighted to see his old centre forward and offered to go down to the buffet and buy a couple of whisky miniatures. As they journeyed, the pair laughed as they recalled the good old days they had spent together at Ipswich. When the train arrived in Ipswich Ted bade a fond farewell to Alf, who informed Ted that it had been great to see him again after all those years. When Ted arrived home, he picked up the local newspaper off the mat and was shocked to see the front-page headline – 'Alf Ramsey Sacked'. At no point during their journey had Alf mentioned he had just been sacked as England manager by the FA. Alf was a gentleman and I should imagine he didn't inform Ted of his summary dismissal for no other reason than he didn't want to embarrass Ted. It was the mark of the man.

Bill Nicholson, like Winterbottom and Ramsey, was quietly spoken and a gentleman. For the most part Bill adhered to the theory that football is a simple game and should be played as such. He was a football purist and liked his teams to pass the ball. Nothing gave him greater satisfaction than seeing a fluid move build from defence and end with a slickly taken goal. Bill was one of the all-time great managers of English football. His Spurs team that won the League and Cup double in 1961 did so with great style and aplomb. What's more, their success was achieved on pitches that in midwinter resembled middens. In that double season Spurs scored 115 goals in the League. Their success contained within it several records. The most victories in a season (31), the most First Division away wins (16), the most consecutive wins at a season's start (11), the most matches involved in the achievement of the double (49) and the record aggregate attendance for a season (Spurs were watched by 2,501,034 spectators at League games).

Bill signed me for Spurs in December 1961 and I was a member of the side that won the FA Cup that season and the European Cup Winners' Cup the following season. Spurs were the first British team ever to win a major European trophy and we also created another record in 1962–3. That season Spurs had eleven different players who were capped by their native country, though oddly for the time we never played together as a Tottenham team. For the record Ron Henry, Maurice Norman, Bobby Smith and myself played for England; Bill Brown, John White and Dave Mackay for Scotland; Mel Hopkins, Cliff Jones and Terry Medwin for Wales; and Danny Blanchflower for Northern Ireland.

Considering his record as Spurs' manager it is little wonder that Bill Nicholson is revered around White Hart Lane to this day. Yet Bill was very modest about his achievements and worth as a manager, to the point of being irreverent. As he once jokingly said, 'When I retired as a player I always knew that if all else failed I could become a manager – and all else failed.' Bill Nicholson never changed his style of management, his manner or his fundamental belief that football is a simple game and the primary job of the player is to entertain. He remains a venerable figure, a manager who treated success, subjugation, fame and fortune with the same level-headed steadfastness. He also accepted minor irritations and major mistakes on the part of officials with dignity and grace. The most controversial thing he ever said to a linesman was 'Are you sure?'

If Bill thought a player was beginning to believe his own publicity he was quick to keep that player's feet on the ground.

A few well-chosen words from Bill were usually enough to make a young player who was getting full of himself take a reality check. Keith Weller was a very talented youngster at Spurs in the sixties. Bill, however, was concerned that the wonderful write-ups Keith had been receiving might have a detrimental effect on him. One morning on the training ground Bill felt Keith was becoming overconfident, to the point of being cocky.

'You should never confuse football talent with fame,' Bill told Keith. 'One is Danny Blanchflower and the other is you.'

To his credit Keith took that message on board and went on to become one of the most talented players of the seventies. One of my favourite Nicholson remarks came during half-time in a game against Aston Villa. Bill's assistant Eddie Baily was frustrated with our centre forward, Frank Saul, who had missed a golden opportunity in front of goal.

'I know, I know, Eddie. I hold my hand up. Sorry, lads. I had the time to put that one away,' conceded Frank.

'Had the time to put it away?' said Bill. 'You had so much time you could have made your own coal!'

This sense of humour is something that is often missing in today's game. Ron Saunders was manager of Aston Villa from 1974 to 1982 during which time he guided Villa to the First Division Championship in 1981. Ron was a lugubrious manager to the point of appearing dour, though unlike Bobby Charlton he had no problem communicating ideas to his Villa players. Ron, however, was given to being taciturn in public, especially at club functions. During a club Christmas party a wife of one of the Villa players went up to Ron in an attempt to engage him in conversation.

'I've got a bet on with my husband', the player's wife informed Ron, brightly. 'My husband says he will buy me a new car if I can talk to you and get more than two words out of you.' Ron offered the lady a characteristic lugubrious look.

'You lose,' said Ron.

Football is seen as such a serious business now managers who indulge in jokes and ready wit, such as Gordon Strachan, Mick McCarthy and Neil Warnock, are an exception. In the fifties and sixties if there was a club where one was almost guaranteed belly laughs it was Fulham. The chairman was Tommy Trinder, a well-known figure from the world of entertainment whose career encompassed that of stand-up comedian, film comedy actor and later that of a television game-show host. Tommy's wit was razor sharp and occasionally directed at the club itself. During one interview, Reg Drury of the *News of the World* said to Tommy, 'Fulham strikes me as being a real family club'.

'Oh, it's a real family club all right,' replied Tommy with a cheesy grin. 'In every room you walk into there's a bloody argument going on.'

During Tommy's reign as chairman, the Fulham boardroom had an 'open house' policy after a game: anyone was welcome to pop in for a drink. On one occasion when Manchester United played at Craven Cottage, after the game the wife of the United chairman, Louis Edwards, fell into conversation with the Fulham groundsman. Their conversation over, Mrs Edwards returned to her husband who was chatting to Tommy. The chairman asked Mrs Edwards if she was enjoying her visit to Craven Cottage. She told him she was but then surprised Tommy by asking him if he could have a word with his groundsman about the language the man used.

'I remarked on the fine state of your pitch,' said Mrs Edwards. 'Your groundsman told me the secret was barrowloads of manure he applied to the pitch when seeding in the close season. I find the word "manure" most distasteful, perhaps you could get him to use the word "fertiliser" instead.'

'You gotta be joking,' said Tommy, his considerable jaw dropping. 'It's taken me six months to get him to call it manure!'

Whether Tommy's wit rubbed off on others at Craven Cottage I don't know, but he wasn't the only one at Fulham to see the funny side of things. Players like Tosh Chamberlain, Maurice Cook, Jimmy Langley, Eddie Lowe and Reg Stratton were always full of fun and witty remarks. Even manager Bedford Jezzard possessed a keen wit. Yet again in the Fulham boardroom, Bedford was chatting to a director of Birmingham City who remarked, 'Bedford? There's a name you don't hear every day.'

'I do,' replied Bedford.

Wilf McGuinness is now in great demand on the after-dinner circuit. Little wonder, as Wilf is one of the nation's funniest sporting after-dinner speakers. Even when he was manager of Manchester United, Wilf was always quick with the jokes. During his time as manager Wilf tried to sign Colin Todd from Sunderland. During a meeting with Todd and Sunderland officials to talk about a possible move to Old Trafford, Wilf asked the player about his personal life.

'I like a drink as much as the next man,' volunteered Todd at one point.

'Not if the next man is George Best, you don't,' replied Wilf, quick as a flash.

Of course, not every manager of the past was like this, far from it. Though generally speaking I think it true to say most had a more light-hearted approach to the game and their jobs than contemporary managers. With the exceptions already mentioned, rarely does one hear a manager today making a joke or expressing wit on the subject of the game. This has much to do with the pressures contemporary managers are subjected to, both in terms of their actual jobs and when appearing before a media that treat football with all the seriousness of a war. It saddens me that the multi-million-pound industry that is football today has bred a culture in which light-heartedness and fun are widely considered an indication that someone is not affording suitable gravitas and reverence to

what one ITV executive informed me 'is now the very serious
business of football'. In 1968 after an 8-0 defeat at West Ham
United, during the post-match interview Sunderland manager
Alan Brown wryly commented, 'It was an even game. We conceded four in each half'. Should a manager make such a
comment today in the wake of such a heavy defeat, he would be
pilloried.

So what's the difference between a good manager and a great
manager? The answer to that is good players and great players.
That may sound overly simple, but in essence it is true and so
we are back to what Bob Stokoe said about it being easy to be
a good manager. A good manager will get the best out of good
players and may elevate them to the category of 'very good'. A
great manager will make a very good player great. How that is
achieved has to do with football nous, technique and man-management, and the ability to communicate ideas. No one can
doubt that Bobby Charlton was a world-class player, one of
the greatest the English game has ever known. But Bobby was
unsuccessful as manager of Preston North End in the mid-
seventies. For all he had a wealth of football knowledge, Bobby
is not the most uplifting of communicators and I think one of
the problems he encountered as a manager was that of getting
his ideas across to his players and motivating them.

Getting ideas across and motivating players has never been
a problem for José Mourinho whose considerable skills as a
manager and coach have reaped benefits for Chelsea and
brought a new dimension and energy to English football. In
2004–5 Chelsea gave their supporters and all genuine fans of
the game a season of football that gladdened the eye. On the
face of it Chelsea appear to epitomise the modern English
top-flight team in that their composition is as cosmopolitan as
a comet. What Mourinho and his team achieved in 2004–5,
however, had a much more positive dimension to it than
simply winning the Premiership title. Chelsea played with

such sagacity, purpose and integrated spirit that their efforts induced admiration and warmth in not just their own supporters, but all genuine lovers of the game. This, in no small way, was down to José Mourinho.

When Chelsea began to assemble their star-studded cast many foresaw problems for Mourinho in trying to keep so many players happy. It was a reasonable assumption that those not playing regularly in the first team would become disenchanted and cause unrest in the dressing room. That this didn't happen maybe had something to do with the level of wages paid by the club, but it also had a lot to do with the management style of José Mourinho.

In Sir Alf Ramsey and Bill Nicholson I was fortunate to play for two of the greatest managers ever to have graced English football, but I would love to have played for José Mourinho. Chelsea's cosmopolitan team responded to the sometimes enigmatic methods of Mourinho in a way few expected. He engendered in his team a hard core of optimism, the can-do factor and more importantly encouraged players to give performances of a standard few thought they were capable of producing, Joe Cole being a case in point. As he did at Porto, Mourinho had proved remarkably effective at inculcating the right habits and attitude among his players. The Chelsea players appear to hang on to his every word, which is understandable as Mourinho had proved himself to be one of the best coaches in the business, a great motivator of players and exceptional at man-management. In football there are basically two types of manager: those who walk into a boardroom and say 'Here I am,' and those who walk into a boardroom and say 'Is it possible to have a word?' Mourinho belongs to the former. Once, during an interview for Central Television, I asked Brian Clough, 'Have you learned from your mistakes in management?'

'What mistakes?' replied Cloughie.

For all his self-confidence, Clough's reply had an element of the tongue-in-cheek about it. Mourinho appears to have a keen sense of humour, but on the subject of his qualities as a manager it is not in the man to be self-deprecating. The spectre of Mourinho is so great, even when he is not present at games he commands much attention from television commentators and the press, if only for reasons of speculation as to his possible location. Banned from the touchline for Chelsea's Champions League matches against Bayern Munich in 2005, football's media appeared obsessed with his whereabouts. In the game against Bayern at Stamford Bridge the press were quick to seize upon a possible story of an absent Mourinho communicating via a mobile phone or radio link with Chelsea's fitness coach on the bench, who may, or may not, have been wearing an earpiece under a woollen bob hat. It is often said that Mourinho is obsessed with his image; seemingly not as much as the media appears obsessed with him. In the course of Chelsea's match in Munich, Mourinho watched ten minutes of the game from the stands before disappearing. During the course of this game the ITV match commentator made twelve references to Mourinho's absence and possible whereabouts. One can labour a point too much, but the constant speculation as to where Mourinho might be watching this game and the purpose of his sudden exit from the Olympic Stadium is indicative of the charisma of the man and the hold he exerts upon a spellbound media.

As for why Mourinho chose to watch ten minutes of Chelsea's game in Munich from the stands then beat a retreat? Here is a man who loves publicity and is so adept at handling the media he knows how to keep himself in the spotlight even when prevented from basking in its glow. There may well be another, more subtle and calculating reason for Mourinho's behaviour in the days leading up to and during Chelsea's games with Bayern Munich. His initial decision not to attend Stamford Bridge for the first leg and to watch only ten minutes of the return ensured Mourinho would gain much publicity in the media. This may have been a calculated action on his part as the resultant publicity he received served to deflect some of the media attention and pressure away from his players.

Great players such as Bobby Charlton and Bobby Moore do not always make for a great manager. Likewise players whose talent was modest, such as Arsène Wenger, can evolve into great managers. Some, such as Bertie Mee, who won the double with Arsenal in 1971, may not have even been a professional player. Personality, an indomitable persona and the ability to communicate ideas are key factors in managerial success. But no one really knows the true secret of successful management and I guess we never will. Though we all have some ideas as to what not do to do. As Jan Molby said on leaving Kidderminster Harriers, 'My mistake as a manager was I couldn't wait for success. So I went ahead without it.'

CHAPTER THREE

Having the ability to score goals is like having power: If you have to tell people you have it, you don't

Centre forward, striker, call it what you will, it is perceived as being the most glamorous position in a football team. It was not for nothing that the hero of the *Tiger* comic, 'Roy of the Rovers', was a centre forward. The on-the-pitch exploits of Roy Race would not have thrilled and captivated generations of young people, should the alliterative Melchester Rovers star have been a centre back or played in midfield. People go to football matches to see goals and it is the job of the centre forward (I shall stick to the traditional term from now on) to do just that.

Owing to their ability to score goals, historically centre forwards have always commanded larger transfer fees than any other position. When I began my career at Chelsea in the fifties there were two types of centre forward. The first was the tall, robust, bull-in-a-china-shop type of centre forward, who was expected to run through a brick outhouse if need be, and knew he would be roundly abused if he shirked that responsibility. Fully paid-up members of that club included Nat Lofthouse (Bolton Wanderers), Arthur Rowley (Leicester City and Shrewsbury), Ted Phillips (Ipswich Town), Bobby Smith (Spurs), Derek Kevan (West Bromwich Albion), John Atyeo (Bristol City), Tommy Johnston (Blackburn Rovers and Leyton Orient) and, though he was blessed with the skills of the most resolute defender as well as of those of the most mercurial inside forward, the great John Charles of Leeds and Juventus. The other type of centre forward common to the era was not tall or well built but equally capable of withstanding tough challenges, of which there was no other type. This type of centre forward relied on speed off the mark, subtle play, mobility and footballing nous, which enabled him to ghost into space and pass rather than blast the ball into the net. Charlie Fleming (Sunderland), Brian Clough (Middlesbrough and Sunderland), Jackie Mudie (Blackpool), Tommy Taylor (Manchester United), Alex Young (Hearts and Everton), Jimmy Murray (Wolves) and Gerry Hitchens (Aston Villa and later Inter Milan) were all fine examples of this type of centre forward.

Of course it was not only centre forwards who were known for their exploits in front of goal. I was what in those days was termed an inside forward. I played off a big centre forward, part of whose job was to create openings for me. I was never a physical player in the sense that Nat Lofthouse or Arthur Rowley were physical; I simply didn't have the build. If anything my role as an inside forward was similar to that of the latter group of centre forwards in that I relied on acceleration and an ability to read situations and get into space accordingly. I scored 357 League goals and if one includes goals scored in Cup matches, for England and other representative teams, my career tally is 491. Of those goals I reckon you could count the number I scored from outside the penalty box on the fingers of two hands, and those from headers on the fingers of one hand! I rarely, if ever, blasted the ball into the net. I would try and see an opening and pass the ball through that gap.

Even in the hurly-burly game that is football today, a forward will have more time than he thinks to score a goal. The secret is to get into space and, on receiving the ball, stay calm and pick your spot. Sounds easy, doesn't it? Of course it isn't, there are eleven guys out there to prevent you doing the job you are paid to do, but by reading the game, anticipating situations, getting into space (ready for a perfectly weighted pass), and staying calm and picking your spot, a forward will score goals. I was not blessed with the physical attributes to rattle defenders. My primary assets were speed off the mark and, on receiving the ball in the penalty area, sharpness in front of goal. If anyone were to ask me the secret of my goalscoring – and they do – that would be my answer.

A good centre forward, like a good inside player, will attack space. That sounds like a technical term from a coaching manual, but in essence it means when your team are in possession, anticipating where the ball will end up inside the penalty area. To a certain extent you can be taught that, but for the greatest exponents of attacking space such ability is instinctive. I firmly believe I was born to score goals. Just like nobody taught Stan Matthews how to dribble past defenders and cross a ball, no one taught me how to score goals. It came naturally to me; it was something I was born with. I think that is true of all great goalscorers. Whether you're talking of Nat Lofthouse or Arthur Rowley, Gary Lineker or Thierry Henry, technique can be improved by coaching and practice, but what makes them great centre forwards is their innate ability to score goals. As Stan Matthews once said of coaching, 'All well and good, but you can't put in what God left out.'

When I began my career as a player the two most lauded centre forwards were John Charles and Nat Lofthouse. John Charles was known as the 'Gentle Giant', a self-explanatory term for a player of Charles Atlas' build, who had the strength of a rugby union forward but whose mark as a player was his grace, dignity and consummate sportsmanship. John was a player blessed with all the treasures of genius, whereas the other stars of his day merely enjoyed the trappings. He was six feet two inches, 13st 121b, as strong as Hercules, and imperious as Caesar, yet he had the balance, skills and dexterity of the most lively of inside forwards. His awesome physique made him a real handful for opponents and he was as effective for club or country as a centre half as he was a centre forward. He could score goals, dribble, tackle, pass and head the ball to great effect and was able to shake off opponents as a dog shakes water off its back. On account of his array of skills, physical presence and indomitable spirit, he would induce fear in the hardest defender and, believe me, there were plenty of those about in John's time. He was the Admirable Crichton of world football who in his pomp shouldered the main burden of Wales' attack. A genial genius of a player wrapped up in such a warm, sporting personality, I think his true greatness was not properly appreciated by some.

John was born in Swansea in 1931, and joined his hometown club at the age of fifteen. When Swansea supporters first laid eyes on him, they were incredulous of his tender age. As one Swansea fan said famously of the young John, 'He can't be fifteen. He was born twenty-eight.' John's ability was such that his time at Vetch Field was brief. A Leeds United scout spotted not so much potential but talent realised in young John, and in a matter of months he was on his way to Elland Road for the princely sum of £10. The fee was so low simply because of the fact that John was still an amateur player while as Swansea. In January 1949 he signed professional terms with Leeds and weeks later made his first team debut as a centre half. A year later he became the youngest player ever to be capped by Wales. His rise in football had been as meteoric as that of his physique.

During the 1952–3 season the Leeds manager Major Frank Buckley switched John to centre forward. (Having mentioned Major Frank Buckley, how I wish contemporary managers held rank from service days. Imagine the press reports: 'Arsenal manager Staff Sergeant Arsène Wenger spoke out at comments made by Lance Corporal Alex Ferguson . . .'). He proved a revelation as a centre forward. In his first season John scored twenty-six goals and the following season, 1953–4, he set a new club record and was the leading marksman in the Football League with forty-two goals. Such was the power of his heading one would have thought he had a boot between his ears. But he could not be ignored on the ground, where his strength was used to power past defenders. Some of them resorted to shabby tactics in an attempt to stop him. It was the mark of the man that John never retaliated. He would simply dust himself down and offer the perpetrator of the foul a look of disdain.

In his pomp John Charles was a formidable opponent and difficult to mark. The former Busby babe Wilf McGuinness tells the story of playing for Manchester United against Leeds. At half-time Leeds were two goals to the good and John Charles had scored both of them. As the United team sat in the dressing room all eyes were on young Wilf, whose job it had been to suppress big John.

'I don't know why you're looking at me,' said Wilf defensively. '2-0 down has nowt to do with me. When Charles scored his goals I was nowhere near him!'

The turning point in the career of John Charles came in April 1957 when he was playing for Wales in the Home International Championship against Northern Ireland at Windsor Park. In the crowd that day was Umberto Agnelli, the president of Juventus. At the time Juventus were a club funded by the Fiat car company – a liaison dating back to the 1930s when Fiat, worried that its workers might turn to communism, had decided to put money into one of the local football clubs in the hope that a successful team would make for happy workers. As a result money was no object to Juventus, and Agnelli entered into negotiations with Leeds United for what was to prove one of the most momentous transfers in the history of the game. In those days it was rare that a British player at the peak of his career should sign for a team overseas. It was a big decision for John and he mulled over the move for some weeks before eventually signing in time to start the 1957–8 season with Juventus. The transfer fee was £65,000, a record for a British player. At the time the maximum wage was in operation in English football – the most a player could earn in this country was £20. Reputedly, John received a signing-on fee of £5000 and a weekly wage of £90. He also had a villa on the Italian Riviera, another in Turin, two cars and in time would be a partner in a restaurant. In less than twelve months he was a star in Italian football and could not walk down a street without seeing cafés empty of fans, all wanting to shake his hand.

In 1958 John scored twenty-three goals to help Juventus win the Serie A Championship. The following year his goals helped Juventus win the Italian Cup and in 1960 they contributed to the Championship and Cup double. He could do no wrong in the eyes of Juventus because he did little wrong on the pitch. In what was a defensively minded game in Italy, John notched twenty-plus goals a season. His star was in the ascendancy. His goals were a key factor in Wales qualifying for the World Cup finals in Sweden in 1958 (the only occasion on which all four home countries have qualified for the finals of a World Cup). Playing against the best players in the world, John proved he was superior to most. His performances helped Wales reach the quarter-finals but an injury prevented him playing against Brazil, who beat the Welsh and eventually went on to be crowned world champions for the first time.

In 1962 John came back to these shores to play for Leeds, who paid £53,000 to see the return of their prodigal son. But John missed the glamour of Italy and the Italian game, and so he signed for Roma. Sadly, his best days were behind him and following a brief stint with the club, he moved back to his beloved Wales and signed for Cardiff City. I always thought it fitting that John's League career ended as it had begun, in his native South Wales. Whenever I hear that old song of Jimmy Dean's, 'Big John', I think of John Charles. As the lyric goes, 'He was a big, big man, was Big John'. John Charles was all that and more.

Nat Lofthouse was a hero of mine as a boy and was still a hero to me when I faced him in a Chelsea shirt and he was rampaging in the lily-white of his only club, Bolton Wanderers. If one ever needed proof that under Sven-Göran Eriksson international matches other than World Cup or European Championship ties have been devalued, it is that Nat Lofthouse's greatest moment came not when he scored both goals to win the FA Cup for Bolton in 1958, but when he scored for England in what would now be called a friendly.

I was in my early teens when, in the spring of 1952, Nat bagged his most famous goal. England had travelled to Vienna to play Austria, then one of the most powerful teams in Europe. Such a fixture today would hardly raise the level of enthusiasm to that one has for watching fish fingers defrost. In 1952, though, it was a different story. It was a war-ravaged Vienna, as depicted in that masterpiece of British film noir, Carol Reed's *The Third Man*. If Newcastle's gnarled, seasoned campaigner Jackie Milburn was Harry Lime, Nat was Joseph Cotton's naive pulp-fiction writer.

'We had played Italy a few days before in Florence,' Nat once told me:

> I'd gone there expecting it to be straightforward, like the English First Division. But the game turned out to be a lot more cynical and calculating than that. The Italians were well organised and knew all the tricks to put you off your game. I mucked it up a bit and we ended drawing 1-1. The press had not been enamoured with my performance and I can understand that because I kind of grew up in that game. I was used to physical play as every player was in those days. But the Italians were very niggly and indulged in all manner of off-the-ball shenanigans. I hoped I would retain my place for the next game of the tour against Austria, but the press were suggesting Milburn should be recalled at centre forward.

Vienna in 1952 was rubble strewn; its buildings were gutted

and a black market was thriving. When the England party reached the British zone, Nat managed a phone call home to his wife, who told him Desmond Hackett of the *Daily Express* was leading a campaign to have Nat dropped for the Austria game and replaced by Milburn.

'Fortunately,' said Nat, 'I kept my place in the team but thought to myself: Nathan, lad, this here's your last chance with England.'

The game was played at the Prater Stadium, which at the time was smack bang in the middle of the Russian-occupied zone. With players such as Oskwirk, Dienst and Huber, Austria were widely considered to have one of the best teams in Europe. They had not lost a match on home soil for twenty years and had scored a staggering 57 goals in their previous 13 international matches. If Nat was going to produce something special, he couldn't have chosen tougher opposition.

It is often said that we British treat war like a sport and sport like a war. There was a large British armed forces presence in Vienna at the time and in the days leading up to the match, the frugality of life in post-war Vienna was forgotten as all conversation centred on the game. The city had an electric atmosphere, and with the British forces present, it was as if home and away fans had four days to stew before the big showdown. All of which, of course, only added to the great air of expectation surrounding this game.

'When we got out on the pitch it was a fantastic feeling,' Nat told me. 'The Vienna Boys Choir sang the national anthems, which both sets of supporters respected as was always the case in those days. As I looked up to the terraces I could see thousands of Tommies from our zone, who had been allowed into the Russian sector by the zonal commander to cheer us on. It were great, just like a home match.'

England got off to a flyer with a goal from Nat himself. It was twenty-yard daisy-cutter that, according to Raymond Glendenning's radio commentary, appeared to bounce every yard. I would soon be made to realise that this particular shot was a speciality of Nat's. (So frequently were Chelsea to be on the receiving end of it, our right back, Peter Sillett, used to refer to it as Nat's 'Barnes Wallis', after the man who invented the bouncing bomb of Dambusters fame.) Sheffield Wednesday's Jackie Sewell sent the Tommies delirious with a second goal, only for Austria to display their mettle and storm back to make it 2-2 at half-time. I remember Glendenning's rich, fruity voice saying England were fortunate to go in on level terms at the interval. After their first goal the Austrians had set about Gil Merrick's goal and England had been reduced to some desperate defending as half-time approached.

After the break the scoreline remained unchanged until there were some ten minutes remaining. It was then that Gil Merrick collected a near-post ball and, looking up, spotted Nat's bulky frame cruising along the halfway line. As the players on both sides began to make their way out of the penalty area, Merrick launched the ball with an almighty throw and Nat was straight on to it. He raced towards goal, the only England player in the Austrian half of the field. As he went he took an elbow in the face from one defender, but characteristically powered his way on. Another Austrian defender came bearing down on him, so Nat upped his pace. He staggered in full flow as the defender's attempted tackle caught him on the ankle, but somehow managed to regain his balance and stormed on. With blood streaming from his nose as a result of the elbow to his face, Nat bore down on goal and the Austrian keeper came racing out to the edge of his box to narrow the angle. As Nat pushed the ball a little too far forward, it was touch and go who would reach it first. Nat drew deep into his reserves of strength to make it first to the ball and coolly rolled it goalbound as the keeper came sliding in to him. Nat was poleaxed, but as he hit the ground injured, he heard the roar of the Tommies.

'I were right down and out,' he said. 'I knew I had hit the ball but never knew it had gone in till I heard those Tommies roaring. I were in right pain, but I lay there looking up at the sky and I felt elated.'

Jimmy Trotter, the England trainer, came out to attend to Nat. As Jimmy applied his magic sponge, he said to Nat, 'Nathan, lad, you've never scored a better one – and you never will.' At the final whistle the England players were chaired off the pitch on a sea of khaki. As Nat recalled, 'After getting changed they took us off to the British barracks. We started in the officers' mess, then supped in the sergeants' mess, then to the privates' mess. It was the finest night of my life, and I don't mind telling you, come the end, I was drunk as a monkey.'

The following day, an unapologetic Desmond Hackett in the *Daily Express* dubbed Nat 'The Lion of Vienna'. And so he was, and so he is (and there's a pub in Bolton to prove it). All these years on, whenever I bump into Nat, following our farewells, as he walks off, John Wayne-like, I know it is all in my mind but for me he does so to the sound of Anton Karas' zither-playing.

Having been denied a Cup winners' medal in what is arguably the greatest FA Cup final of all – that of Blackpool and Bolton in 1953 – Nat returned to Wembley in 1958 when his beloved Bolton faced Manchester United. Bolton were in a no-win situation. United, devastated some three months earlier by the Munich air disaster, which claimed over forty lives including those of eight players and three club officials, had reached the final on a wave of public sympathy and their own resolution and inspiration. Bolton were as sympathetic to United's plight as anyone, but on the day proved themselves to be consummate professionals. Two goals from Nat gave Bolton the Cup. His second effort was clouded in controversy but was also indicative of football at that time and of the man himself.

Early in the second half the ball was played into the United penalty box. Goalkeeper Harry Gregg seemed to collect it comfortably, but there arrived Nat like some lion stalking its prey. As the becapped Gregg took the ball, Nat turned sideways on so that he was shoulder to shoulder with the United keeper. As Nat's burly frame made contact, Gregg's cap was comically dislodged from his head and the ball ended up in the back of the net. The goal was given for 'a fair shoulder charge', an anachronism in football today. No one disputed the legitimacy of a shoulder charge in those days, but controversy raged, as some believed Nat's shoulder, rather than making contact with the shoulder of Harry Gregg, had thumped into the back of the United keeper. Television coverage and press photographs of the incident failed to prove this one way or the other. All I know is such a challenge would be deemed a foul today, albeit that particular standpoint has not been changed in the rulebook but by way of interpretation.

I shudder to think what the reaction of Sir Alex Ferguson would be should such a challenge result in Manchester United losing a Cup final. There was, however, little in the way of resentment or hard feelings in those days. Centre forwards gave a knock to goalkeepers and took a knock or two in return, and had a pint afterwards. That's how I remember it being and I don't think I'm mistaken. Incidents like these, controversial though they may have been, were also vehicles for humour. Such was the game in those days. When Nat retired as a player, for a time he was the licensee of the Castle Hotel in Bolton. In the bar was a photograph of Nat scoring his second goal of that 1958 Cup final and underneath it was a poem, which read:

> *Harry Gregg after t'final*
> *Went into Nat's for a beer*
> *Who returned his money and telt 'im*
> *We don't charge goalkeepers here!*

I make special mention of Nat Lofthouse, and in particular those two stories, because to me they crystallise what a centre forward is all about. The heroics of Nat in Vienna and his shoulder charge on Harry Gregg are vignettes from another age of football, when physical play was part and parcel of the game, and the lot of a centre forward was to dish it out but also to take it and never complain. I am not saying that football was better in Nat's time than the game we know today, only that it was very different. As a consequence, so too were the players. Or was it a case of the players influencing the game? I say that because Nat's generation were a hardy lot. They endured economic depression in the thirties. That was followed by a world war, after which there was more frugality. Everybody of Nat's generation had either lost a loved one to the war, or knew someone who had. Yet somehow Nat's generation managed to sustain emotional sensibility. A tough life bred tough. On the morning of the day Nat made his debut for Bolton Wanderers he had worked a half-shift down the pit. Like many of his peers, Nat never thought he was badly done to because he and his like had never known any different. So when it came to taking an elbow in the face, as he did in that game against Austria, he never went down because it was not in him to do such a thing. Likewise, when the second Austrian defender whacked his ankle. Only when the Austrian goalkeeper poleaxed him did Nat eventually go to ground; by then glory was his. It is worth noting that not one player was booked in that game between Austria and England. Referees were more tolerant of robust, physical play, as were players themselves. Having endured an upbringing of hardship, then a world war, a whack on the ankle or even an elbow in the face, as unpleasant as it was, were placed into perspective. The life of a professional footballer was eminently more preferable to life down a pit or in a cotton mill. Working-class lads aspired to be footballers because the game represented an escape from the daily drudgery of working life, whereas today football is not so much an escape as a vehicle for lifestyle aspirations.

Society has changed much since the days when Nat Lofthouse shoulder charged Harry Gregg into the net to win the Cup for Bolton, as has football. Bolton is no longer the chimney-filled, cotton-spinning centre of an Empire, but the mark of Nat Lofthouse as a centre forward is that over forty years after his retirement as a player, he is still the city's most famous son.

Henry Cooper was a great British heavyweight boxer. In a career that spanned from 1954 to 1971, Henry was British and Commonwealth Heavyweight Champion for eleven years and was thrice European Heavyweight Champion. Ask most people today what they remember about Henry, however, and they will tell you of two fights he lost, against Cassius Clay and Joe Bugner – both of which were travesties of justice. Likewise, the career of Jeff Astle as a terrific centre forward is similarly and unfairly overshadowed by one miss of his. During that classic match between England and Brazil in the 1970 World Cup, Jeff Astle had an opportunity to cover himself in perpetual glory. Having come on as a substitute with the game 1-0 in favour of Brazil, Jeff was presented with what we forwards called a gimmee. The Brazilian goalkeeper and a defender got in a muddle, and the ball broke to Jeff Astle with the goal at his mercy. Jeff stubbed the ground as he shot and, uncharacteristically, he put the ball wide of the gaping net. It was late in the game and in all probability if Jeff had scored England would have had the draw their play so richly deserved. The fact that England lost to Brazil by the only goal of the game had no bearing on either team qualifying for the next stage of the finals – Brazil went through as group winners and England as runners-up. That being the case, one might have expected Jeff's glaring, and once again I must emphasise uncharacteristic, miss to have been forgotten along with all the other golden opportunities spurned by England centre forwards over the years. That match, however, was such a superlative game of football it seeped into the national consciousness of both Brazil and England, and is still talked of in reverent tones to this day.

As such, Jeff Astle's miss has never been forgotten. He was a great lad, a courageous and free-scoring centre forward but, as with Henry Cooper, Jeff Astle is now remembered more for the one negative aspect of his career as opposed to the many, many positives.

Jeff Astle was much loved by West Bromwich Albion fans. He made his name as a prolific centre forward with Albion in the sixties, though he began his career with Notts County (as did that other formidable centre forward of the sixties, Tony Hateley, the father of Mark). Jeff was somewhat of an anachronism to sixties football. In keeping with most young men of that era, footballers had become very fashion-conscious and had taken to wearing their hair a little longer in the style of the day. Jeff, in contrast, always sported a short back and sides, like some forward of the forties or fifties. More often than not it would also be kept in place with Brylcreem, another throwback to a bygone era. All this was in keeping with a player whose brave, bustling style was akin to that of Lofthouse and Jackie Milburn. Like all good centre forwards, Jeff was consistent when it came to scoring goals. In 1967–8 he scored twenty-five for West Brom to finish as the third highest goalscorer in the First Division behind George Best and Ron Davies (Southampton), who tied in top place with twenty-eight goals apiece. The following season Jeff scored twenty-one goals, again making him one of the leading marksmen in the First Division. In the 1969–70 season he topped the First Division goalscoring chart with twenty-five goals.

Some centre forwards achieve a reputation for scoring goals but when you analyse their records many of the goals scored were not vital to the team. Now, there is an argument for saying every goal is vital. But, while I think every goal, irrespective of how and when it is scored, is important, not all goals are vital. Some players score a good number of their goals when a match is won and the opposition are at their least effective. For example, a team may win 4-0 and a player may have scored his side's third and fourth goals somewhat late in the game – his name appears in the goalscoring charts and generally most people assume that player is a good goalscorer. But the real key to being a good goalscorer is how often a player notches one when his team really need him to. Jeff Astle scored a lot of goals when West Bromwich Albion really needed them from him. In the late sixties Jeff secured many a one-nil victory for West Brom, and his most memorable was in the 1967–8 FA Cup Final against Everton. On paper Everton had the better team, and what's more they outplayed West Brom for long periods of that Cup final. If it weren't for a combination of resolute defending by the Baggies and profligacy on their part, Everton would have had the match tied up long before big Jeff struck with the game into extra time. In what was a rare moment of West Brom pressure, the ball cannoned off an Everton defender to Jeff who was just outside the penalty area. When shooting at goal Jeff always favoured his right foot, but the ball came to him on his left and there was no time to readjust his positioning. Jeff met the ball on the half-volley with his left boot and it went like a rocket into the roof of the Everton net. The Everton keeper, Gordon West, had no chance. Jeff had had what for him was a quiet match. He had been well marshalled by Everton's Brian Labone and chances had been few. The one real opportunity to come his way, he put away. That's another mark of a good centre forward: give him but a single opportunity and he will punish you for doing so. Jeff had one real opportunity at goal in that FA Cup final and he took it, when it really mattered.

In keeping with every player of his generation, Jeff Astle never made a fortune from his career as a footballer. For all he played the majority of his football in the First Division, was often among its leading goalscorers, won both FA Cup and League Cup winners' medals, and was capped by Sir Alf Ramsey for England, when Jeff Astle hung up his boots he became a window cleaner. For years Jeff had his own window-cleaning business and his wonderful sense of humour was evidenced in the company's advertising which read, 'Jeff Astle, window cleaner – I never miss corners.'

I don't go along with the notion that contemporary English football does not produce great centre forwards any more. There may be an argument for saying Gary Lineker cannot be bracketed as a contemporary player, but his career is recent enough to be a part of the living memory of most. Gary was a fine leader of the line and no British player of his generation was better at attacking space. Lineker's 48 goals in 80 appearances for England, and career tally of 322 goals in 631 senior games, is highly laudable and indicative of his prowess in the opposition's penalty area. Of his contemporaries, Mark Hughes may have scored more spectacular goals but, unlike Lineker, Hughes did not score anywhere near the amount of bread-and-butter goals. That is, goals of the unspectacular variety where the ball is tapped in or bundled over the line. They all count and come May when you examine the records, they all look the same.

Gary Lineker was tall and slim for a centre forward, given to finding space and able to thread his way through defences and tuck the ball away neatly. He gave the impression of coasting through a game, until the ball was within playing distance. Then there was that sudden burst over two or three yards which distinguishes the great from the good. I previously stated that my prime assets as a goalscorer were speed off the mark and sharpness. These were Lineker's too, but what elevates good to great is that first yard, which is in the head. Gary was also a menace in the air, which has been overlooked by some. His anticipation, plus one of the neatest foreheads in the business, was quite capable of doing the rest, whether it be attacking the goal or laying the ball off for players coming up in support. Above all, he showed a tremendous appetite for the game that many of his contemporaries seemed to lack. The real mark of Lineker as a great centre forward was the damage he could do in his opponents' penalty area. Anyone who calls himself a centre forward has to do the business where it counts, and Lineker was never afraid to dive in where it hurts – that gave him the edge. With centre forwards such as Nat Lofthouse, Jeff Astle, Bobby Smith (Spurs), John Toshack (Liverpool) and to a certain extent Ruud van Nistelrooy (Manchester United), everything starts from physique, but with Lineker it started from the brain.

The nearest the contemporary game has had to what I would term an old-fashioned centre forward is Alan Shearer. His record as a goalscorer stands for itself. Along with Andy Cole he shares the record for having scored the most Premiership goals in a single season – thirty-four – albeit in achieving that Shearer played two more matches than Cole. Alan Shearer is, however, far and away the leading all-time goalscorer in the Premiership, with over 250 goals, nigh on a hundred more than the Premier League's second highest goalscorer, Andy Cole. Shearer is a throwback to the old style of centre forward in that he is rumbustious and barnstorming. He doesn't possess the physical build of Lofthouse or Charles, but he is strong and very difficult to knock off the ball, and he is devastating in the air, where immaculate timing enables him to beat taller defenders and direct the ball with power at goal. Target man is a glib phrase that rolls off the tongue these days, but Alan made for a superb one, in much the same way as Geoff Hurst did. Like Hurst, Shearer has perfected the role of an attacker running free to latch on to balls played out of midfield, before turning goalwards to inflict maximum damage. It sounds easy, but you need to be a special type of player to do this. For a start there is a vast amount of running involved in being available at all times for passes out of midfield or defence. Once on the end of a pass, the first touch is crucial. Shearer's first touch is excellent, and his ability to get the ball under control and played in front of him, all in one swift movement, has given him the edge over defenders. There are some forwards who run for the sake of it, but Shearer knows just how and where to run to upset the equilibrium of a defence. This is an invaluable asset in that it provides a great many opportunities for team-mates.

Sometimes footballers think they can't win with the press. Should they commit a misdemeanour journalists lambaste them. Should a player live a quiet family life and have an unstained character, as is the case with Shearer, he suffers from being labelled a bore and is accused of having no character. Because of the saturation coverage of football by the media, supporters tend to think they know players. Invariably, they don't. This is very much the case where Alan Shearer is concerned. Alan was once referred to in one national newspaper as being 'the Steve Davis of English football', an epithet as unfitting as it was unwarranted. Personally speaking, I have never found the former World Champion snooker player to be boring, and I feel the same about Shearer.

Alan has also often been accused of having no sense of humour. A Geordie without a keen sense of humour? That would be a first. He possesses a ready and incisive wit as evidenced during an incident in 1997 when, after at one stage having enjoyed a twelve-point lead at the top of the Premiership, Newcastle United finally succumbed to the challenge of Manchester United.

Alan Shearer was walking towards his car at the Newcastle training ground, fielding questions from a local reporter. Displaying sycophancy and optimism in equal measure, the local journo made an oblique reference to Newcastle blowing the Championship but also to the resolution of the club by saying to Shearer:

'If at first you don't succeed . . .'

'That's the end of you skydiving,' replied Shearer, quick as a flash.

When conducting interviews as a player Shearer is often guarded, although I think his caution has as much to do with not wanting to run foul of club PR policy as it does any mistrust of the media (after all, television can't misquote you). Clubs today demand that players 'toe the party line' because anything a player says that is even mildly controversial or that is deemed to be detrimental to his club can affect the club's share price, or cause concern among supporters. Fans need to be kept 'onside' not just with regard to attending games but if they are to patronise the many commercial activities generated by clubs these days. I think Alan Shearer has always been mindful of his responsibilities in this respect. If you only tend to get the truth from politicians after their retirement, or when they have given up all hope of achieving a post in the cabinet, so it is with footballers, who only tend to come out with the real story once they have hung up their boots. It is to be hoped that following his retirement Alan Shearer will be less guarded and more truthful when asked for his opinions on the game.

Being a centre forward is one of the few areas in life where it is acceptable to be selfish. All good centre forwards have a selfish streak in them. They may well be team players at heart but their head tells them when an opportunity for a shot at goal arises, you have to go for it. Confidence is another key element to the role. Ron McGarry was a centre forward with Newcastle United in the mid-sixties but had served several other clubs as well. McGarry was so confident in his ability to score goals he had business cards printed and handed them to opponents. Written on the card was his name followed by the catchphrase 'Have Goals Will Travel' – a phrase borrowed from a television Western series of the time featuring a bounty hunter called Paladin, who brandished cards that bore the line, 'Have Gun Will Travel'.

I wonder what today's press would make of a sixteen-year-old centre forward who scored fourteen goals on his debut for Manchester United's youth team? That happened to a lad called Tommy Spratt (you couldn't make it up) who, during the 1957–8 season, scored fourteen on his debut in a 25-0 victory for United's youth team. Spratt never made the grade at Old Trafford and spent his career in the lower divisions. All of which goes to prove that in football early promise is no indicator of a pro in the making. Young players who scored a huge number of goals when playing in a club's junior team was not unusual years ago. In 1956–7 I scored 122 goals in a single season for the Chelsea youth team. In the sixties Dominic Sharkey made his name as a centre forward with Sunderland. Nicky Sharkey, as he was to become known, scored 140 goals in a single season for the Sunderland junior side in 1961. He also equalled the club's individual scoring record in League football when netting five times in a 7-1 victory over Norwich City in 1962–3 – a club record he shares to this day with the great Charles Buchan.

If a sixteen-year-old of today scored as many goals in a season as Sharkey – or myself – agents would be beating a path to his door with promises of a Porsche and a celebrity lifestyle. At the end of the season in which I scored 122 goals, the Chelsea manager Ted Drake told me he was deliberating as to whether or not to offer me professional terms. I was by no means certain that he would, as in the previous season Ted had released a young centre forward by the name of Joe Baker. The rule of thumb is that those who play in the same position as that occupied by a manager in his days as a player will improve as players. This is simply because the manager will know from personal experience more about what is required to play in that particular position than any other in the team. When Ted Drake told me he wasn't sure about me I was more than a tad concerned. Many thought Joe Baker had a great future ahead of him as a centre forward – a view not shared by Ted, who up to that time had been one of the greatest centre forwards English football had ever produced. In the event Ted was proved wrong about Joe who, on leaving Chelsea, signed for Hibernian and went on to play for Torino, Arsenal,

Nottingham Forest and Sunderland, and won eight caps for England.

The fact that Ted Drake did sign me as a professional had much to do with the scout who had taken me to Chelsea. That was Jimmy Thompson, the best scout since Baden-Powell who, on learning of Ted Drake's indecision about me, stormed into the manager's office and demanded he sign me. Football history contains numerous instances of young centre forwards having been rejected by one club, only to go on to achieve considerable success with another. The most notable example is that of Geoff Hurst. Geoff was told by Fulham manager Bedford Jezzard that he was releasing him because, in the opinion of Jezzard, Geoff didn't have 'the necessary' to make it as a professional at Craven Cottage. Geoff left Fulham and was taken on at West Ham United and the rest . . . well, I think you know the rest.

Rodney Marsh began his career at Fulham in the early sixties. The Fulham manager of the time, Vic Buckingham, was watching Fulham reserves against Birmingham City reserves, a game in which Rodney Marsh had been given to displaying one or two party tricks. At half-time Buckingham tore a strip off Rodney, asking his young centre forward what the hell he thought he was playing at.

'Just trying to entertain the supporters,' replied Rodney.

'If I wanted players to go out on the pitch and entertain, I'd go to Billy Smart's and sign two clowns,' said Buckingham.

'You've got a first team full of them, what would you want two more for?' Rodney asked.

Needless to say for all his abundance of talent, after that remark to his manager Rodney found first-team opportunities for him at Fulham rather limited. A few weeks later he was again turning out for Fulham reserves in a Football Combination game on a Wednesday afternoon. There were only a few hundred spectators in the ground, one of whom was the football writer Tony Stratton-Smith. Tony spotted the QPR manager Alec Stock sitting alone in the stand. Stock was as always in relaxed mode, his arms casually draped across the back of the empty seats either side of him. Smelling a story, Tony approached Stock.

'Got your eye on anyone in particular, Alec?'

'No,' said Stock casually.

'Come on, Alec, there must be some reason for you being here. Managers don't take time out to watch Fulham reserves for no reason at all,' ventured Stratton-Smith.

'Ah, that is where you are wrong, Tony. I do,' replied Stock. 'If you can spend a perfectly useless afternoon in a perfectly useless way, you have learned how to live.'

On hearing that reply, Stratton-Smith gave it up as a bad job and left Stock to his seemingly pointless musings. Three days later Alec Stock signed Rodney Marsh for Queens Park Rangers. He developed into a fabulous ball-playing centre forward who possessed the nous, vision and skill of the most cerebral of players, and was to become one of the most gifted and entertaining players of his generation. Marsh became a legend at Loftus Road, ending up the most revered and celebrated player in the history of the club. Alec Stock saw potential in Rodney Marsh, as he later said in his autobiography: 'When I first saw Marsh I immediately saw a great player in the making.' Seemingly, Vic Buckingham didn't. Alec Stock left Queens Park Rangers in 1968 and became manager of Luton Town, and later Bournemouth. As for Vic Buckingham, he left Fulham to manage Barcelona. Funny old game.

Continuing the Fulham theme, one of the greatest larger-than-life characters ever to grace English football was the Fulham centre forward Trevor 'Tosh' Chamberlain. I got to know Tosh during my days at Chelsea. They broke the mould when they made Tosh. He had a heart as big as a bucket, knew no fear and was what one used to term a robust centre forward. Tosh was a decent goalscorer for Fulham with an average of just under a goal every other game. However, he also displayed an errant clumsiness and a penchant for verbal faux pas. It was as if Tommy Cooper had met Sam Goldwyn on a football pitch. Tosh was never an automatic choice for Fulham at centre forward, but throughout his career at Craven Cottage he rarely missed a game for the first team or reserves through injury. A fact taken up by Desmond Hackett of the *Daily Express*, who once asked Tosh his secret: 'I eat a piccalilli and mustard sandwich,' said Tosh. 'When you have eaten one of those, it takes your mind off a tweaked hamstring, I can tell ya.'

Tosh Chamberlain's humour was legendary. In 1957–8 Tosh scored 13 goals in 27 appearances for Fulham. It was the era of the maximum wage, which at the time was £20 a week. Needless to say, Tosh wasn't on the maximum wage at Fulham and the fact that he played in a little over half of Fulham's first-team matches that season meant he and his family often existed on meagre reserve-team money. At the time the skiffle clubs that were once prominent around Fulham and Chelsea had given away to blues singers. Tosh was talking wages one day with Fulham team-mate Eddie Lowe, bemoaning his financial situation.

'You know them blue singers, Eddie?' said Tosh. 'I'm on such poor money here, they come round to my house when they've got writer's block!'

Fed up with the wage he was on, Tosh asked for a meeting with the Fulham chairman Tommy Trinder, with a view to getting a pay rise.

'All the time I've been at this club, I've asked you for nothing,' said Tosh.

'Yes, and still you ask more,' replied Trinder, quick as a flash.

Tosh Chamberlain made for what reporters call great copy. Moments into the second half of a game against Leeds United, the ball landed just outside the Fulham penalty area. Tosh, back to help his defence, was the first to react. He sprinted towards the bouncing ball as the Fulham goalkeeper Tony Macedo left his line. Tosh's speed won the day and he reached the still bouncing ball just before Macedo. Normally in such a situation one of two things would happen: the outfield player would either lift the ball into the hands of his goalkeeper with a deft touch of the foot, or he would turn sideways on to the advancing keeper and put it into Row G. However, Tosh, on reaching the ball, bent his head forward, jumped six inches off the ground and, mustering all his weight, strength and technique into one combined effort, blasted the ball into the midriff of Macedo, who by then was only two feet away. The crowd let out a collective gasp, but it was nothing compared with the one emitted by Tony Macedo, who hit the ground like a bag of hammers, unable to breath as the air left his body in one cannonball rush. The Fulham trainer took to his toes, and the St John Ambulance men in their long black coats began what was always their comic waddle of stifled urgency. Fulham's Bobby Keetch, however, was first on the scene.

'What the hell you doing?' asked Keetch.

Tosh stood confused and bewildered, arms out wide, the palms of his hands turned upwards.

'I looked up, saw the goal and me head went. I thought I'd have a go,' opined Tosh. 'I forgot we'd changed ends.'

Football has changed irrevocably since I began my career at Chelsea. The game itself has changed and so too have the roles of the individual positions. In the era of Nat Lofthouse and John Charles the job of a centre forward was to score goals, more than any other member of the team. The passing of judgement on the worth of a centre forward was informed simply by how many goals he scored. Throughout the forties and fifties the leading four or five goalscorers in each division were invariably centre forwards. The First Division's leading marksmen were all centre forwards: Ronnie Allen (West Brom), Gordon Turner (Luton), Bobby Smith (Spurs), Jimmy Murray (Wolves), Tommy Taylor (Manchester United), Jackie Mudie (Blackpool) and, of course, Lofthouse.

In 1958–9 English football experienced a change in the make-up of its goalscorers. It was in that season that I, an inside forward, topped the list of leading scorers in the First Division. I wasn't to be the only inside forward to overtake centre forwards in the goalscoring stakes. Others, such as Peter Dobing (Blackburn Rovers), Johnny Fantham (Sheffield Wednesday), Len White (Newcastle United) and Denis Viollet (Manchester United), were all prolific marksmen, but I was the first inside forward of the post-war years to become the leading goalscorer in the First Division. The following season, 1959–60, Dennis Viollet emulated that achievement. I was then the leading goalscorer in the First Division for four of the following five seasons (1960–1 to 1964–5). In 1965–6 another inside forward, Roger Hunt of Liverpool, topped the list of leading marksmen in the First Division.

The change in emphasis from centre forwards to inside forwards becoming leading goalscorers was all down to the 'Revie plan'. In the mid- to late fifties, Don Revie formed a highly effective partnership at Manchester City with Ken Barnes in which Revie fulfilled the role of a deep-lying centre forward, allowing Barnes to exploit the space in front of him. The ploy was nothing new. It was in effect a version of the tactic Hungary had deployed to such devastating effect against England in 1953. The Hungarian centre forward Nandor Hidegkuti had played a very deep role, while Ferenc Puskas, ostensibly an inside forward, pushed on. The tactic was simple enough but to an England team that played in a straitjacket 'WM' formation of two full backs, three half backs and five forwards, in which the job of a defender was to mark his opposite number, it caused chaos. The England centre half Harry Johnston didn't know who he should be marking because the guy he had been allotted to pick up, Hidegkuti, came nowhere near him.

The Revie plan came to fruition in the 1956 FA Cup final between Manchester City and Birmingham City. Don Revie's inclusion in the Manchester City team was in itself indicative of another age. He was a last-minute replacement for Bill Spurdle, who was the hapless victim of boils. When was the last time you ever saw someone with a boil, let alone a plethora of them? I wonder what sort of story today's press would make of, say, Chelsea's Frank Lampard missing a Cup final due to boils. An attack of boils is suggestive of another age, as is the fact that Manchester City were upfront in revealing the real reason for Spurdle's omission. I suppose the reason for this is simply down to the fact that boils at that time were common and nobody thought anything untoward of it. If a player of today missed a Cup final due to such an ailment it would have comic overtones.

So, thanks to boils, Don Revie played in the 1956 FA Cup final and seized the opportunity with both hands. Adopting a role similar to that of Hidegkuti, Revie chose the occasion to give one of the finest performances of his career. Playing as a deep-lying centre forward, Revie's skilful assortment of long and short passes, timed and measured to perfection, probed ceaselessly into the Birmingham defence; while his shrewd positioning in midfield enabled him to collect, relabel and redispatch the long throws of his goalkeeper Bert Trautmann to his fellow-conspirators lurking deep in the Birmingham half of the field. Manchester City's triumph was that of Revie and his plan.

As I have previously intimated, in the fifties English football came of age. Just as in society, changes were taking place, but they didn't happen overnight. It took a year or two before the role of the centre forward was to change from that of the swashbuckling, robust, 'run through a brick wall' ace goal-getter to that of a more measured and cerebral player, whose contribution was to the team ethic. In 1958–9 centre forwards were still expected to score goals, but that was only a part of their new-found role. They were also expected to hold the ball and lay it off, or run and create space for other forwards. And so inside forwards such as myself, Dennis Viollet, Johnny Fantham and Peter Dobing assumed the role of goal-getters. There was another reason for this and that was to do with the fact that in the fifties the build and strength of players had become more standardised. Around that time food became plentiful and more varied. Generally people had more money to spend on what were termed essentials, and soon we would have 'disposable income'. The diet of the nation changed, and as a result so did that of the footballer. In schools football the biggest lads tend to get picked for the football team; those with exceptional talent also. A slight lad who possesses a modicum of football ability can be overlooked in preference to a bigger, stronger lad who is able to cope with other big strong lads. In many respects that was true of centre forwards in professional football in the thirties, forties and early fifties. As previously stated there were two types: tanks, who sent centre halves bouncing off them, and wee 'uns in the tradition of Hughie Gallacher, who liked the ball given to them 'on the carpet'. But the basic function of both kinds of centre forward was the same: to score goals and plenty of them.

In the late fifties the old-time centre forwards of the 'WM' formations, who were lighthouses of the forward line, were asked to be deeper-playing stylists that could help to direct operations. Of course, they were still expected to score goals themselves, but the sole burden for that was no longer on their broad shoulders. With tactics a growing influence in the sixties, the centre forward was often part of three strikers in a 4-3-3 formation or a deep-lying player in a 4-4-2. And so the role evolved. In the seventies centre forwards hunted in pairs. Working in tandem, they usually combined the attributes of big 'un and a little 'un, as in the cases of John Toshack and Kevin Keegan at Liverpool, and Joe Jordan and Jimmy Greenhoff at Manchester United. It is a combination that has proved durable throughout the myriad changes that have taken place in the game in recent years. One of its most effective recent examples is that of Niall Quinn and Kevin Phillips at Sunderland who, up to Quinn's retirement in 2002, formed a highly useful partnership.

Faced with the speed of the game today I have heard it said that centre forwards need to be quicker of mind and foot, and more mobile in order for them to cause 'maximum disruption to organised defences'. I don't think that is anything new. Drogba of Chelsea or Wayne Rooney of Manchester United, albeit different in their individual styles, fulfil roles not dis-similar to those of the centre forwards of yesteryear, in that they look to run into space and receive the ball. Sometimes that is in a forward position, at other times it is deep-lying. They are both great naturals. Naturally born centre forwards shoot and score at a least-expected moment, when many a player would be looking to lay the ball off or for an opening in which to shoot. They do that because the mark of a good goalscorer is that he always expects the unexpected and is primed and ready to exploit.

There are still great centre forwards in the game today, such as Thierry Henry, Wayne Rooney, Didier Drogba, Michael Owen and Ruud van Nistelrooy. Each has his own individual style, and each will perform a specific role for his respective club. In the final analysis football is a simple game and, irre-spective of the role a centre forward is asked to fulfil, he is still expected to score goals. As for his role in the team, that will be the brainchild of the coach, or the result of a theory. It's like my old Spurs team-mate Alan Gilzean once said: 'As forwards, we are subjected to all manner of tactics and theories as to what we should be doing in a game. But the measure of a good tactic is, it should be easily explained to a barmaid.'

CHAPTER FOUR

He was 'a goalkeeper in the flower of youth' – I suppose they meant a crocus, as he only came out once a year and then only briefly

In 1990 there were two foreign goalkeepers on the books of clubs in what was then the First Division, and neither was a first-choice. In 2005 there were thirty-nine foreign goalkeepers with Premiership clubs. Of the twenty first-choice goalkeepers in the Premiership in 2005, seven were English and one (Shay Given) was Irish. It concerns me that less than a third of the first-choice goalkeepers in the Premiership in 2005 were eligible to play for England. And you hear people ask, 'Why can't England produce great goalkeepers any more?'

Some countries are renowned for producing certain quality: France for cuisine, Italy its fashion, Germany its cars. British, in particular English, football was noted for the quality of its goalkeepers. Sadly, that is no longer the case. The dearth of top-quality goalkeepers today can be attributed to a number of factors. As we've seen these days many managers hold down a job at a club for two, perhaps three years. Most pay lip service to youth development simply because the average manager knows he is unlikely to see the young players come to fruition. Directors and supporters, and even the media nowadays, demand instant success. Some managers may lay down plans for the long term, but the majority opt for the 'quick fix'. As a result, managers are reluctant to give young players a chance. This is especially true of goalkeepers, occupying as they do a crucial position in a team.

In my day as a player and throughout the seventies and eighties, managers would take a chance on a young goalkeeper at the end of a season. In 1966–7 the Leicester City manager Matt Gillies played three youngsters in the final four games of the campaign. One of those young lads was a seventeen-year-old goalkeeper – Peter Shilton. (Peter had actually made his Leicester debut in the previous season when only sixteen years old.)

The reason why Peter Shilton was given that opportunity at such a tender age was all to do with how international matches were organised at that time. At the age of sixteen, Peter had established himself in the Leicester City reserve team. The Leicester first-team keeper was Gordon Banks, who was also Alf Ramsey's number-one choice for the national side. England played home international matches on a Wednesday evening, or, in the case of the Home International Championship, on a Saturday afternoon. Alf's squad would arrive at the England headquarters on the Sunday preceding the match, so had either three days or a whole week to prepare. Should a club have a match in that time it went ahead in the absence of their international players, English or otherwise. There was one famous incident in 1966: when hearing of the England squad for a forthcoming international, West Ham manager Ron Greenwood telephoned Alan Hardaker, the dreadnought secretary of the Football League. Greenwood pointed out that three of his players – Bobby Moore, Geoff Hurst and Martin Peters (hardly lightweights in the West Ham team) – would be on England duty, and requested that their League game that day be postponed.

'Postponed? Because you have three players out?' said Hardaker incredulously. 'What the bloody hell do you think you've got a reserve team for?'

Hardaker's hard-line approach to requests for games to be postponed because of players' international commitments was actually beneficial to young players. With Gordon Banks on duty for England, the young Peter Shilton was given an early opportunity in the Leicester City first team to show what he could do. For the record, Peter made his debut in 1966 against Everton, the FA Cup winners that year, and kept a clean sheet.

The sixties and seventies were a golden period for British goalkeeping and one of the reasons for that was young keepers were given these early opportunities. Pat Jennings made his name with Spurs and Arsenal but his League debut came at the age of seventeen with Watford, and Ray Clemence was eighteen when he first played in goal for Scunthorpe United. Pat and Ray were exceptional goalkeepers, as were Shilton and Banks. Other keepers who can be classified as 'very good' also made their League debuts when in their teens – Peter Bonetti (Chelsea), Jim Montgomery (Sunderland), Peter Grummitt (Nottingham Forest), Gary Sprake and David Harvey (both Leeds United) and Phil Parkes (QPR) are all examples. A goalkeeper will reach his peak around the age of twenty-nine, but in order to do that he must have been playing first-team football for at least seven years. That was the case with Shilton, Bonetti and Co., but it doesn't happen now because managers are reluctant to take a chance on a young keeper.

While in the past League fixtures took place on the occasion of an England game, now the Premiership will take a sabbatical for a fortnight (and many Championship games will be postponed as well). English cricket and rugby union continue as normal when players are on international duty. This gives youngsters a chance in the first team and makes for a more open league. Unlike the Premiership, domestic cricket and rugby union are not dominated by one or two clubs.

Football managers today will look for an easy answer. It is less bother and is safer to pay £400,000 for an experienced goalkeeper from Italy or Estonia than spend time and money on the development of a home-grown keeper. An experienced pro will rarely, if ever, have a really bad game. On occasions he may not play to his usual standard, but he won't have a stinker.

That's not true of young players, who are notoriously fickle, on song one game, virtually anonymous the next. Knowing young players to be inconsistent, with so much at stake in every game, managers today are not as willing to risk playing a young goalkeeper. That is why many opt to buy experience, and if the keeper comes from Eastern Europe the fee involved is usually within the means of most clubs.

The easy availability of experienced goalkeepers from overseas has resulted in many clubs not only acquiring them as first-choice keepers, but as cover as well. Hence another door is closed to young home-grown goalkeepers, many of whom find they can't even get a game in their club's reserve team. Who are Jon Masalin, Kevin Ellegaard, Yves Makalambay, Cedric Berthelin, Martin Herrera, Jeremy Ban, Patrice Luzi-Bernardi, Raman Shaaba, Cristian Ricardo, Arni Arason, Harald Wapenaar, Lars Hirschfeld, Shwan Jalal and Simon Miotto? Even the most ardent football fan would be hard pressed to recognise that all those players were foreign goalkeepers on the books of Premiership clubs at the start of the 2004–5 season. They total fourteen keepers and the list is by no means comprehensive. Not one of them was first choice at their respective clubs and it is extremely doubtful whether any will establish themselves in the Premiership. Is English football so impoverished of talented young goalkeepers that we have to import players even to act as cover for the first-choice? Their presence is a bar to young English goalkeepers, and, I say it again, people wonder why this country doesn't produce quality goalkeepers any more. Young English keepers are not being given the chance to play first-team football, or even reserve-team football, and as long as that situation is allowed to continue, we shall not see the likes of Banks, Shilton and Clemence again.

Though the standard of goalkeeping in English football today leaves something to be desired, generally speaking keepers are of a much higher calibre than in the fifties. The level of goal-keeping in English football was at its zenith from the late sixties to the eighties. Gordon Banks was the first goalkeeper to really study the position. Banksy didn't have a coach to help him and much of what he achieved in the game was down to his own dedication and hard work. Gordon made a concerted effort to analyse the role and in effect turned the art of goalkeeping into a science. I played against and with Banksy on many occasions and, having seen him conduct his personal training, one thing stood out for me. When normal training is done many players stay behind to indulge in personal practice of skills. Invariably, this only involves practising the things they are good at. Rarely do players spend countless hours working at those aspects of their game which they consider weak. Banksy was different. He would spend untold hours on the training pitch working at the parts of his game he thought needed improving. In many respects Banksy's quest to become the best goalkeeper in the world was a rite of passage. There was no template to follow, and no specialist goalkeeping coaches to offer him advice. Most people recognise Gordon Banks as being one of the greatest goalkeepers in the world, if not the greatest, but he was also a goalkeeping pioneer, setting the standard for all others. It is no coincidence that Peter Shilton was once the understudy to Banksy at Leicester City. Credit to Peter, he learned from Gordon and, through his own ideas and dedication, took the science of goalkeeping on to another threshold

When I first made it into the Chelsea team the goalkeeper was Reg Matthews. Reg was a decent keeper for that time. He won five caps and has the distinction of never having played on a losing side with England. Reg was a good shot-stopper, but I have to say he was the worst kicker of a dead ball I ever came across. When taking a goal kick on a muddy pitch Reg would grunt and groan as he put everything behind the kick. Occasionally the ball would bounce before it left the penalty area. When it did leave his penalty area it did so by a matter of a few yards. It was pointless forwards like Ron Tindall and myself waiting on the halfway line for one of Reg's kicks to come our way. Instead we had to drop so deep to receive the ball we were only just outside our own penalty area. After Reg had kicked the ball all hell would break loose about twenty-five yards from our goal, as players from both sides fought for possession. Despite constant complaints Reg insisted upon taking goal kicks himself, but these put us under so much pressure that the players finally resorted to ganging up on him in the dressing room. Only after lengthy protestations was Reg eventually compliant. He agreed to let our full backs, Peter and John Sillett, take goal kicks for him.

When I was first picked for the England team during a tour of South America in 1959, the goalkeeper was Bolton's Eddie Hopkinson. He was a good goalkeeper, as can be seen by his performance in the first game of that tour, against Brazil, when he pulled-off four excellent saves to deny Pele. I watched the game from the stands, unaware that I would be making my England debut in the next match against Peru. Brazil beat England 2-0, but had it not been for Eddie's heroics they might have won by six or seven. Towards the end of the game the Brazilian forward Julinho was put clear through on goal. Eddie came racing out to narrow the angle and, in a forerunner to the Macedo–Chamberlain incident, was poleaxed when Julinho let fly with a thunderbolt only three yards from him. At the time Brazilian radio commentators were supported by colleagues near the touchline and it was acceptable for these additional commentators to come on to the pitch when play was halted and get comments from players. As Eddie lay there gasping for breath, a bevy of these supplementary radio men joined England trainer Harold Shepherdson in rushing on to the pitch. While Harold administered treatment they tried to interview Eddie. It was just as well they couldn't understand his direct comments, delivered in broad Lancastrian. As one of the commentators later asked Walter Winterbottom during the post-match press conference, 'Your go'lkeeper, Horp-kinsun. What he mean when he say "Blue-dee Nor-ah"?'

When playing for Bolton Wanderers against Manchester United at Old Trafford, Eddie Hopkinson was involved in an incident that resulted in what must be one of the most fortuitous goals ever scored in football. Unfortunately, it was against him. A Manchester United attack had broken down and with the ball safe in Eddie's hands, his team-mates and the United forwards turned their backs on him, as they started to make their way towards the halfway line. Eddie slipped as he kicked the ball upfield and instead of it sailing deep into the United half of the field, it shot like a bullet towards the United centre forward Alex Dawson, who, his back turned to Eddie and blissfully unaware of anything untoward, was beginning to make his way out of the Bolton penalty area. The ball left Eddie's boot like a house brick fired from a cannon and hit Alex square on the back of the head. His two crowned front teeth shot from his mouth as he was lifted off his feet and propelled forward. Having hit Alex on the back of the head, the ball flew in the opposite direction and sailed over Eddie Hopkinson, stranded near the edge of his penalty area, before looping into the net. For a split second the goal was treated with silent disbelief by the 63,000-strong Old Trafford crowd, as they got their heads round what had happened. Then the roar went up. Alex, meanwhile, lay prostrate, face down in the Old Trafford mud, his legs and arms splayed wide. On hearing the roar of the crowd, the only movement he was capable of making was to raise a hand six inches off the ground to acknowledge the cheers of the United supporters.

There is a postscript to this tale of goalkeeping woe and it involves a young lad who was on the Manchester United groundstaff at the time. The lad in question was none other than George Best. One of George's duties was to clean the boots of the senior pros and the following morning he was doing just that when Alex Dawson entered the room. George

nodded good morning but was too embarrassed to say anything to Alex. He couldn't very well say, 'Great goal last night,
Alex', because it had been farcical, especially as they had only
been able to find one of Alex's front teeth. So George busied
himself cleaning Alex's boots while the United centre forward
read the morning newspaper. Eventually, Alex looked up from
his paper.

'Aren't you going to say "Well done", for my goal last night?'
asked Alex.

'Yeah, of course,' said George, feeling even more embarrassment. 'You took it well.'

George expected Alex to say what a lucky goal it had been,
but that wasn't Alex. 'Yeah, well, when you've been in the
game for as long as I have you get an instinct for things,' said
Alex drily. 'You don't even have to be facing the ball to score.'

Facing penalties is all part of the job of a goalkeeper but one
Chelsea youth-team keeper made a habit of it – in a single
match. Willie Brewster was a junior with Chelsea in the mid-
fifties. In 1955 when playing for Chelsea's youth team against
Dunstable Town, Willie faced five penalty kicks in the course
of the game and saved four of them. Chelsea won the match
4-3, but to the best of my knowledge Willie Brewster was never
offered pro terms at the club and drifted into non-league football.

There have been plenty of unusual and humorous incidents
with goalkeepers and penalties. One such involved Walsall
centre forward Tony Richards. He was playing for the Saddlers
at Swindon Town in 1958 when his side won a penalty.
Richards stepped forward to take it and duly scored. A few
minutes later the Walsall goalkeeper John Savage was injured
and had to leave the field. As there were no substitutes, Tony
Richards went in goal. He had only been deputising for ten
minutes when Swindon were awarded a penalty. It was really
Richards' day because, fittingly, he saved the Swindon spot

kick. An outfield player scoring a penalty then saving a penalty all within the space of fifteen minutes? Who wouldn't pay good money to see that?

On the subject of goalkeepers and penalties, I once incurred the wrath of Gordon Banks. Actually it is not strictly true to say I did it once. It was twice. The first was on the eve of Banksy's England debut against Scotland at Wembley in 1963. On the Friday morning before the game we trained at Stamford Bridge. At the end of the session Alf Ramsey ordered everyone on to the team coach, but the press and TV boys wanted a shot of England's new goalkeeper in action, and asked Alf if Banksy could stay behind just for a few minutes for a photo call. Alf agreed to this, and I volunteered to put Banksy through his paces. The manager said there was only time for one shot, and it was agreed that I would take a penalty so the media could have their shot of Banksy in action.

'I'll place the ball to your right, at about waist level,' I told Banksy. 'Do the spectacular bit; it'll make for a good photograph.'

Just as I made contact with the ball Banksy dived somewhat dramatically to his right. I can still see the look of surprise and horror on his face as I placed the ball to his left. As soon as it hit the back of the net Alf was on the pitch calling for us to join the rest of the lads on the team coach. I turned and walked, leaving an embarrassed Banksy forlorn on the ground. To be fair to Banksy he took it all in good part. Most photographic editors cropped the photograph to omit the ball, but a couple of Saturday-morning newspapers ran with a picture of Banksy flinging himself to his right and the ball entering the net to his left.

'It makes me look a right prat', Banksy told me on seeing the photographs.

'Lesson learned', I told him. 'Never expect a forward to do what you expect him to do.'

In 1964–5 Spurs played Leicester City on the final day of

the season. Neither side had a chance of winning the Championship and, as both were well clear of relegation, the two teams took it upon themselves to entertain what was a decent end-of-season White Hart Lane crowd of 33,000. Spurs were leading 5-2 with about ten minutes of the match remaining, when we were awarded a penalty. Cliff Jones had helped himself to a hat-trick; I'd scored one and fancied another, so I stepped up to take the penalty. As I did, I noticed Banksy had his back to me. He was by his left-hand post, wiping the palms of his hands on the grass inside the goal. For a bit of a laugh, I stepped up and dinked the ball with the toe-end of my boot into the opposite corner of Banksy's goal. The crowd saw the joke in this and, when the ball crossed the line, offered an ironic cheer. To everyone's amazement, however, the referee blew his whistle and awarded the goal. Peals of laughter swept down from the terraces and the players of both teams fell about laughing; all except for one, that is. Banksy was livid. He sprinted up the pitch in pursuit of the referee, and it didn't take long for Banksy to catch him.

'You can't give that. I had my back to the play. I wasn't ready. It's a bloody ridiculous decision,' remonstrated Banksy.

'Goal given,' said the referee.

'How can you give a goal?' asked Banksy.

'I played advantage,' explained the referee.

'Played advantage?' said Banksy incredulously. 'From a penalty?'

'Played advantage,' reiterated the referee. 'Best law there is. Allows a referee to ignore all the other rules for the good of the game.'

As a forward whose prime job it was to score goals I experienced goalkeepers at close range. I appreciated the technique and talent of a top-class keeper, and their worth to a team, but I am not so sure some leading managers always did. One man who did appreciate the value of a top-quality goalkeeper to his side was the Stoke City manager Tony Waddington, who signed both Gordon Banks and Peter Shilton. Waddington once said that having Banks in his team was worth 25–30 goals to Stoke in terms of the number not conceded. He signed Banks and Shilton in an era when many managers would happily spend considerable amounts of money on outfield players, but were reluctant to spend what, in relative terms, would be a modest fee on a top-drawer goalkeeper.

That was still largely the case throughout the seventies and eighties, and to some extent it still applies today. One only has to look at the goalkeepers fielded by Arsenal and Manchester United as they battled with one another, and subsequently Chelsea, for the Premiership title for proof of that. When Arsenal met Manchester United in the Premiership in February 2005 they produced a classic game of football. United won 4-2 and the level of technique, skill and application from both sides was of the highest order, except where the respective goalkeepers were concerned. In comparison to the high quality of the outfield players, United's Roy Carroll and Manuel Almunia of Arsenal, both goalkeepers, appeared decidedly ordinary. Given the performance of the goalkeepers on the night, some might consider the description of them being 'ordinary' a little flattering. In this particular game Arsenal's Denis Bergkamp cut in from the right and beat Carroll at his near post. Much was said on television and written in the press about how Carroll was beaten at his near post and that Bergkamp's shot had gone through the keeper's legs. As far as I can tell no one mentioned the fact that in coming out to face Bergkamp, Carroll, rather than spreading his body, came out feet first. The mind boggles at the thought of a goalkeeper doing this at such a level: it is, in my opinion, poor goalkeeping technique.

Towards the end of what was a pulsating game, United went ahead when Giggs broke clear on the right. The Arsenal keeper Almunia came racing from his line to meet Giggs when there was no need – Arsenal defenders were already bearing down on the United winger. This left the keeper in no man's land and the Arsenal goal unprotected behind him. Almunia offered a despairing dive in an attempt to block Giggs' cross, but never had an earthly of doing so, such was the gap between him and the United player. With the Arsenal defenders trying manfully to get back and offer cover, Giggs' cross found Ronaldo unmarked at the far post and it was a bread-and-butter tap-in. Neither Roy Carroll nor Manuel Almunia covered themselves in glory that night. Far from it. The performances of these two players were, in fact, indicative of the dilemma both Arsenal and Manchester United faced that season, and in previous years, of having top-quality outfield players but suspect goalkeepers; their respective ages aside, goalkeepers in the 'flower of youth'. Their dilemma was to work in Chelsea's favour as José Mourinho's side went on to win the Premiership. Chelsea boasted a squad with incredible strength in depth, but should one look for another pointer as to why they would win the title that season, rather than Arsenal or Manchester United, it is Carlo Cudicini – a reserve-team keeper better than any goalkeeper Arsenal or Manchester United could call upon.

I played in front of two world-class goalkeepers: Gordon Banks with England and Pat Jennings at Spurs. Playing in front of a top-quality keeper instils confidence in a team. Players are more relaxed because they have implicit faith in their goalkeeper. I also know from personal experience that facing a world-class shot-stopper is problematic for a forward because you know you have to produce something special to beat him. However, it is not only his ability to produce a top-drawer save that gives a quality goalkeeper an edge. It is how few opportunities he presents for a shot at goal. Goalkeepers of the quality of Banks, Shilton, Clemence and Jennings would organise their defences in such a way opportunities for a shot at goal were limited. When you did create that chance for a shot they had worked their angles and lines out to such exactitude in relation to the position of the forward that they offered few, if any, opportunities to shoot into a gap. In such circumstances forwards would usually pass the ball, in the hope of finding a team-mate with a better view on goal.

In 2002 Gordon Banks met with the Brazilian legend Jairzinho. It was the first time the pair had met since the epic game between England and Brazil in the 1970 World Cup, when Banksy produced that miraculous save from a Pele header, which, by the way, was the result of a cross from Jairzinho. The pair recalled that World Cup match and in particular Banksy's save from Pele, which had afforded him worldwide fame. At one point in the conversation Jairzinho said to Banksy, 'People the world over talk of that save. But what they never mention is how many times you thwarted Pele, Tostao and myself by taking up positions so we could not fire a shot at goal. We had never come across such fantastic goal-keeping before.' I told Banksy that for all the plaudits he has received for his goalkeeping, that was the highest praise of all.

As I've said, playing in front of a top-class goalkeeper fills a team with confidence. Players aren't riddled with anxiety or worrying that should they make a mistake it could result in a goal against them. When a team has concerns about their goal-keeper it concentrates the mind wonderfully, but brings uneasiness to every player's game. It also has an adverse effect on the attacking potential of a side because players become wary of pushing up if there is a question mark about the ability of their keeper. Supporters aren't stupid, they quickly suss out players who are not up to the mark. In the case of Arsenal in the 2004–5 season, the ironic cheers occasionally offered by their supporters when Manuel Almunia or Jens Lehmann saved a simple shot should have sent a clear message to Arsène Wenger.

Goalkeeping is arguably the greatest test of character within a team. The goalkeeper is either a hero or a villain, depending on his performance and the presence he exerts in his penalty area. To play at the highest level a keeper must know that he is trusted completely. I cannot see how a number of goalkeepers in the Premiership are able to believe such trust exists among their team-mates, manager or supporters, and I cite Almunia and Carroll as cases in point. I find the fact that two of the top three clubs in the Premiership continued to contest the title with goalkeepers of questionable ability to be mystifying. I am a big fan of Sir Alex Ferguson, who deserves his place in the pantheon of managerial greats, but find it curious that he appeared not to have learned from Manchester United's past in relation to goalkeepers.

Throughout the seventies and eighties Manchester United strove to repeat their 1967 Championship success and subsequent European Cup victory. They boasted outfield players of the calibre of Lou Macari, Gordon McQueen, Sammy McIlroy, Gordon Hill, Martin Buchan, Steve Coppell, Joe Jordan, Jimmy Nicholl and Jimmy Greenhoff, to name but a few. Yet for years United persisted with Gary Bailey in goal. He was a good keeper, but in goalkeeping terms not one of the best, and certainly not in the class of Peter Shilton, Ray Clemence or even Phil Parkes (QPR and West Ham United). Twice during his career, Shilton was in talks with United regarding a move to Old Trafford, and on the second occasion United baulked at the fee being asked by Stoke City. Brian Clough fully realised the benefit of having a top-class goalkeeper and, although Nottingham Forest did not have the financial wherewithal of United, he persuaded his directors at Forest that £275,000 would be money well spent on Shilton.

Manchester United had paid that and more for a number of outfield players, and it still puzzles me why they would refuse to consider such a fee for a goalkeeper such as Shilton. During this period Nottingham Forest went on to win the Football League Championship, the European Cup twice, the League Cup and the World Club Championship, and Clough admitted that the success Forest enjoyed had much to do with their having a world-class goalkeeper in Peter Shilton.

In the eighties when Manchester United contained the likes of Bryan Robson, Ray Wilkins, Kevin Moran, Arnold Muhren, Norman Whiteside, Frank Stapleton, Remi Moses and Gordon McQueen – most of whom were acquired for large fees – Gary Bailey kept goal, before being succeeded by Jim Leighton. United had a succession of quality teams that were assembled at some cost, and yet their holy grail of the Championship remained elusive. I believe it did so because they never invested in a really top-class goalkeeper, and I think it no coincidence that when they did eventually win the League title in 1993, they did so with Peter Schmeichel, a truly out-standing keeper, between the posts.

Since the departure of Schmeichel, Sir Alex Ferguson has called upon the services of various goalkeepers, such as Mark Bosnich, Raymond van der Gouw, Massimo Taibi, Paul Rachubka, Andy Goram, Fabien Barthez, Roy Carroll and Tim Howard, not one of whom, in my eyes, could be termed a real top-quality keeper. Likewise, Arsène Wenger has a galaxy of talent at Arsenal except, that is, where goalkeepers are concerned. While Sir Alex has never found a truly suitable replacement for Schmeichel, neither has Wenger for David Seaman. This is in part because England, for the reasons I have given, is not producing world-class goalkeepers any more.

One of the reasons for the standard of goalkeeping in England not being as high as it once was is down to the type of ball used today. In my day as a player, and in subsequent years, the type of football commonly used was the Mitre Matchplay. When that ball was hit at goal it travelled more or less true; there was very little deviation through the air. Should a goal-keeper's positioning and angles be correct, he would be able to judge the flight of the ball and execute a save. From the fifties through to the eighties, the standard weight for a ball was set at exactly sixteen ounces – the equivalent of 0.45kg. Over the years the weight of a football has gradually decreased. The ball used in the Premiership in recent years, the Nike Total 90 Aerow, is far lighter than the footballs used years ago.

A prototype of the Nike ball was tested at Arsenal some years ago. Under the supervision of their goalkeeping coach Bob Wilson, the Arsenal keepers of the time, David Seaman and John Lukic, were put through their paces. When asked for their opinion of the Nike ball, they said, 'These are joke balls'. Despite reservations, this type of ball was given official approval. Since then the Nike balls have been subjected to further developments and now make life even harder for the modern keeper.

One only has to see a camera view of a shot from behind a goal to see how much the Nike ball swerves and dips through the air. That causes goalkeepers to be constantly adjusting their position and, as this kind of ball deviates in the air so much, it places modern goalkeepers at a disadvantage. So there is an argument in saying that for all the standard of goalkeeping in the English game not being as good as it was, the role of the keeper has been made more difficult by the type of ball being used nowadays. That said, the majority of shots at goal do not come from distance and through the air. I scored the vast majority of my goals by simply passing the ball into the net; the old type of Mitre ball or the new lightweight Nike Total 90 Aerow, it wouldn't have mattered to me.

On more than one occasion my speed took me past defenders and into a one-on-one situation with the opposing goalkeeper, but I always kept something back in the way of pace for those situations. As he came out to dive at my feet I would do one of two things: I would hit the accelerator, and that sudden increase in speed would be enough to take me past the keeper who, having committed himself, could not readjust; or at speed I would drop a shoulder, giving the impression that I was going to check a certain way, and when the keeper changed his positioning I would swerve the other way.

I did this kind of thing countless times, but if the keeper's flailing arms made contact with me not once did I ever think of going to ground. Today I see numerous players who take a dive when presented with a similar situation. The likes of Gordon Banks (Leicester and Stoke), Peter Bonetti (Chelsea), Jim Montgomery (Sunderland), Ron Springett (Sheffield Wednesday), Bob Wilson (Arsenal) and Pat Jennings (Spurs) wouldn't think twice about diving in among the boots of an opponent. However, modern goalkeepers do have to think about it because, whether they make contact or not, there are too many players who will throw themselves forward in the hope of winning a penalty (and invariably they do). Nowadays it is common practice for a forward to dive over a sprawling keeper, which can result in a penalty and the hapless keeper receiving his marching orders. I can't ever remember Pat Jennings, Bill Brown (Spurs) or Gordon Banks taking a player out in such a way, but should they be playing today the chances are they would miss half a season due to dismissals.

Having said the general standard of goalkeeping today is not as good as that of the sixties, seventies and eighties in defence of current goalkeepers the penchant of forwards to dive over a keeper, changes in the laws of the game, such as outlawing the back pass, and the lightweight ball have all served to make keepers more vulnerable. The current trend of rotating squad players doesn't do a goalkeeper any favours, either. Rotation is not good for a keeper as it induces insecurity and anxiety. We all know that an outfield player can make a mistake and get away with it, but a mistake on the part of a goalkeeper will often result in a goal. Rotation compounds anxiety in a keeper because he knows that the slightest error could see him on the bench for the next game and replaced by his rival, who no doubt will be just as jittery. There were several examples of this in the Premiership in 2005: Chris Kirkland and Jerzy Dudek at Liverpool (who also had to contend with the arrival of Scott Carson); Manuel Almunia and Jens Lehmann at Arsenal; Roy

Carroll and Tim Howard at Manchester United; and Richard Wright and Nigel Martyn at Everton. Competition for places is a good thing – it keeps players on their toes – but goalkeepers who know one howler will result in them losing their place in a team end up short on natural confidence. They need this to survive. When Peter Shilton and Ray Clemence played alternate games for England under Ron Greenwood it was because they were world-class goalkeepers and Greenwood wanted to keep the two of them involved. Such was their quality it mattered not one jot to England which one kept goal; they were both superb. Rotating Shilton and Clemence in this way was not ideal, neither keeper was happy with the situation, but it meant both were a part of the England setup. Unlike the situation when Don Revie was England manager and he opted for Clemence rather than Shilton, who got really cheesed off with always being on the bench. Come the 1982 World Cup finals in Spain, Ron Greenwood knew he had to go for continuity to instil one with complete confidence, and opted for Shilton.

When my career began, what I call the old order of goalkeepers was giving way to a new, more athletic and studious breed of keeper. As a teenager I remember playing against Gil Merrick of Birmingham City. Gil was one of the old school, who had won twenty-three caps for England. He had been shattered by the Hungarians, shipping thirteen goals in two games against Puskas and Co. I suppose it says much about the FA selection committee that, having conceded seven against Hungary in Budapest, Merrick retained his place in England's next game, their opening match of the 1954 World Cup finals (a 4-4 draw against Belgium). Though Gil had let in eleven goals in two games (nineteen in five matches), he still kept his place for England's following World Cup match against hosts Switzerland. For the life of me I can't imagine that today an England goalkeeper who had conceded eleven goals in two matches would retain his place in the team. If he did, the mind boggles at what the response of the press would be. To emphasise how quixotic the FA selection committee was, after England's 4-4 draw against Belgium, the selectors had made four changes to the five-man forward line for the match against the Swiss, and yet, barring Bill McGarry for Syd Owen, stuck with the same defence. In fact the back line that conceded four against Belgium had remained unchanged from that of England's 7-1 defeat in the game against the Hungarians.

Given the number of goals Gil Merrick had conceded, one wonders what other goalkeepers of the time, such as Bert Williams (Wolves), Ray Wood (Manchester United), Jim Sanders (West Bromwich Albion) and George Thompson (Preston North End), thought they had to do to be called up for England. With his Brylcreemed short back and sides, and dapper moustache, Gil gave the impression of being a Scotland Yard detective in an English B-movie. Complete with heavy, green turtle-neck jumper and baggy shorts, he appeared to me an anachronism in the late fifties. Yet Gil was a very good goalkeeper in his era, which makes we wonder about the ability of goalkeepers in the forties and early fifties. I didn't start my career in football until the late fifties, but Stanley Matthews, who began his in 1930, once told me that the one area of the game that improved greatly from the forties to his retirement in 1965 was the standard of goalkeeping:

'The goalkeepers who were around when I hung up my boots, such as Gordon Banks, Tony Waiters, Peter Bonetti, Gordon West, Alan Hodgkinson and Ron Springett,' Stan once told me, 'they were all of a much higher standard than those considered to be top keepers in the thirties, forties and fifties. The general standard of goalkeeping improved considerably in my last ten years in the game.'

The level of goalkeeping continued to improve after Stan's retirement in 1965, but until the emergence of Gordon Banks, keepers simply did the same training as every other player. Banksy couldn't excuse himself from daily training but felt that much of it was of little benefit to him. Goalkeeper is a specialist position and Banksy realised he needed specialist training if he was to develop his personal game.

In his early days with Leicester City Banksy used to cajole Frank McLintock and Davie Gibson into helping him train on a Sunday morning. On Sundays the Leicester groundsman Bill Taylor would redress the Filbert Street pitch following the previous day's game. He would start by replacing divots in one goalmouth, then cut the grass and finally roll it, gradually working his way down to the other goalmouth. Bill agreed to allow Banksy, McLintock and Gibson to practise in the goalmouth he wasn't attending, and so the study of the science of goalkeeping began. McLintock and Gibson would put Banksy through his paces for ninety minutes every Sunday morning. Banksy had them fire shots at him from every angle around the penalty area, after which they would shoot from a certain position and a given angle. Banksy made a mental note of the angle at which the ball came towards the goal from the given position and, after a time, found he'd learned the best position to take up for making the save. He also worked on his footwork and realised that the best way to move up and down his line was sideways. That way he didn't lose a vital second adjusting his feet when needing to turn to execute a save.

Having worked on angles and positioning Gordon set about improving his reactions. He'd ask McLintock and Gibson to half-volley the ball at him from about five yards without telling him which side of the goal the ball was going. Banksy discovered he had to position himself differently, according to where in the area the ball had been struck, to make each type of save. He also worked on crosses from both sides, and practised punching the ball under pressure, discovering half a dozen different ways to punch a ball, depending on the circumstances.

The more Banksy learned about goalkeeping, the more he knew there was to learn. On his way to daily training he used to call into a newsagents and buy a morning paper. He always handed the newsagent a pound note and made sure he got plenty of silver in his change. Banksy used that money to pay Leicester apprentices to stay behind and work with him on an afternoon. During one such session he realised that just about every goalkeeper, himself included, stood on or near the goal line, watching a situation develop to which they might suddenly have to react. Working with the apprentices, Banksy learned he could dictate to opposing forwards, rather than have them dictate to him. Having instructed an apprentice to play the ball into the penalty area for a team-mate, he would anticipate the cross or pass by quickly adjusting his position, causing the opponent to change his mind. With Banksy off his line, having taken up a position on the edge of his six-yard box and in front of the intended receiver, the player putting the ball into the area was forced to hit a much wider pass to another team-mate to ensure his side kept possession. That done Banksy would readjust his position accordingly, which made it difficult for the next player to hit a telling ball to a team-mate. Gordon put all this into practice in matches and, believe me, it was revolutionary stuff. Banksy not only became Alf Ramsey's number-one choice for England, but the number-one keeper in the world.

Other goalkeepers watched Banksy in action and began to ask themselves how they too could develop their personal game along such lines. The sixties were a revolutionary time and there was definitely a goalkeeping revolution in that decade. Yet it would be overly simplistic and indeed wrong to imply that there were no good goalkeepers around prior to Banks and Co. There were, but Banks, Shilton and others elevated the standard of goalkeeping to a level hitherto unknown.

When I was growing up the biggest name in goalkeeping was Frank Swift, which was somewhat fitting, given that, at six feet four inches, Swift was himself a big man. Frank was a spectacular goalkeeper, Swift by name and by nature. He was immensely popular with supporters, not least because he often played up to them. He had hands the size of shovels and would pick up the ball one-handed, before throwing it further than I went on my holidays as a boy. After signing professional forms for Manchester City in 1932, he made his debut in 1933 and proved so successful that he didn't miss a match for the next five years. He played in the Manchester City team that won the FA Cup in 1934 and the League Championship in 1937. Frank was only twenty years of age when he played in the Cup final, and ensured his place in football folklore after fainting from what was diagnosed as nervous exhaustion when about to ascend the steps at Wembley to receive his winners' medal. If such a thing happened today there would be chaos. People would be flapping about riddled with concern, as if someone had shot the goalkeeper with a gun, and it would be analysed and debated on television ad infinitum. Matt Busby was in the Manchester City side that day, and he used to tell the story of how, when Swift fainted, the City trainer rushed to his side with a bucket of water. As the trainer lathered Frank's face with a sponge sodden with cold water, the City winger Eric Brook entered the scene.

'Get up!' ordered Brook. 'There's a hundred thousand people here, we've just won the Cup and you're making us look fools.'

No sympathy there then. Brook's attitude to Swift fainting is different to that displayed today when a player is down. Now attitudes have changed, but then it was typical of the era and such an attitude continued into my days as a player. Men of Swift and Brook's generation were the product of harsh working lives and were not readily given to displays of emotion. Football then and in my time was overly physical, and both players and supporters alike considered it 'a man's game'. Should a player be injured he was told by his team-mates to get up and get on with it. If a player was to roll around on the ground following a tackle, his own supporters would give him the bird. They did so because they felt their team was an extension of themselves, their community and their lifestyle. Any player who was thought to display weakness, by succumbing to injury, or fainting, was considered to be a slight on his team-mates and supporters alike. It was as if their pride had been dented, hence Eric Brook's terse reaction to Swift fainting on City's big day.

Frank Swift was a big man in every sense of the word and quickly put the fainting incident behind him. Despite his successes in the early stages of his career, he didn't win international honours until being selected for England in 1943. With wartime games deemed 'unofficial international matches', it was 1946 before he won his first cap for England (when coming up to thirty-three years of age). In 1948 he became the first goalkeeper to captain England, in what was a famous 4-0 victory over Italy in Turin. It is a little-known fact that after the previous match for England – against Scotland at Wembley – Swift had again collapsed. On that day England beat the Scots 2-0 but the game was a personal triumph for Frank Swift, who recovered to play on after being knocked unconscious in a clash with Liverpool's 'Flying Scotsman', Billy Liddell. Following the game, Swift travelled back to his Manchester home by train, but on leaving his train he collapsed on a platform. The stationmaster and his staff were quickly on the scene. While someone was dispatched to telephone for an ambulance, the stationmaster and his colleagues loaded Frank on to a station trolley and, somewhat ignominiously, wheeled the England captain-elect to the station forecourt to await the ambulance. As they waited, the heavens opened and there followed a downpour straight from the Book of Genesis. One member of the station staff removed his coat and draped it over the prostrate Swift, and a well-meaning porter took off his cap and placed it on the goalkeeper's head. Picture the scene as the ambulance finally arrived: the England goalkeeper and captain-elect, lying on a station trolley, draped in an overcoat and wearing a porter's hat on his head . . . and David James thought he suffered humiliation in 2004 in the wake of England's game against Austria.

Before long Frank was rushed to hospital, where it was discovered that, as a result of his clash with Billy Liddell, he was suffering from concussion and had two broken ribs. Such was the humour of Frank Swift he saw the funny side to the trolley incident and would often regale players and press alike with the story. Frank was in his era a great goalkeeper. When he finally retired from football in 1949 after seventeen highly entertaining years at Manchester City, he was a licensee for a time, before becoming a football journalist with the *Empire News*. Sadly, Frank died in the Munich air disaster of 1958. His tragic and untimely death was a source of deep emotion to all who knew him and a matter of sad regret to everyone who appreciated goalkeeping at its best and most entertaining.

I always found it curious that having chosen to play in the most specialist position on the field, many goalkeepers jumped at the chance of playing out in five-a-sides. Conversely, quite a few centre forwards were quick to take their place in goal. Even with England, Gordon Banks enjoyed playing out in practice games, while Bobby Charlton was always first to volunteer to take Banksy's place in goal. Whenever a movie deals with football, even if the actors are decent players, they never look right playing the game because it is very difficult to truly replicate a professional. It's something like this when outfield players take over in goal following an injury to the goalkeeper. I recall one Spurs game when Mike England took over in goal from Pat Jennings. Although Mike threw himself about, came for crosses and didn't let us down that day, he didn't look a goalkeeper, which is a specialist position and for that reason goalkeepers have empathy with one another. There is an unofficial union of goalkeepers in football and always has been. They are aware that one mistake on their part can lose a match and sometimes result in criticism being heaped on their shoulders, so they sympathise with one another's plight. Each understands the unique pressures they face and as a result goalkeepers share a common bond of fraternity that does not exist between, say, strikers or midfield players. Most keepers are quiet and unassuming because they are very much aware that in their position from hero to villain is but one small step. Some, like Peter Schmeichel, are very assertive and will lambaste defenders they feel have exposed them. Occasionally the game will produce a goalkeeper outwardly confident enough in his own ability to the point of being pushy, which reminds me of Bob Dennison, manager of Middlesbrough from 1954 to 1963. A local football reporter once asked him what was the best piece of advice he had ever been given in football.

'To sign Peter Taylor as our goalkeeper,' said Dennison.

'Who told you to do that?' asked the reporter.

'He did,' replied Dennison.

One aspect of the game that has changed little over the years, if at all, is the way goalkeepers get away with murder when challenging for the ball. In jumping to collect a ball in front of an onrushing forward, invariably a goalkeeper will do so with one leg raised and studs showing. Rarely, if ever, is a keeper penalised for this. It was the same in my day as a player and it is still the case now. If an outfield player challenged in such a way, he would be literally brought to book. Goalkeepers will no doubt decry what I have just said, and will cite the many times they have to dive at the boots of an onrushing striker as proof that it is they, rather than opposing forwards, who are not afforded sufficient protection. They have a point, as I feel I do. All of which alludes to something I have always believed about football, namely that the game, rather than being played to a strict set of rules, is played according to a vague consensus of what is and is not acceptable. Goalkeepers who challenge for a ball with a boot raised and studs showing are accepted by players and match officials alike; not so when an outfield player does this. Thus exists one of the many dichotomies of professional football.

That said, the position of goalkeeper is potentially the most dangerous on the field. Many is the keeper whose career has been terminated early by a debilitating injury collected when flinging himself at the boots of an oncoming forward. Tragically, some have even died as a result of such bravery. Goalkeepers expect a buffeting from an opposing forward when challenging for a ball, but such is the way the laws concerning challenges on a goalie are interpreted nowadays, a forward need only brush against a keeper to have a foul given against him. The former Spurs centre forward Bobby Smith used to take delight in making chips of goalkeepers by shoulder charging them into the back of the net. Referees wouldn't tolerate such challenges today, and neither would self-righteous television commentators and pundits. I played alongside Bobby Smith at Spurs and on occasions he was told to go out and purposely 'hit' the opposing goalkeeper, with a view to ruffling his confidence. This was a command that Bobby dutifully carried out, and he wasn't unique in this, as most forwards of yesteryear set out to unsettle the opposing goalkeeper. It was part of the job of a centre forward.

For their part, goalkeepers could dish it out, too. The most extreme case was that of the West Germany goalkeeper Harald 'Toni' Schumacher who, in the 1982 World Cup semi-final against France, made a terrible challenge on Patrick Battiston. The French substitute went for a through-ball on the edge of the West German penalty area, only for Schumacher to go straight through him. Schumacher appeared to make no attempt to play the ball, yet went unpunished while Battiston left the field on a stretcher. Well before this, Brian Clough's career as a player effectively ended on Boxing Day 1962 in a clash with Bury keeper Chris Harker. In what appeared to be a tragic accident, the two collided when competing for a

through-ball. While I am not for one moment saying Harker
set out to intentionally injure Clough, it ended the career of a
gifted centre forward. The point is this: goalkeepers, whether
challenging fairly or unfairly for the ball, can really hammer an
opponent, if not actually cause a serious injury.

Goalkeepers consider the penalty area as their domain and
the good ones like to boss their area. Many of them will even
consider it their job to deal with an opponent who is making a
nuisance of himself in the box. One of the most celebrated
cases of this is that of Gordon West, who kept goal for
Blackpool and Everton. In the late sixties, Leeds United's Jack
Charlton gained notoriety for a certain tactic that he deployed
whenever Leeds won a corner. Jack caused a stir throughout the
game by taking up a position on the goal line and standing
right in front of the opposing goalkeeper. When the corner was
played into the penalty box, Jack would position himself in
such a way as to make it difficult, if not impossible, for the
goalkeeper to reach the ball. This tactic was highly controversial at the time. It was debated at length in the media,
particularly on BBC TV's *Match of the Day* programme where
Jimmy Hill echoed the thoughts of many, saying that although
taking up a position on the goal line in front of the goalkeeper
was not in breach of any rule, Jack's action was 'not in the
spirit of the game'. Arguments raged, but Jack continued with
this tactic and to some effect. With opposing goalkeepers
unable to bypass Jack and reach the ball from a corner, Leeds
would position players on the edge of, or just outside, the
penalty box, ready to rifle a shot at goal if their forwards didn't
win the ball and it was headed out by the opposing centre
backs. The fact that Leeds scored several goals off the back of
Jack's 'legal obstruction' of the opposing goalkeeper only
served to make this tactic – and Jack himself – even more controversial. The tactic, however, finally came unstuck at
Goodison Park when Jack came up against Gordon West.

West, like everyone else, had seen Jack put his obstructive

goal-line tactic into practice courtesy of *Match of the Day*. When Leeds came to town, Gordon West was determined no member of the opposition was going to dictate to him in his own penalty area and, in the event of a Leeds corner, had devised a tactic of his own to counteract Jack's presence on his goal line. The first half was some twenty minutes old before Leeds won their first corner of the game. To hisses and whistles from the Goodison faithful, big Jack trundled upfield to take his by now customary position on the goal line. Only Gordon West didn't do what all the other goalkeepers had done and stand right behind Jack. Instead, much to the surprise of Jack, West took up a position just beyond his far post.

When the Leeds winger Eddie Gray took the corner and floated the ball just under the Everton crossbar, Jack thought he was going to be treated to an easy 'good morning' goal, whereby a simple nod of the head would be enough to direct the ball into the net. But, according to Jack, as soon as Gray crossed the ball, Gordon West took off from his position by the far post and launched himself at the flighted ball. Having gained the necessary momentum and height, West reached over the top of Jack and punched the ball clear, in so doing embedding his knees in Jack's back. The ball sailed towards Row G, while Jack went down like a bag of hammers.

'I guess that's the end of that,' suggested West, as Jack lay on the Goodison turf in some considerable pain.

It was.

CHAPTER FIVE

They were the softest, most lily-livered team ever. When the manager's son sang 'Ding Dong Bell, Pussy's in the Well', six of them fainted

I wasn't aware that Billy Bremner was behind me. If I'd known that, I would have been on my guard. In fact I would have moved away and double-quick. I was just about to take to my toes when suddenly there was a sound as if someone had whacked a settee with a carpet slipper. A searing pain shot across my right calf. I swung around and there was Billy Bremner.

'And that's just for starters, Jim,' Billy said, his face as menacing as a nest of vipers.

I always accepted physical play as part of the game. I even put up with downright dirty play, but in purposefully kicking me on the calf, Billy had overstepped the line of what is and is not acceptable in football. We were, after all, still in the tunnel at Elland Road. The game had yet to start, and both Leeds and Spurs were waiting for the signal to take to the pitch.

Billy Bremner, his Leeds team-mate Norman Hunter and Chelsea's Ron 'Chopper' Harris are some of the legendary hard men of football, and no chapter on hard men would be complete without mention of Liverpool's Tommy Smith either – an opponent whose face always reminded me of that of a clumsy bee-keeper. These men were hard, but there were harder players around. It all depends on your definition of 'hard'. Ron Yeats (Liverpool), Charlie Hurley (Sunderland), Arthur Rowley (Leicester City, Fulham and Shrewsbury

Town), Maurice Setters (Manchester United and Stoke City), and the Spurs pair Dave Mackay and Maurice Norman were all different types of player, but all were as hard as teak.

I had the dubious distinction of playing against Liverpool's Ron Yeats many times. Ron was a colossus of a centre half, a man mountain who was so tall and broad across the shoulders and chest the red shirt of Liverpool stuck tighter to his torso than bark on a tree. When Bill Shankly signed Yeats from Dundee United in the summer of 1961 so taken was Shanks with the imposing stature of his new recruit he invited the press to 'take a trip around our new centre half'.

When Shankly signed Ron he was in the army doing the fag end of his national service and playing for Dundee United whenever he could be released. Soon after the deal was completed Ron gained his release from the Army and arrived in Liverpool during the summer of 1961. It was a time when many players still took on a 'summer job' to supplement the close-season retainer they received from their clubs. As Ron was a new recruit at Liverpool the club set about trying to find him gainful employment until pre-season training began at Anfield.

One day the Liverpool chairman T. V. Williams approached Shankly saying there was a possibility of Ron getting a temporary job in a local garage.

'No need,' said Shankly. 'I had a word with a friend of mine. Yeats has got a job. The boy's working as a lifeguard on Southport beach.'

The Liverpool chairman offered Shankly a look of surprise. 'But he can't swim,' said Mr Williams.

'No,' said Shanks, 'but he can wade out for two miles!'

In a more contemporary vein, Bryan Robson, Paul McGrath, Graeme Souness, Vinnie Jones, Tony Adams, David Batty, Paul Ince and Kevin Muscat all earned a reputation for being fully paid-up members of the hard school. Each player has to be placed in the context of the era in which he played, and, again, it all depends on your definition of what constitutes a hard player. Vinnie Jones courted trouble on the football field and off it as well. In one well-publicised incident involving a dispute with a neighbour, Vinnie was sentenced to 120 hours of community service, though this was reduced to 80 hours as a result of an appeal – probably by the community.

While I played in an era when football was overly physical, I was anything but a physical player. Irrespective of the era, every pro, if not hard himself, has to be able to cope with robust and physical play, and every player has a different way of coping with it. Some give it back; others rely on speed to avoid physical challenges. Some players depend on team-mates to protect them, and there are those who, having been on the receiving end of a bad tackle, will take it out on another member of the opposition.

Hunter, Harris, Smith and Bremner gained reputations for being hard men in football because by and large they were open and honest about what they did. Opponents didn't like it, but accepted it as part of the game. What really riled a player was when an opponent was snide and sneaky. It is the player who kicks you off the ball, or smashes an elbow in your face when play is down at the far end of the field, that induces anger and fear. Not fear of him as a man, but fear of what he might take upon himself to do when no one is looking.

The school of hard knocks has a long and illustrious roll of honour. Supporters of every generation believe the players they watched as youngsters were far harder than those they watch now. That is not as fanciful as it may seem because what was acceptable in the way of physical play has changed over the years. I was, as I have said, never a physical player but given football's current climate I wouldn't last ten minutes in a game these days, never mind Norman Hunter or Ron Harris. What the football of today has in common with the game of the past is that it is not always played according to the rulebook. Yet football mirrors society, and in society attitudes are constantly changing: what was perfectly okay in the game in the fifties may not be tolerated now. While in society we pride ourselves on being more open-minded nowadays, on the football field I feel we are less tolerant than years ago. The contemporary game is less willing to allow overly physical play, or sledge-hammer tackles. Both television and the game's governing bodies are keen to present football as a 'family game', just as it was in the days before hooliganism did its worst in the seventies and eighties. I am all for football as a family game, but the price it has had to pay for courting such support, and for it to be accepted into people's homes, is the loss of its rough edges.

Televised live football is broadcast before the nine p.m. television watershed, and broadcasters and the game's governing bodies don't like to see players squaring up to one another, or even being at odds with each other. When such a thing does happen on the pitch, television commentators and the game's administrators invariably take the moral high ground. They proffer distaste if not outrage at such and such a thing happening on a football pitch. The media's protestations inevitably act as a catalyst to the FA which, aware that players have not been in breach of any actual rule, evokes the woolly charge of 'bringing the game into disrepute'. I find it odd that despite the commercial departments of clubs being at pains to urge supporters to ' feel the pride and the passion' of football, whenever footballers do display overt passion, such as in games between Arsenal and Manchester United, they are brought to book by the authorities.

Ever since English football got into bed with television for the inception of the Premiership, broadcasters and the sport's administrators have slowly been turning it into the type of game it never was and was never intended to be. Their penchant for decrying physical challenges and tetchiness between players has resulted in the disappearance of the so-called hard player. The way the game is played now, tackling is so infrequent it is in danger of becoming a lost art. The player who took it upon himself to 'sort things out' when things got heated in a game is now as rare as men who thatch roofs or mine coal. In the Premiership Roy Keane is the rare exception.

As someone who was not a physical player and was often on the receiving end of sledgehammer tackles, and on more than one occasion subjected to intimidation, you might be given to thinking that I wouldn't mourn the passing of those players who could dish it out. But I do. As the great French goalscorer Just Fontaine once said, 'A football team is like a concert pianist on tour. There has to be a creative, an orchestrator, a conductor to the string section who play the tune, but there also must be piano shifters.'

Every team used to have piano shifters. The game I knew as a player was very physical, and every player had to look after himself on the pitch because, metaphorically speaking, a piano hurts when it hits you at speed. Tommy Smith, Ron Harris and Norman Hunter earned renown for being hard men, but in the fifties, sixties and seventies just about every team had its own Smith, Harris, or Hunter. Some, such as Bolton Wanderers and Newcastle United in the fifties, had a bevy of them. In Jimmy Scoular, Frank Brennan and Bob Stokoe, Newcastle United had a half-back line that took no prisoners, ever. All of them could play a bit and dish it out more than a bit. Jimmy Scoular lived up to his name. I remember the Chelsea captain Peter Sillett meeting with Scoular for the pre-match coin toss between the two skippers.

'I think we might have to mix it today, lads,' said Peter, on returning to our ranks. 'I've just shook hands with Scoular and he gave me the sort of look he'd give on seeing a skidmark on a hotel bedsheet.'

Jimmy Scoular went through games with a perpetual look on his face that was a mixture of determination and menace. There are some fortunate people who, when in their forties or fifties, look little different from how they looked when in their twenties. Cliff Richard, Paul Newman and (though it pains me to say this) Ian St John come to mind. There are others who look old when in their twenties, yet curiously never seem to age beyond that. Of these, I can think of the star of the *Carry On* films Sid James, Jimmy Hill and Jimmy Scoular. The Newcastle player looked fifty when he was twenty-five. He was built like a Coke machine with a bald head, the sides of which boasted thick wedges of black hair that were always unkempt. The most striking parts of Jimmy's countenance were a forehead hammered flat through contact with a thousand muddy caseballs and a nose that made Karl Malden's look like that of Kylie Minogue. If Tom Waits' voice could ever be turned into a face, it would be that of Jimmy Scoular.

Playing Jimmy was like coming up against a bag of hammers: in addition to Exocet tackling, every part of his body seemed capable of jutting out whenever necessary to inflict jarring pain. In his days at Newcastle, Jimmy, Bob Stokoe and Frank Brennan formed an iron curtain across the pitch. Once you got past them there was the likelihood of scoring, but getting past that trio was a big problem. Jimmy was a formidable opponent, but one who could also play the ball around. His passing had Swiss-watch precision and his astute vision enabled him to set up many a Newcastle attack. He was an awesome sight in full flight. Many was the player who learned that the best defence against Scoular was not to be there when he did surge forward.

We live in uncertain times, but personally I don't fear terrorism, because I played against the half-back line of Hennin, Higgins and Edwards. They were part of the hardest team I ever came across in the fifties: Bolton Wanderers. In an era when managers chose what they believed was their best eleven, and teams only changed due to injuries or lack of form, the Bolton defence ran off the tongue like a litany: Hopkinson, Hartle, Banks, Hennin, Higgins, Edwards. If that wasn't enough to put the fear of God into opponents, at centre forward Bolton boasted 'The Lion of Vienna', Nat Lofthouse.

Of all the players in the fifties, in my opinion Tommy Banks was the hardest. He was born and bred in Bolton. He won his place in the Bolton first team in unusual circumstances, in that he did so at the expense of his brother, Ralph. Off the pitch, Tommy was a warm, friendly guy with a wonderful wit; on the pitch, he was fearsome. I remember one blockbuster of a tackle Tommy made on my Chelsea team-mate, Micky Block. As Micky lay there writhing on the ground, Bolton's right back, Roy Hartle, came up to Banks.

'You're losing your touch, Tommy,' Hartle told him, pointing to Micky. 'He's still wriggling.'

To my mind there are two situations in which it is impossible to look cool: in a go-kart, and when lying injured on a football pitch. Micky Block was a handsome young lad and a favourite with female supporters. Today he might be referred to as 'cool', though he appeared anything but as he lay there in agony following that characteristic Tommy Banks tackle.

Tommy was as hard as iron, and he was an excellent left back – one good enough to play for England. In the World Cup finals of 1958 England met Brazil in the qualifying group. The England manager Walter Winterbottom was giving his pre-match team-talk and wanted Tommy to deal with the Brazilian winger Zagalo.

'Zagalo will be yours,' Winterbottom told Tommy. 'Keep him quiet. First tackle, hit him hard. Hurt him. Is that clear?'

'Not really, boss,' said Tommy. 'When thou sayest "hurt" him, does't tha mean temporarily like, or permanent?'

For the record England drew 0-0 with Brazil and Tommy Banks never gave Zagalo the opportunity to weave his magic. The draw against England was the only game in the World Cup finals in which Brazil failed to score. England's performance, and that of Tommy Banks at left back in particular, prompted the Brazilian manager to ring the changes. For their next game, against the USSR, Zagalo switched to the right and Brazil introduced Garrincha on the left wing. Vava replaced Mazzola at centre forward, with his place at inside left being taken by a relatively unknown seventeen-year-old – Pele.

On a football pitch Tommy Banks was as sharp as a razor blade and just as accommodating. Tommy, however, also displayed a razor-sharp wit. In the late fifties the England captain, Billy Wright, became engaged to Joy Beverley, who was one of the Beverley Sisters, a very popular and glamorous trio of singing siblings. In an era when the media were comparatively reserved, Billy and Joy were the 'Posh and Becks' of their day.

Before a game against Russia, England manager Walter Winterbottom concluded his team-talk by saying, 'Apply yourselves fully. Go out, play the way I know you can play. Win the game, and afterwards you can all feel joy.'

'Bloody hell,' said Tommy, 'that's one bonus I never expected from playing for England. Reet sporting of you that is, Billy, lad.'

The whole team, Billy Wright included, fell about laughing.

Throughout the sixties and early seventies no team relished playing against Leeds United. Don Revie's team were a terrific footballing side, but there was another aspect to their play that made them difficult to handle: Leeds were arguably the most physical team of the post-war era (and that's saying something!). The style of their play was physical in the sense that they were hard, but they also indulged in some cynical play that was snide and sly. Leeds had no qualms about intimidating opponents; I have already mentioned that I was kicked by Billy Bremner in the tunnel at Elland Road and how Jack Charlton's presence on an opponent's goal line was considered not to be in the spirit of the game. Yet, for all Leeds gained a rightful reputation for being overly physical, cynical and intimidatory, they played super football and possessed players of real class, none more so than Bremner himself.

They didn't come much smaller in stature and bigger in

heart than the Leeds skipper. Billy Bremner was a bubbling, bouncing package of football industry encased in a chalky white skin and topped off by a curly mass of flaming red hair. I don't know what it is about players with red hair, but they always seem to be real firebrands. If Bremner didn't have the ball at his feet there was something wrong, and he would go in search of it, seemingly affronted by the very idea that the game, any game, could actually be proceeding without his immediate involvement. 'Hunger for the ball' is a cliché often used in foot-ball, but with Billy, far from being hungry for the ball, he always appeared to me to be on the point of starvation. However, if there was nothing subtle about his tackling, there certainly was about his passing. For a player with such a fear-some reputation as a hard man, Billy's distribution was deft, fluent and executed with all the precision of a BMW engine. He was very much the driving force of the Leeds midfield.

Billy symbolised an era of football known for cynicism and overt physical play, but also for flair. After Leeds won promo-tion from the Second Division in 1963–4, the following season they took the First Division by storm, finishing runners-up in the League and beaten finalists in the FA Cup. Nevertheless, they won few friends outside the city of Leeds itself. In a par-ticularly tempestuous match against Everton at Goodison Park, at one point the game degenerated into a free-for-all. Everywhere they played Leeds seemed to rile the opposition with their hard-nosed play and tactics; though it has to be said that their captain during this season, Bobby Collins, produced such stylish football that he was voted Footballer of the Year by the Football Writers' Association. Collins was a fine player, but in my opinion he was more dangerous and certainly more devious than Bremner. Billy was, for the most part, upfront about what he did to you, whereas Bobby Collins indulged in a lot of off-the-ball ragging. A tackle from Bremner was a thing to behold because it was crisp and upfront, but on more than one occasion I saw Bobby Collins make a tackle, only to 'leave his foot in'. Bobby's career was terminated early when he sustained a broken leg playing in a European match. The cynics were of the mind that 'he who lives by the sword dies by the sword', but I feel such a view to be ungracious, crass even. Bobby Collins could dish it out, on occasions cynically, but, like Billy Bremner, he was also a fine footballer.

Nobody looked forward to playing against Leeds. Opposing teams knew they would be in for a battle, that there would be antagonism and some cynical play, but credit where it's due, Don Revie's side could really play, and there was a period when they were indisputably the best footballing team in England. But teams gain reputations, and invariably they never see themselves as others see them. I think this was very much the case with Revie's Leeds. To this day Don Revie does not enjoy widespread acclaim. His name was sullied when he walked out on England. Revie took up a coaching appointment in the United Arab Emirates. The FA, incensed that he had walked out on the national side, banned Don Revie from any involvement in football in this country. He took the FA to court and had the ban revoked, but he didn't come out of the court with his reputation intact, let alone enhanced, and the judge referred to him as 'untrustworthy'. It was a sad end to what had been a marvellous managerial career. Like Bill Shankly, Don Revie took a struggling, mid-table Second Division club and turned it into one of the best the country had ever seen. Don Revie's detractors point to the number of times Leeds faltered at the final hurdle to justify him not being held in similar esteem to Shankly or Matt Busby. While it is true Leeds were dubbed 'eternal bridesmaids', to set the record straight, under Revie they won two First Division Championships, both the FA and League Cup, the Fairs (UEFA) Cup twice and the Second Division Championship. The bridesmaid tag came from the fact that Leeds lost five major Cup finals and were also First Division runners-up on five occasions. Under Revie Leeds were rarely out of the top four of the First Division and were often only a point or two from taking the title. To place Leeds' title challenges into perspective, just another eleven points gained at the right time, and spread across five seasons, would have won them an additional five League Championships.

Following England's World Cup success of 1966 (more of which later) managers and coaches aped Alf Ramsey's 4-4-2 and 4-3-3 team formations. English football changed after our success in the World Cup, and the emphasis was placed on not conceding goals, rather than scoring them. It led to many dour battles conducted in midfield and as a result far fewer goals. When Leeds United won the First Division Championship in 1969 their sixty-seven points beat by one the record set by Arsenal in 1931. That title-winning Arsenal team scored 131 goals. Leeds in 1969 scored sixty-six goals, less than the number of points they accrued. This tally of goals was also the lowest of any team to have won the First Division Championship prior to the number of games being extended to forty-two and the change in the offside law in the early twenties. Conversely, Revie's team only conceded twenty-six goals, fewer than any previous champions in the forty-two-match season (although runners-up Liverpool conceded two fewer). Mick Jones was Leeds' leading goalscorer in the 1968–9 season, with fourteen goals, the lowest leading goalscoring tally of any club to have won the Championship. Leeds' critics, of whom there were many, labelled their Championship side of 1969 as defensive, destructive and dour. But only two clubs in the First Division scored more goals than Leeds that season. England's World Cup success meant managers and coaches copied Alf Ramsey's 'wingless wonders'. It wasn't Alf's fault that the emphasis in English football changed. He picked players to suit a system he felt could win the World Cup. Months later, Alf had England playing to another system, but post-1966 managers and coaches slavishly used 4-4-2 and 4-3-3 systems because what better example was there to follow than that of the world champions? Leeds were crowned champions in 1969 on the back of some mean football, a mean tally of goals scored, a mean defence and a mean midfield, but Revie's team were not alone. Come 1968–9 every club was producing mean, ultra-defensive football.

In these days of Chelsea's multi-million-pound squad it's worth noting that of the Leeds Championship side of 1969 only three players in their sixteen-man squad cost a fee – Johnny Giles (£32,500 from Manchester United), Mick Jones (£100,000 from Sheffield United) and Mick O'Grady (£30,000 from Huddersfield Town). Since the fifties Manchester United had received plaudits for their youth system, and in the sixties clubs such as Burnley, Sunderland, Leicester City and West Ham United were famous for producing home-grown talent, yet few ever applauded Don Revie for his youth policy. Leeds United were just not liked beyond the boundaries of their city. Praise, if ever forthcoming, was usually of the grudging variety, and when Leeds failed to lift a major trophy, there was smug satisfaction. Talk to former Leeds centre forward Alan 'Sniffer' Clarke and he will tell you the club was often the victim of its own success.

'It makes me laugh when Arsène Wenger says his Arsenal team play too many games,' said Alan:

I remember one season at Leeds when we played seventy-six matches and all told, used twenty players. Those who did come into the team did so because of enforced changes due to injury or suspension and only featured in a handful of matches. Otherwise, I am sure we would have fielded the same eleven players. Paul Madeley, Norman Hunter and Peter Lorimer were ever-presents. Jack Charlton and Billy Bremner only missed one game apiece; and Gary Sprake, Johnny Giles and myself missed about half a dozen.

When we won the FA Cup in 1972 we didn't get to cele-brate because we had a League game on the Monday night. We only needed a point at Wolves to do the double, but lost

2-1. We lost against Wolves because we were knackered. There was no reason why that game could not have been played on the Wednesday night rather than the Monday, which would have given us sufficient time to rest after the FA Cup final.

In the seventies Manchester United had great players but they were never a great team. Leeds United were. The most infamous Leeds player of the Revie era was Norman 'Bite yer Legs' Hunter. His reputation as a hard man ranks alongside that of Tommy Smith and Ron 'Chopper' Harris. Most supporters recall Norman only for his reputation as a hard man, and many forget that he was a member of Alf Ramsey's 1966 World Cup squad. He won twenty-eight caps and would, I am sure, have played many more times for England had it not been for the peerless Bobby Moore. Hunter was a linchpin of the Revie era and became a legend for his virulent tackling. For all that, Norman has the distinction of having been the first recipient of the Professional Footballers' Association's Footballer of the Year award in 1973 – proof, if ever it were needed, of the high esteem in which he was held by his fellow professionals.

Today the name Norman Hunter is synonymous with that of a hard man. Don Revie loved Norman and would play up to his reputation as a hard man. Talking of Norman on one occasion Revie was given to saying, 'Hunter left the pitch with a broken leg; try as we might we couldn't find who it belonged to!'

Norman was fearsome and formidable, yet he never missed a game for Leeds for five seasons. He played 543 games for the club and over a hundred for Bristol City, and was sent off only once during his career and received just four bookings. Those statistics are indicative of just how tolerant referees and the game's administrators were of physical play in the sixties and seventies. The harder Norman tackled, the more maniacally friendly the smile he bestowed upon his victim. Norman

Hunter may have been hard but he was not what you would call a dirty player. Nevertheless, because of his style of play, I doubt he would last longer than ten minutes in a game today.

There was a history of bad blood between Leeds and several teams, none more so than Sunderland. The bad feeling between these two clubs dated back to 1962 when the Sunderland inside forward Willie McPheat sustained a broken leg in a game against Don Revie's side at Elland Road. It was an injury that all but ended the playing career of the young Scot. In 1963–4 Leeds and Sunderland were vying with one another for promotion to Division One, and the two sides met over the festive period. They drew 1-1 at Elland Road and met again a few days later at Roker Park. Sunderland won that match 2-0 in a game the *Daily Express* said 'should have been given an X-certificate as it was not suitable viewing for children'.

The two clubs continued their feud throughout the sixties and it came to a head in 1967 when they were paired in the fifth round of the FA Cup. The tie took place at Roker Park and was marred by a broken leg sustained by Sunderland's teenage winger Bobby Kerr, following a tackle from Norman Hunter. The game ended in a 1-1 draw and the replay drew a record crowd of 57,892 to Elland Road. That tie also ended in a 1-1 draw after extra-time, and so the teams travelled to the neutral venue of Hull City's Boothferry Park, where a capacity crowd witnessed another dogged fight that at the time broke out into a football match.

Leeds triumphed 2-1 at neutral Hull in a game that should have been the first match to carry a government health warning. The winning goal came from a highly controversial penalty, awarded when Jimmy Greenhoff was adjudged to have been fouled by the Sunderland full back Cec Irwin. The Sunderland players were of the mind that Greenhoff had indulged in gamesmanship, purposefully throwing his body across the penalty area as Irwin committed himself to the tackle. What followed was little short of mayhem. While some Sunderland players argued with referee Ken Stokes, others squared up to Leeds players. Sunderland's Jim Baxter and Leeds' Billy Bremner were team-mates in the Scotland side, but that didn't stop the pair exchanging heated words. At one point Bremner grabbed Baxter by the throat, which brought an irate Sunderland supporter on to the pitch, who attacked Bremner with a haversack. As players jostled one another and some Sunderland team-members continued to argue the toss with Ken Stokes, something must have been said between the Leeds winger Albert Johanneson and the Sunderland captain George Kinnell, because Johanneson suddenly broke rank. The crowd were then treated to the sight of Johanneson zig-zagging around the pitch, with Kinnell in hot pursuit. Referee Ken Stokes and his linesmen, Fred Barr and Al Jenkins, were too preoccupied with the main body of dissenting players to be bothered about Johanneson and Kinnell's private feud that now, having started in the Sunderland penalty area, was continuing across the Leeds half of the field. George Kinnell, a cousin of Jim Baxter, was a gnarled, rugged Scot who took no nonsense from anybody. It was a good job Albert could run.

When order was finally restored after a five-minute hold-up, George Mulhall of Sunderland was sent off, Leeds scored from the penalty, which only prompted another Sunderland player, George Herd, to voice his protestations too vociferously to referee Ken Stokes, and receive his marching orders. With their noses in front, Leeds did what they had to do, and 'killed' the game, as Sunderland attempted to kill them. When the players left the field there was a fracas in the tunnel. When that was broken up order was restored, but for all of a few seconds, as Bremner and Baxter then had a set-to outside the dressing rooms. It was said that Baxter hit Billy Bremner three times, though when asked for his opinion of Baxter's actions, Sunderland skipper George Kinnell is reputed to have said, 'I admire Jim's restraint'. This still wasn't the end as the Leeds centre half, Jack Charlton, and the Sunderland centre forward, Neil Martin, had to be pulled away from one another by officials of both clubs when they bandied words of a non-pacifist nature. The referee was eventually called from his dressing room to help restore order. When Ken Stokes arrived on the scene, Jack Charlton said, 'I dunno what you've come out for. If any more of this continues, we won't need a referee, we'll be needing a priest!'

When Sunderland, then of the Second Division, sensationally beat Leeds in the 1973 FA Cup final, the euphoria of their supporters at winning the Cup was only matched by the sense that at last they had gained revenge on Leeds for all their feuding throughout the sixties, particularly that second replay in the fifth round of 1967. Should such a game occur today between two Premiership clubs it would evoke an indignant response from both the game's administrators and the media. A volatile match like that would be analysed and debated endlessly, and no doubt former players-turned television pundits would be up in arms about it, probably referring to such behaviour as 'outrageous' and 'despicable' and calling for 'action to be taken to restore the game's reputation'.

In 1967 the response was altogether different. Reporting on the game at Boothferry Park, the *Daily Mail* said, 'Such was the tension and passion in this game, understandably there were times when it boiled over'. The Newcastle *Journal* was a model of restraint, saying, 'Another testy encounter between these two clubs resulted in the dismissal of two Sunderland players'. The *Daily Mirror* wrote approvingly, 'Tempers flared in what was a blood and thunder tie in the tradition of the Cup'. The indifference of the press and the matter-of-fact way in which they reported this game were typical of the time. The media didn't get too worked up about tempestuous games that, on occasions, saw players squaring up to one another. Although games like the one between Leeds and Sunderland were an exception, generally speaking most of the contests Leeds were involved in during that era got rather heated. The *Journal* described the Leeds–Sunderland game at Boothferry Park as testy and in the eyes of most that is what it was. Nobody called for legislation to be brought in to prevent such a thing happening again. It was accepted that football was both a physical and a passion-fuelled game, and as such there would be games like the one between Leeds and Sunderland.

Should one ever need evidence of how much the game, media and attitudes have changed, one only has to look at the way the media and the FA have reacted to the culture that has developed between Arsenal and Manchester United in recent years. During twelve seasons, from 1992–3 when the Premiership was introduced, to Arsenal's historic success as unbeaten champions in 2003–4, only Blackburn Rovers (1995) managed to break the United–Arsenal domination of the Premier League. Encounters between these two sides finally resulted in the FA in 2005 calling representatives of both to a meeting, with a view to putting an end to 'the feud that exists between the two clubs'. But while the FA must be seen to act on incidents like that of Sir Alex Ferguson being showered with soup (and that was just for starters) one feels their time could be taken up tackling more important issues within football.

The so-called feud between Arsenal and United is nothing more than the product of a game which has evolved in such a way that only a few elite clubs have a chance of winning the Premiership. For over a decade the battle for the Premiership title was a private party between United and Arsenal. Both clubs knew the winning of the Championship was basically between them, and when they played each other the fixture took on totemic relevance. Arsenal versus Manchester United was more than a three-pointer: a win offered the victors a great psychological advantage, and also fuelled club pride by way of one-upmanship on their sole rivals for glory. The tetchy rivalry between Arsène Wenger and Sir Alex Ferguson, and the players of both teams, was simply the by-product of the standing these two clubs occupied in English football for a decade and more. Although the public relations and commercial departments of clubs encourage supporters to experience the pride and passion of football, when matches become truly impassioned and bubbling with conflict and drama, the FA wants to stamp it out.

Let's get back to the hard men. Players like Norman Hunter, Billy Bremner, Ron Harris and Tommy Smith gained notoriety, but in my opinion during that era there were players who were even harder. Spurs' Dave Mackay is one such. To my mind, Dave Mackay was not just the hardest player of his generation, he is also the greatest player ever to have worn a Tottenham shirt. Dave had everything – power, skill, drive, strength, stamina and, above all, infectious enthusiasm. He was really hard, and a man of action, but he never got a reputation because he was always scrupulously fair.

There is a famous photograph of Dave holding Billy Bremner off the ground during a game between Spurs and Leeds at White Hart Lane. In it Dave's teeth are gritted and Billy's elevation is due to the fact that Dave has picked him up by his shirt-front, most of which is concealed within a clenched fist that looks as big as a ham shank. Billy Bremner had been a naughty lad that day. He had gone over the top on me for a start. When Billy executed a similar tackle on Dave, he took exception to it. The challenge put Dave on the deck, but on regaining his feet he didn't run towards Bremner with a red mist in his eyes. He simply strode across the pitch, brushing a Leeds player who was in his way to one side, and took hold of Billy. The story goes that Dave was so mad he butted Billy in the face and the referee, Norman Burtenshaw, gave Dave his marching orders, only for Dave to respond to Norman with, 'If you send me off, fifty thousand fans here will come and lynch you!' Norman Burtenshaw is then reputed to have said, 'Er, okay, but any more of that and you will be off.'

It makes for a good tale, but I played in that game and it isn't my recollection of events. I never saw Dave butt Billy, neither did Terry Venables, nor anyone else who played for Spurs or Leeds that day. In fact I could never believe Dave Mackay capable of doing such a thing, no matter how angry he was. Dave adhered to a strict code of conduct. He put everything behind every tackle, but always played the ball and expected similar treatment himself. If an opponent went outside the rules, either written or unwritten, Dave took exception. On such occasions, as the one with Billy Bremner, Dave would quite literally take matters in hand. He was a lawmaker rather than a lawbreaker.

Dave Mackay arrived at Spurs in March 1959 from Hearts. In a way it was befitting of the man that he should have started his career with Hearts, for, as players go, he had one the size of a bean bag. At Spurs – like the cockerel that forms the Tottenham badge – Dave's puffed-out chest became his trademark. The club is one of those that used to be known by a number of nicknames – Spurs and Lilywhites being two – Dave Mackay too revelled in a variety of monikers: Iron Man, Granite Guy, Indestructible and Mac the Knife, all of which bear testimony to the fact that he was a player of great strength and fortitude. You could almost hear the bagpipes playing when Dave went into action. He was not a big guy, but when he pulled on a football shirt he visibly grew. He played for Scotland at schoolboy, Under 23 and full international level, and twice made startling comebacks after breaking his leg. Curiously for a hard man, Dave never wore studded boots. Like me, he always played in rubbers, simply because he found boots with rubber-moulded soles and studs more comfortable. Should Dave have ever worn studded boots I don't think it would have made much difference: he wouldn't have injured anyone, even unintentionally, because the timing, precision and strength of his tackling were immaculate. Dave was a formidable opponent but it would never cross his mind to leave his foot in when committing himself to a tackle. He was, as I say, a lawmaker not a lawbreaker.

No chapter on hard men can ignore Liverpool's Tommy Smith. Fate tried to conceal the man by naming him Smith, but anonymity on the football pitch was never going to be the destiny of a player Bill Shankly boasted he'd not signed, but quarried. Tommy was revered and feared, but off the pitch he was the most good-natured and friendly guy you could ever wish to meet. On one occasion when Spurs visited Anfield, we were making our way from the dressing room and met the Liverpool team as they walked towards the steps you descended to the pitch. I found myself alongside Tommy, who pushed a piece of paper into my hand. I was totally perplexed as to why he should want to give me what I believed was a letter, and I unfolded the sheet of paper and glanced at it. The reason for Tommy pressing the piece of paper into my hand became immediately apparent – it was the evening menu for Liverpool Royal Infirmary! I have to say that when Tommy handed me that piece of paper, he did so with a smile on his face. He wouldn't have done anything to me to merit my ending up in the infirmary; handing me the menu was simply black humour, although there was an underlying message to the act.

Tommy Smith joined Liverpool in 1960 as a fifteen-year-old groundstaff lad. His father had died the previous year and throughout his time under Bill Shankly's management, I think Shankly became a father figure to Tommy. He was offered professional terms on his seventeenth birthday and made his debut in the first team at the end of the 1962–3 season in a 5-1 victory over Birmingham City. After the game Tommy's mum and stepfather met him, saying, 'Come on, let's go home for a cup of tea', but Tommy wanted to savour the moment a while longer. While his mum and stepfather headed for home, Tommy walked the streets around Anfield, alone with his thoughts. He later told me, 'I wanted to taste the atmosphere for as long as I could. Even though all the supporters had gone home, something of the match still lingered about the streets. I loved it; I could have died that night and been quite happy.'

To paraphrase Michael Caine, not a lot of people know that Tommy first began to establish himself in the Liverpool team as a centre forward. In 1964–5 Bill Shankly decided to play Tommy up front, in place of the injured Ian St John. Despite scoring twice in four matches, the manager knew already where Tommy could be best employed. When Liverpool played Belgian champions Anderlecht in the European Cup, Shankly played Tommy Smith in defence and from that moment on he became a fixture in the Liverpool team. For the next thirteen seasons, his name became synonymous with Liverpool and, of course, as that of a fearsome hard man.

For all his fame and reputation, though, Tommy remained down-to-earth and – off the pitch at least – congenial, warm and friendly. A reporter from the Liverpool *Echo* once asked Tommy during an interview, 'What about this reputation of yours as the hardest player in English football?'

'I didn't know I had such a reputation,' replied Tommy. 'The only time a Liverpool player realises he has a reputation is when Bill Shankly tells him he isn't living up to it.'

Tommy, as I say, is a down-to-earth guy. He was Liverpool through and through, and gloriously happy just to be 'one of the team'. He also disliked players who were full of self-admiration and had a long-running feud with Alan Clarke that began during Sniffer's days as a Fulham player and carried on when Clarke joined Leicester, then Leeds United. There was no love lost between Tommy and Sniffer, whose mutual dislike was such that when they clashed on the pitch, gaining possession of the ball was of secondary importance. The other player Tommy never warmed to was his own captain, Emlyn Hughes.

Spurs' Danny Blanchflower was a captain in every sense of the word. A cerebral player who understood the heart of the game. *(Getty Images)*

Matt Busby's tactical nous foxed Blackpool in the 1948 FA Cup final. Matt loved his Players, as can be seen from this photograph. *(Offside)*

Manchester United players after their 1957–8 European Cup quarter-final against Red Star Belgrade. In front is the great Duncan Edwards: 'They've built battleships on the Clyde that are smaller and less formidable'. *(L'Equipe)*

In the past surfaces in winter resembled molasses, like in this shot of West Ham playing at Upton Park. *(Action Images)*

Peter Sillett's search for his contact lens is interrupted as Reg Matthews and Mel Scott
fail to stop Chelsea conceding. Goals were plentiful in the fifties;
in 1958–9 Chelsea scored 77 but let in 98. (*Action Images*)

Burnley chairman and
Football League president
Bob Lord supported the
PFA's fight for the
abolition of the maximum
wage. Here he is seen
buying a ticket for a
Burnley FA Cup tie at
Brentford. The turnstile
operator obviously
recognises him!
(*PA/Empics*)

Most newspaper photographs of football today show a close-up of two players contesting the ball. By contrast this shot of Wolves v West Bromwich Albion from the sixties epitomises football as 'the working man's ballet'. Left to right: Don Howe (WBA), Jock Wallace (Albion's keeper), Chuck Drury (WBA), Barrie Stobart (Wolves), Stan Jones (WBA), Jimmy Murray (Wolves) and Bobby Robson (WBA). *(PA/Empics)*

England v Hungary, 1953. Even as the two teams took to the field it was apparent from their respective strips and boots that England belonged to another age. That day England woke up to the fact that we were no longer masters of world football. *(Getty Images)*

Football in the sixties was far more physical than the game of today. One of the toughest players was Liverpool's Tommy Smith. In this match Tommy's left leg has been severed at the knee but as you can see, he simply carried on playing. *(Getty Images)*

Dave Mackay was a great player and one of the bravest the game has ever produced. In this match, Leeds' Billy Bremner had 'gone over the top' on me and then perpetrated a similar tackle on Mackay before Dave quite literally took matters in hand. *(Mirror Pics)*

The 1975 European Cup final. Bayern Munich's Franz Beckenbauer warily eyes Leeds' Billy Bremner – and with good reason. *(L'Equipe)*

In the seventies even the most creative players were not averse to overt physical challenges. Here Chelsea's John Hollins 'plays the ball' via the body of Stoke City's Jackie Marsh, while an unconcerned Ian Hutchinson and Alan Hudson look on. *(Colorsport)*

Charity was nowhere to be seen in the 1974 Charity Shield between
Leeds United and Liverpool, the first to be broadcast 'live' on
television. Following their dismissal, Billy Bremner displays
a rare moment of charity by offering his shirt
to Kevin Keegan. *(Colorsport)*

In the past sendings off were rare. West Germany goalkeeper Toni
Schumacher makes a terrible challenge on Patrick Battiston (France)
during the 1982 World Cup. Battiston was knocked unconscious;
Schumacher escaped without punishment. *(Colorsport)*

Up to the late sixties it was commonplace for spectators to overflow from packed terracing on to the perimeter track. In this shot from the late twenties at Craven Cottage what appears to be Mussolini (front row, below exit staircase) gets in on the act. *(Offside)*

Only at football matches are men given to wearing the most ridiculous of hats, believing them to be the height of football fashion. An Arsenal fan sports Giorgio Armani's 1971 catwalk success – 'stovepipe and indefinite article'. *(Colorsport)*

I think it fair to say Tommy never got on with Emlyn, whom he thought self-regarding. Being a member of a football team is like any other work situation, in that a group of people come together for a common aim. It's like most people's work situation: there you will make good friends with some workmates, others you will simply 'get on with', and there might even be the odd one you dislike. Things are the same with a football team. The players have been assembled by the manager and, we humans being what we are, there will be players who, for whatever reason, simply don't get on with one another. The best a manager can hope for in such a situation is that the professionalism of the players will come to the fore. A player may not like one of his team-mates but he will make an effort to respect that person as a footballer. In my opinion that was very much the situation with Tommy Smith and Emlyn Hughes. Tommy respected Emlyn for what he did on the football field in the name of Liverpool, and for his leadership qualities on and off the pitch, but seemingly that is as far as it went. Regarding his reputation as a hard man, unlike other robust players of his era Tommy Smith adhered to a certain code of ethics. Tommy played it hard, but always by the book even though 'leaving your foot in' was a common feature of the game in the sixties and seventies.

There was a whole generation of 'difficult' forwards: Alan Clarke, Derek Dougan (Wolves), Wyn Davies (Newcastle), Bobby Gould (Coventry and Arsenal), Martin Chivers (Spurs), Andy Lochhead (Burnley and Aston Villa) and Peter Osgood (Chelsea) all knew how to look after themselves. It was the same with midfield players, including the Leeds trio of Bremner, Collins and Johnny Giles, and Frank Munro (Wolves), Jimmy McNab (Sunderland), Johnny Morrissey (Everton), Peter Storey (Arsenal), Terry Hennessey (Nottingham Forest and Derby), Jim Iley (Newcastle), Mike Summerbee (Manchester City), Nobby Stiles (Manchester United) and Maurice Setters (Man United, Coventry and

Stoke). Every team had its share of hard men and you will notice from this brief list that I have not even mentioned defenders! The only team that didn't seem to possess a couple of players who could 'mix it' were West Ham United, whose penchant for purist football was enough to get them through the majority of games.

Tackling hard and fairly was an acceptable part of the game, but doing it slyly, or indulging in what we used to call 'Italian off-the-ball' antics', was not. Tommy Smith was the embodiment of the 'hard but fair' school. I have never heard a player say that he went over the top. Such was Tommy's fearful reputation, a few words from him were usually enough to quell the exuberance of any opponent who might give him a basting on the pitch. Having said that, I am not so sure the same could be said of another Liverpool great, Graeme Souness.

Steve Kindon played for Burnley and Wolves – amongst others – and Steve was so quick he could have raced pigeons. At one time he had the Olympic qualifying time for the hundred metres, so it stands to reason that his pace was problematic to defenders. Steve was a teenager when he first played for Burnley at Anfield and on that occasion his pace began to get to Tommy Smith. Time and again Steve would push the ball on the outside of Tommy, take to his toes and leave the Liverpool player in his wake. This had happened a few times when Tommy finally decided to take matters in hand. With the play deep in the Burnley half of the field, Tommy walked up to Steve.

'You go down the outside of me again and I'll break your leg, son,' snarled Tommy, his words more of a psychological threat than any statement of intent.

Tommy's advice, however, rattled young Kindon, who made a beeline for the referee, Clive Thomas.

'Ref! Ref! I've been threatened,' said young Steve. 'That Smith says to me, if I go on the outside of him again he's gonna break my leg!'

Clive Thomas was a very experienced official, who had been around long enough to know the ins and outs of the professional game, and was well versed in banter between players.

'Really?' said Clive. 'In that case, I wouldn't go down the outside of him again, if I were you. It's pro football, son. Get on with it.'

Steve Kindon's naivety came from the fact that he was a young lad and, at the time, inexperienced in the ways of the pro game. Bill Shankly had a quirky phrase for a naive, young player such as Steve: 'Green around the gills and a stranger to the lavatory,' Shankly would say. Though I doubt many young footballers who played against Tommy Smith were strangers to the lavatory.

Supporters used to eagerly await the meeting of two players who enjoyed renowned reputations. The clash of two opposing players known for being hard, or brilliant in the air, or who possessed outstanding ball skills, would often take on greater importance than the game itself. Outside grounds, newspaper hoardings or notices pinned to lamp-posts would extol supporters to read the next day of the 'titanic' (they were always titanic) clash between John Charles and Charlie Hurley (the Giant meets the King); Mike England and Tony Hateley; Tommy Smith and Mike Summerbee; or Nobby Stiles and Billy Bremner. Such a meeting of minds would put thousands on the gate, especially if it involved two players of notoriety. As Joe Mercer said, in his days as manager of Aston Villa, 'I don't like the idea of football being played on red grass, but the prospect of it ensures packed terraces.'

It certainly did in 1962–3 when Chelsea entertained Stoke City. A crowd of 66,199 packed Stamford Bridge, with an estimated 10,000 locked out. Both clubs were contesting promotion from Division Two, in addition to which a sell-out crowd was ensured because the teams were diametrically opposed. Chelsea were a young, trendy team managed by the outspoken and flamboyant Tommy Docherty. They contained a bevy of youngsters, who would go on to become big names in the game and legends at Stamford Bridge, such as goalkeeper Peter Bonetti, Ken Shellito, Eddie McCreadie, Terry Venables, Bobby Tambling, Barry Bridges, Bert Murray and Ron Harris. Stoke City were managed by Tony Waddington, a quiet and unassuming manager – the very antithesis of Docherty – and if Chelsea were young and on the up, Stoke City comprised, in the main, veteran pros in the twilight, if not the dusk, of their careers. These included Stanley Matthews, Jackie Mudie, Dennis Viollet, Eddie Stuart, goalkeeper Jimmy O'Neill, Don Ratcliffe, Jimmy McIlroy, and one of the hardest, no-nonsense players ever to have graced – and disgraced – the game: Eddie Clamp.

The match took place in May and the meeting so late in the season of two teams locked in a battle for promotion to the top flight was always going to produce a bumper attendance at Stamford Bridge. But this game had the added essence of a number of clashes of the titanic nature. There was the unfailing attraction of the forty-eight-year-old Stanley Matthews pitting his wizardry against the teenaged Ron Harris, who, though in his first season in the Chelsea team, was already on his way to earning the epithet of 'Chopper'. What added spice to the meeting of Matthews and Harris was the presence of Eddie Clamp.

Stan Matthews first joined Stoke City in 1930, in the days of the legendary Everton centre forward Dixie Dean, and played his final game in the equivalent of the Premiership in 1965 (at the age of fifty), in the era of George Best. For all he achieved in the game, Stan Matthews was not a man given to boasting, though the fact that he was never booked or spoken to, by a referee in his thirty-five years as a player was always a matter of great pride to him. That exemplary record is testament to Stan's great sportsmanship and unbelievably cool temperament, because in his time he came in for some torrid treatment from defenders. The only way some could think of stopping Stan was to attempt to kick him up hill and down dale, and not once did he ever retaliate to shabby treatment. In what was Stan's second spell with Stoke City, Eddie Clamp appointed himself as the maestro's minder.

'Don't you worry about anyone sticking it to you, Stan,' Eddie told Matthews. 'You just play your normal game. You're a gentleman and a sportsman, Stan, but should ever anyone kick you, they'll find out I'm not.'

Clampy, as he became known, was a tough and rugged wing half who belied the position he played by never doing anything by halves. In addition to being one of the most aggressive players of the post-war era, he was also a great character. By the time he retired, Clampy had amassed a wealth of great and comic stories from his time in the game, and became a very popular after-dinner speaker. One of his favourites concerned his time as a player at Highbury. Eddie had twelve successful seasons with Wolves, during which time he won two First Division Championship medals, an FA Cup winners' medal and four caps for England, and he joined Arsenal in 1961 for a fee of £12,000. However, he never settled at Highbury. At a loss as to why he wasn't reproducing his Wolves form in an Arsenal shirt, especially when playing at fantastic, spacious grounds such as Goodison Park, Old Trafford, Maine Road and Stamford Bridge, Clampy's Arsenal team-mate Dave Bacuzzi suggested to him that he might be agoraphobic.

'Me? Afraid of fighting? Never!' replied an indignant Clampy.

Clampy only spent ten months with Arsenal before signing for Stoke City, where he forged a formidable partnership with another hard man, his former Wolves team-mate, Eddie Stuart. Before Stoke's big game against Chelsea in 1963, Clampy reiterated to Stan Matthews that he would look after him and it wasn't long before he had to do exactly that.

Chelsea had two tough left-sided players in Eddie

McCreadie and Ron Harris, and in the game Ron was given the job of marking Stan Matthews. Within minutes he had left his mark on the veteran winger, and as the game progressed, he kept hitting Stan with sledgehammer tackles, at one point unceremoniously dumping him on his backside. Stan could cope with robust tackling – he had, after all, been the subject of it for thirty-odd years – but Ron upped the ante, and his tackling became foul rather than fair. Referee Arthur Starling intervened and gave Ron a ticking off, warning him as to his future conduct, but such was football at the time, and the tolerance towards physical play, that the official decided Harris' conduct did not merit a booking.

Minutes later Ron Harris hit Stan from behind and his legs were taken from under him. Stan fell awkwardly, injuring his elbow in the process. Grimacing in pain, he opened his eyes to see Ron standing over him. As Stan lay there waiting for the Stoke trainer to arrive all of a sudden it was as if a dark cloud had passed over Stamford Bridge and blotted out the sun. Next to Ron Harris stood Clampy. The two of them had played against one another during Eddie's brief spell with Arsenal, and seemingly on that occasion the pair had been involved in a ding-dong.

'Listen here, you little sod,' said Clampy menacingly, 'if I see you clobber our Stanley again, you'll be taken out of this game. On a bloody stretcher. What I said to you last season at Arsenal wasn't a threat. It was a bloody promise.' At which point Mr Starling intervened.

'Now, now, lads. Football's the game, not boxing,' he said.

Clampy's team-mates Dennis Viollet and Don Ratcliffe, seeing Clampy was livid and concerned the big man might kick off and even be sent off, led him away from the scene. As they did this, Eddie came out with one of the best lines ever heard on a football pitch.

'That's the trouble with you referees,' said Clampy, speaking over his shoulder, 'you don't care which side wins!'

With order restored, and treatment administered to Stan Matthews, the game got under way again. Ten minutes later, Stan received a pass from Bill Asprey and set off down the wing, only for Ron Harris to hit him with one of his more humane tackles – at about thigh height. Stan saw it coming and tried to jump to avoid Ron's lunge, but to no avail: the legs of the legendary winger waggled in the air like those of Old Mother Reilly, and he was pitched headfirst across the ground. Mr Starling was quickly on the scene and, having had enough of Ron's antics, booked him. In that era a booking was the mark of serious action on the part of a referee. Unlike today, when bookings in matches are two a penny and as such seem to have lost meaning, in the early sixties they were not common, and sendings-off were rarer still. In fact I used to think that the only way a player could be sent off was if he shot someone with a gun.

With Ron Harris' name in the book, and Stan Matthews limping awkwardly, play resumed. Just before half-time Harris received a pass from Chelsea centre half John Mortimore and brought the ball out of defence. As Ron progressed up field, he started to gain speed and was some five or so yards from the halfway line, when Eddie Clamp got him in his sights. Eddie was looking in Ron's direction, but his eyes seemed to be transfixed on some point in the distance beyond the Chelsea player's shoulders. The closer Clampy came to Ron, the faster Clampy ran and the more transfixed his eyes became, until they appeared to bulge from his head like golf balls. When he was about three yards from Ron, Clampy took off, his right leg, like a bag of concrete jutting out in front of him. Airborne for a moment, Eddie completed his descent with a deep grunt and his right leg came down hard first on the ball, then on various parts of Ron's anatomy. In television cartoons whenever there is a fight, it is often depicted by swirling blurs, with arms and legs protruding at various times and moving in a circular motion. That's how it appeared when Clampy hit Ron. He rose into the air as if he was on a springboard and diving into some distant pool below, only there was no grace or technique to his movement. Clampy's legs splayed in the air, gravity did what it does and Ron ended up carving out his own niche in the pitch. With his chin!

Even in thirty years at the game Stan Matthews reckoned he had never seen a challenge like it. Such had been the force of Clampy's tackle, the ball had shot from under Ron Harris and out for a throw-in on the far side of the pitch, some twenty yards away. When the ball disappeared into the crowd, which parted like the Red Sea, it was still rising! Stoke's Don Ratcliffe was on the left wing when the ball flew past him.

'The ball was like a meteor going through the air,' Don later told me. 'It went past me so fast I feared I might get sucked into its slipstream and end up in the crowd myself.'

Meanwhile, Clampy's momentum had carried him under Ron Harris and beyond the Chelsea player, but no sooner had he applied the brakes than he was up on his feet and sprinting back to tower over a prostrate Ron.

'I telt you what would happen, lad,' snarled Clampy. 'Next time I won't play the ball first and they'll just slide the stretcher under thee. I always keep a promise.'

From that moment on Stan Matthews never had another spot of bother from Ron Harris, who settled down to play the football he was so eminently capable of. I too was often on the end of some less than humane tackling from Chopper Harris, and I didn't have Eddie Clamp to do the sorting out. Spurs did, though, have Dave Mackay, who was always quick to, as he put it, 'nip things in the bud'. For all we were adversaries on the pitch (Ron Harris was my adversary, but by no stretch of the imagination was I ever his), Ron and I became good pals off it, and these days we will often appear together at theatres or as after-dinner speakers. Although he was only a teenager at the time, for this book I wanted to get Ron's take on the Eddie Clamp incident.

'Even by the standards of the day, Clampy's challenge on me was a humdinger. In all my years of playing the game, I was never on the receiving end of one like it,' said Ron. 'No one ever thought there was anything malicious going on that day. It was how it used to be. After the game Clampy and I shared a beer, Stan had a tomato juice and we had a good laugh about it. I was still laughing – and limping – when I made my way home.'

When Stan Matthews and Eddie Clamp eventually hung up their boots they remained the best of friends. Even when into his late seventies, Clampy would always tell people he was still Stan's 'minder', and Stan loved Eddie's company as his comic stories and sharp wit always made Stan laugh. In 1997 the good people of Stoke erected a statue of Stan in the centre of Hanley, the place of his birth. It's a wonderful bronze erected on a plinth, and it captures Stan perfectly. Despite being embarrassed by the tribute, he went along to the unveiling as he didn't want to offend his own folk, and he asked Clampy to accompany him and his wife, Mila. When the statue was unveiled Stan turned to Clampy and asked his opinion of it. Eddie surveyed this fine statue mounted on a plinth, before offering his opinion.

'It's perfect, just perfect, Stan,' Clampy told him. 'You're not so high that pigeons will crap on you, and you're far enough off the ground so that dogs can't piss on you!' Stan guffawed with laughter.

When the Premiership began in 1992, hard men in the mould of Clamp, Smith, Hunter and Harris were already a dying breed. Their aggressive, raw style of play would not be tolerated in today's game, which has gradually been sanitised by the likes of television executives, the game's governing bodies, coaches, referee committees, and the influence of overseas players and managers. We have a game now in which players shave their heads but wear gloves in an attempt to keep warm. (If

Eddie Clamp or Billy Bremner were around to see it, I can just imagine what they would have to say about players wearing gloves.) The eighties and early nineties still produced their share of bad boys, and Mark Dennis (Southampton and Birmingham City) and Julian Dicks (West Ham and Liverpool) were cases in point. However, the physical style of play of the two players, and others, was far different from that of the likes of Smith, Hunter and Harris. There seemed to be a greater tendency towards petulant play in the new breed of hard player. Sledgehammer but fair tackling looked to have given way to tackles that were clearly outside the rules – hence the story that when Julian Dicks signed for Liverpool from West Ham, on his debut he picked up the number-nine shirt because he saw it had 'Fowler' written on the back. Not true, of course, but the very fact that such a story did the rounds in football is indicative of the point I am making, that the hard school which had existed in football for decades was producing an altogether different type of graduate.

The game is even more different today, and so too are the players and those with a reputation for being hard. Roy Keane is a wonderful footballer, one of the few around now who knows how to tackle, and Robbie Savage too is an aggressive player, but only by today's standards of what constitutes aggressiveness. Should Keane be transported back in time to play his football thirty or forty years in the past, he would stand out because of his football talent. With all due respect I don't think the same can be said of Robbie Savage. Even his aggressive style of play would simply blend in to that of most other players of that time and he wouldn't, as such, stand out.

With players of the style of Norman Hunter or Nobby Stiles no longer in the game today, too much time and energy is taken up addressing petulant infringements like pushing, shoving and the raising of hands, all of which are now deemed to be 'violent conduct'. You often hear managers or commentators say 'Raising your hand to an opponent is an immediate send-ing-off offence', and yet nowhere in the football rulebook does it say this, which brings me back to the point made earlier, that football today is played according to a vague consensus of what is and is not acceptable. To my mind this consensus is led by the game's administrators and by television.

Irrespective of the era, no one wants to see a player's career ended as the result of a robust challenge, but it seems to me that in the absence of what we used to term hard play, the game's authorities are jumping on incidents of mild provocation and fits of anger, considering them violent conduct. We have all witnessed players being carpeted for a fit of pique while another who has perpetrated a damaging tackle on an opponent gets away with it. I think what the FA and other bodies must do is adopt the Mikado's lead and let the punishment fit the crime. In short, common sense should prevail at all times. That, however, I feel is too much to ask.

The perception of the game's governing bodies, television and coaches as to how football should now be played has meant that many of the old skills are disappearing for ever. Some of these skills are the minutiae of how the game was once played, such as being able to pass the ball across a muddy surface or execute a fair shoulder charge. One whole area of football, however, has changed completely over the years, so much so that I think it has become a forgotten art – that of defending.

CHAPTER SIX

In the late fifties the Chelsea defence was like Jordan's shoulder-straps. They knew they had a job to do, but were incapable of doing it.

In the 1957–8 season Chelsea scored eighty-three League goals, but conceded seventy-nine. The following campaign was a little leaner as far as scoring goals was concerned – we notched seventy-seven but let in ninety-eight. The season after that seventy-six goals were scored and ninety-one shipped. Chelsea were, as the football journalist Tony Stratton-Smith once said, 'prolific at both ends'.

To be fair Chelsea were not alone, as just about every First Division club rattled goals into the net, only to concede plenty at the other end. In 1960–1 Newcastle United scored eighty-six goals, eight more than Sheffield Wednesday, who were runners-up in the First Division. Newcastle, however, conceded 109 and were subsequently relegated. It all made for royal entertainment for the supporters. Goals were what they and reporters wanted to see and, believe me, in that era of football they all saw plenty – at both ends of the pitch.

From 1956–7, when I first began to establish myself at Chelsea, to my first success as a Tottenham player in 1963, plenty of goals were scored in the First Division. There wasn't a season when at least one team netted in excess of a hundred. For three successive seasons (between 1957–8 and 1959–60) Wolves scored in excess of a hundred League goals (103, 110 and 106 respectively). In 1957–8 they were joined by Preston and Manchester City as goalscoring centurions, while Spurs and West Bromwich Albion both managed in excess of ninety.

That this was an era when teams scored and conceded a lot of goals is borne out by Manchester City who, in 1957–8, scored 104 League goals but conceded 100. At two bob (ten pence) a time to watch a game from the terraces, supporters who saw every Manchester City League game that season would have witnessed 204 goals for a total price of four pounds and four shillings (£4.20). That's what I call value for money.

I think it fair to say that supporters in that time were as fanatical in support of their clubs as they are today, but first and foremost they were supporters of football. If their team lost, they were disappointed, but such feelings would be tempered if it had been an entertaining game. Many would rather see their team lose an end-to-end game 4-3 than win a drab, soulless match 1-0. That is one of the many differences between football then and now. Today winning is everything and supporters will willingly endure games of stupefying boredom as long as their team manage to eke out a win.

We all know what Disraeli said about statistics. These can be interpreted in different ways, depending on how you look at them. However, the following statistics of goals scored in the First Division in my first five seasons as a player, compared with the last five of my career (i.e. after England had won the World Cup in 1966), make for significant reading.

Year	Goals Scored	Year	Goals Scored
1957	1612	1967	1387
1958	1721	1968	1398
1959	1692	1969	1203
1960	1790	1970	1211
1961	1725	1971	1089

These figures show a marked decline in goalscoring post-1966. In fact there were 701 fewer goals scored in the First Division in 1971 than in 1960. When one compares the aggregate number of goals scored in the fifties with those scored in the ten years following England's World Cup success, the difference is startling. The total number of goals in the First Division between 1950 and 1959 was 15,420. Between 1967 and 1976 that figure dropped to 12,880 – in essence 2,540 fewer goals were scored in the ten years after England's World Cup victory than were scored in the fifties.

This was a pattern repeated throughout the divisions of the Football League in this time. In 1961 Peterborough United were promoted from Division Four, having scored 134 goals. The runners-up that season, Crystal Palace, scored 110 goals, and Hartlepool United, who finished second bottom in the division, scored 71 goals. In 1968–9 Halifax Town won promotion from Division Four, having scored 53 League goals. To emphasise further how goals became scarce after 1966, when Peterborough United won promotion in 1961, their centre forward Terry Bly was the club's leading marksman with 52 League goals. That's just one less than the entire Halifax team managed in their promotion season of 1969. For me the thing is that the decline in the number of goals scored in my first five seasons in the game, compared with my last five, happened in the top flight, where it matters most since that is where fashions and trends are, or should be, set.

No one would argue that Liverpool had a fantastic team in the seventies. For a time Bob Paisley's side were the best in Europe, and they dominated the domestic scene throughout that decade. Yet when Liverpool won the First Division Championship in 1977, the year they also won the European Cup, they scored only sixty-two goals in the League. The previous season they had also been League champions, having scored sixty-six goals, but such a record of goals would have been considered pitiful in the early sixties. As I said earlier, Newcastle United were relegated in 1961 when they'd scored eighty-six, and the season before that – 1959–60 – Leeds

United were relegated, in spite of getting sixty-five goals. That is just one goal less than the Leeds teams that won the First Division Championship in 1969 and 1974 managed to score.

So why did teams score far fewer goals after England's World Cup success in 1966? Equally to the point, why did sides concede fewer goals? Was it simply a matter of having better defenders? Well, yes and no. It has already been established that the standard of goalkeeping in the sixties and seventies was much higher than that of the fifties, so that was a contributing factor to fewer goals being scored – goalkeepers like Gordon Banks, Peter Shilton and Ray Clemence marshalled their defences so well that opportunities for a shot at goal were limited. But the most telling factor post-1966 was the way managers and coaches slavishly followed the tactics deployed by Alf Ramsey in the World Cup, despite in most cases not having the players capable of executing such systems successfully.

I can readily recall Spurs' first training session in the wake of England's World Cup win. After our victory I had taken my family on holiday. The close season had been short because of the tournament and, after the holiday, I flew out to join the Spurs team, who had assembled in Malaga, Spain, for a pre-season get-together. Our first session astounded me: Bill Nicholson and his assistant Eddie Baily spent the best part of an hour talking theory with the aid of a blackboard, and by the time we took to the pitch I realised what an effect England's World Cup win and, moreover, Ramsey's tactics were going to have on the game. Bill Nicholson and Eddie Baily were like men possessed. They had defenders marking space, as opposed to their opposite number, with each of them given an area in our half of the field that was to be his responsibility. It was the first time I had ever experienced zonal marking at Spurs. Bill Nicholson, who had always encouraged Spurs players to 'go out and express yourselves, enjoy the game and play the football you love to play', was suddenly full of coaching sound bites and buzz-phrases: 'We have to be as good at executing a move as initiating it'; 'We must restrict the opposition's capacity to score'; 'The full backs must occupy the spaces on the flanks, as well as marking space that is part of their normal duties'; 'More goals are conceded through fatigue than any other factor. To compensate this, we have to increase our on-the-field work ratio. Create an aura of open-air claustrophobia for the opposition around our penalty area'; and 'We're going to play from the wings not on the wings'.

I listened in disbelief. Was this the manager I admired greatly, not just for what he had won, but for the fact that his teams had done so in such style? Bill Nich's adherence to what was a new way of thinking in football was typical of that of every manager and coach at the time. Wingers were out, and two-man forward lines were in. Players had to 'squeeze' the opposition in midfield. Defenders had to 'hold the line'; and why not? England were world champions, after all; but while Alf Ramsey had developed his ideas, domestic football did not go beyond this, and stuck to 4-4-2 or 4-3-3 in the style that won us the World Cup.

Hungary in 1953 and Real Madrid in 1960 had demonstrated to English football that individual talent was far more effective when deployed collectively. Teams had become more organised, and the emphasis was put on stifling opponents and not conceding goals. Winning the 'battle in midfield' became the mantra of almost every team, and having an organised and resolute defence was a priority. To concede a goal was almost blasphemy. A team might win 2-1 but a manager would bemoan the fact that his side had let in what he considered to be a 'cheap goal'.

Along with this came more analysis of matches, something that was 'helped' by television's increased coverage of the game. The 1970 World Cup saw ITV give birth to the television pundit. I should know, I was one of them. Looking back at old tapes now, what the likes of George Best, Derek Dougan,

Pat Crerand and I had to say about matches amounted to little more than plain common sense. There was even a certain irreverence in much of what we said. I talked simply about the game because that is what it is, a simple game. Although one would be hard pressed to believe that listening to the pundits and summarisers of today.

With games and incidents subject increasingly to analysis, television naturally wanted an opinion from the coalface, and the contributions of managers and coaches when interviewed served only to make football seem even more complicated. They were naturally more guarded in what they had to say; they had, after all, their jobs to protect and so teams were praised for their 'professional' attitude, which was a way of saying they applied themselves to the job in such a way as to deny the opposition opportunities to play. When a side scored as much time was devoted to discussing the mistakes the opposition had made as to praising the build-up that led to the goal. Slow-motion replays allowed the mistakes of defenders to be highlighted, and a culture of fear crept into the game. Managers and their teams set out not to concede goals instead of trying to score as many as they could.

This was the climate in English football post-1966. The flair players of the seventies, such as Alan Hudson, Stan Bowles, Tony Currie and Rodney Marsh, were branded 'mavericks' and, for all their skill and technique, found themselves frozen out of England teams. Players had to be professional which meant fitting into a rigid system of play and being a good team player, rather than a gifted individualist. Little wonder George Best became bored, disillusioned and disenchanted with it all. He was an artist who threw away his brushes and canvas, and with them his inborn genius to entertain and excite.

There have been times in my life when I have thought about what fate might have had in store for me, had I not been injured in 1966, and played in the World Cup final. However, I can honestly say I haven't thought about that as much as I have about how English football would have developed had we not won the World Cup. As we've seen, in the fifties conceding goals was largely acceptable, as long as you scored one more than the opposition, and this attitude changed after England's World Cup success when teams, in particular in defence, became better organised. Of course, there is a case for saying defenders became better players because they let in fewer goals, but whether or not they became better footballers is a moot point. The game changed considerably in the late sixties and seventies: players were fitter than in the fifties – though no fitter than they had been in the sixties – and defenders certainly did improve, though their cause in this was helped by the fact that much of the rest of the team had to help them defend. 'Work rate', 'effort and commitment' became bywords for good play, and that is still largely the case today. How many times does one hear a contemporary manager explain away a defeat by saying, 'I don't think you can fault the effort and commitment of the players today'? When I hear that I always think, You could have taken eleven of your supporters out of the crowd and played them. They wouldn't have been able to play football, but you couldn't have faulted their effort and commitment.

When a player is being paid thousands of pounds a week for playing the game, the very least you expect from him is effort and commitment.

The game has changed so much over the years that comparisons between the defenders of yesteryear and those of today are meaningless. Modern English football contains some of the best defenders ever to have graced the game: Sol Campbell, Ashley Cole, John Terry and Kolo Touré would have been outstanding defenders in any era of football. If there is an area in which the current England team can be said to be well blessed, it is in the heart of defence. Over the decades central defenders in English football were seen as players with great prowess in the air, and as players who dug in, gritted their teeth and clenched their fists. As ursine warriors with limited skills, in fact, but that's not strictly true. England could boast Bobby Moore, and players like Colin Todd, Roy McFarland and Paul Madeley were as skilful as the most cerebral of midfield players. These notable exceptions apart, though, generally speaking central defenders did have their limitations, whereas English football today possesses a number of central defenders who are more than simply prosaic artisans capable of heading a ball out of defence and kicking it like a comet through the atmosphere.

While I've said the true value of having a top-quality goalkeeper is still not appreciated by some managers, English football seems to have woken up to the fact that the contribution of a top-quality centre back is as crucial to winning trophies as that of an Henry, Giggs, or a Lampard. Before the arrival of Arsène Wenger, Arsenal's success was built on a rock-solid back four. Lee Dixon, Tony Adams, Steve Bould, Martin Keown and Nigel Winterburn were, at various times, the mainstays of that back four. When Wenger took over as manager at Highbury, he realised age was against his defence, and gradually replaced them all. The players Wenger brought in were of a different type, but superb defenders all the same – Sol Campbell, Kolo Touré, Etame Lauren and Ashley Cole replaced the old guard in a way that was to prove seamless.

Wenger, I am sure, appreciated the worth of Adams, Bould and Co., and knew he would need a resolute defence of cultured players, if he were to build on past successes. Likewise, in 2001, Sir Alex Ferguson needed an outstanding central defender to replace Jaap Stam. Manchester United won the Premiership in each of the three seasons Stam was at Old Trafford, but the player's undoing was to make less-than-favourable remarks in his autobiography about Sir Alex's dealings in the transfer market. Stam's departure, however, was not the undoing of Manchester United. Sir Alex went out and bought Rio Ferdinand as a replacement for the Dutchman, and subsequently the Premiership title was wrested from Arsenal. José Mourinho continues to add to the galaxy of talent at Stamford Bridge. Few players seem guaranteed a place in the Chelsea first team, with the exception, that is, of John Terry. It says much for Terry's quality and contribution that Mourinho plays him consistently in a team that appears to change as often as the moon. Perhaps an inkling as to what Mourinho thinks of Terry can be gleaned from something he said to the press when questioned about the central defender.

'He plays because when you build a house, you don't start with the roof but the foundations,' said Mourinho.

The interesting thing about some current central defenders, such as John Terry, Sol Campbell and Rio Ferdinand, is how they have become as much superstars in the game as players like David Beckham, Ryan Giggs and Thierry Henry. Terry, Campbell and Ferdinand have just as much kudos when it comes to their cultural appeal as Beckham, Henry or Giggs. In the past centre backs like Jack Charlton, Mike England, Dave Watson, Terry Butcher and Tony Adams enjoyed respect and reverence, but were never considered to be among the cultural elite of football. Today Sol Campbell, John Terry and Rio Ferdinand capitalise on their standing as *galacticos*, and their Prada-clad shoulders can be seen in magazines like *Esquire* and *Loaded* just as often as they appear in *Shoot* or *FourFourTwo*. That England have an embarrassment of riches when it comes to central defenders can also be shown from the fact that in 2004 Real Madrid signed Jonathan Woodgate, a central defender who is so far down the pecking order when it comes to a place in the England team as not to be there at all.

While Wenger, Mourinho and Ferguson appreciate the worth of top-class defenders to a team as much as the managers of yesteryear, seemingly football writers are still seduced by goalscorers and creative midfield players. I say that because it is over twenty years since a defender was voted the Football Writers' Association Footballer of the Year. Steve Nicol won the award in 1989, but he played more in the Liverpool midfield than he did their defence. One has to go back to 1977 and Emlyn Hughes to find a recognised defender as Footballer of the Year, although there is a case for saying Hughes too spent a chunk of his Anfield career in midfield. Goalkeepers apart, the last out-and-out defender to be voted Footballer of the Year by the FWA was Nottingham Forest's Kenny Burns in 1978 who, I should say, had been converted from a striker to a central defender by Brian Clough and Peter Taylor. From that I can only surmise that for all the plaudits awarded to Terry, Campbell and Ferdinand, when it comes to appreciation of worth, our top football writers prefer attacking zeal.

Not that there is anything wrong in that, of course.

For me the best defender English football has ever produced is Bobby Moore. What elevates Bobby above the likes of Tony Adams, Sol Campbell and John Terry is that he had an abundance of style. Bobby and I were great mates – our friendship dated back to his early days with the England team in 1962 and continued unabated until his untimely death in 1993. Bobby began his career as an amateur with West Ham in 1956 and signed as a professional two years later. He made 642 League and Cup appearances for the Hammers, captaining them to victories in the FA Cup (1964) and the European Cup Winners' Cup the following season. Bobby joined Fulham in 1974 and went on to add a further 150 matches to his domestic career, one of which involved him leading Fulham in the FA Cup final of 1975 when, as fate would have it, they lost to his old club West Ham.

Bobby made a record eighteen appearances for the England youth team – I used to josh him that he must have been the only twenty-eight-year-old ever to play youth-team football –

and went on to win 108 caps for England at senior level. Ninety of those were as captain. He was voted Footballer of the Year in 1964, when it was not unusual for defenders to win this prestigious award. The runner-up to Bobby that year was the Sunderland centre half Charlie Hurley. Sunderland were then a Second Division team, though they did win promotion that season, but for the life of me I can't imagine a defender in the Championship these days ever being voted runner-up as Footballer of the Year. This is basically because I'm not so sure some of our top football writers know the Championship exists.

Bobby, of course, will always be remembered for having skippered England when we won the World Cup in 1966. Our victory was always a matter of great pride to him, and it was the mark of the man that in winning the World Cup he felt greater satisfaction for his country, and English football in particular, than for any sense of personal achievement. When Bobby announced his retirement from football in 1977 it came as something of a surprise to me. So effortless and easy did he make the game look that deep in the back of my mind I had the notion he could go on playing for ever.

Bobby Moore possessed any amount of laudable qualities, one such being the higher the stakes, in terms of world-class opposition, the higher he was able to raise his game. He played football effortlessly, with élan and panache. Owing to the economical way he played, some might be forgiven for thinking he was not always in top gear, but I doubt whether any of Bobby's opponents ever questioned his commitment. When lesser players had to run around to be effective, Bobby's considerable cerebral qualities as a player enabled him to be a highly effective defender while moving only the minimum number of yards. Pitched against the best players in the world (of which he was one) such as Pele and Eusebio, he produced defensive football of the highest level.

Bobby seemed to be able to read a pass before the idea

occurred in the mind of his opponent, and I think this was one of the secrets of his success. When a footballer plays in a deep position, as Bobby always did, his first responsibility is to defend, but that may be doing the great man injustice. Bobby Moore was not your archetypal defender, far from it. He played in an era when the England shirt was pristine, and carried no sponsors' logos or politically correct messages on behalf of kit manufacturers, and that was in keeping with an England captain whose football was of the purist type. Long ball or short ball, it was always the right ball from Bobby. His passing or 'possessional distribution', as Chris Kamara once referred to it on Sky Television, was immaculate. A naturally two-footed player, such was Bobby's creativity and accuracy when passing the ball other players despaired of emulating him.

I found Bobby a very easy defender to play alongside. He would pass the ball to a point where an opponent found it hardest to perpetrate a tackle on the receiver. He never belted the ball, but always seemed to stroke it gently towards a teammate so that your next move was simplified. I have heard some people say that if Bobby had any weakness as a defender, it was that he tackled like a wet lettuce. All I can say is I played against him on many an occasion and I can assure you that a tackle from Bobby Moore was anything but a pleasurable experience. He wasn't among the hardest tacklers of his era, but he didn't have to be. Bobby's timing was such that he stole the ball, rather than won it off an opponent. If the ball broke loose in the penalty box, it would prompt players from both sides into a frenzy. They would jostle one another for possession like late-night revellers scrambling to get on the last bus home, but above the chaos would be Bobby Moore. When confronted with such a situation, invariably out of the panic he would emerge, elegant, poised, dignified and graceful, with the ball at his feet. It would never occur to him to alleviate the pressure by whacking the ball up into Row G. Instead that incredible football brain of his would see an opportunity for a pass and the ball would glide across the pitch to the intended recipient.

As a captain Bobby operated more by example than by inspiration or by shouting words of encouragement. He was always cool, calm and collected, which instilled in us fellow England players a feeling that all was well and that there was no way the opposition were ever going to rattle him. It was that superior level of calm that rubbed off to England's advantage when we won the World Cup.

Bobby was a sixties icon. His face became the face of English football and was also emblazoned on adverts for suits, deodorants, shoes, shirts and even pubs and gravy. Little wonder that when England travelled to Colombia prior to the 1970 World Cup finals in Mexico, it was Bobby who was subjected to a trumped-up charge of shoplifting a bracelet. As Alan Mullery said at the time, 'It stinks because it's all rubbish. Bobby steal a bracelet? With his money he could buy the whole shop.' The judge agreed, and Bobby rejoined the England team in Mexico. He played so assuredly throughout England's involvement in the tournament that Pele was moved to say, 'He's the best defender in the world'. Praise doesn't come any higher.

It was said of James Whistler (probably by himself) that he mixed his paints with brains. That is what Bobby Moore did with his football. Tony Stratton-Smith told me he once offered a complimentary ticket to see England play Northern Ireland to a colleague of his at the *Daily Mail*, only for his fellow journo to turn down the offer.

'Bobby Moore's playing,' said Tony.

'But *Coronation Street*'s on the telly,' said Tony's colleague.

Anyone who could ever pass up the opportunity to see Bobby Moore play in an England shirt would, I am sure, pull the blinds down when passing the Taj Mahal at sunset.

Another great defender I had the privilege to play with was

Danny Blanchflower. Without wanting to give further emphasis to my point about football writers being seduced by
attacking flair for the past thirty years, it should be noted that
Danny was voted Footballer of the Year twice (1958 and 1961).
He was one of the most creative and authoritative players ever
to grace British football. Danny was a born leader who, as well
as captaining Tottenham Hotspur through the 'Glory Glory'
years of the early sixties, captained the Northern Ireland team
that reached the quarter-finals of the World Cup in 1958. He
won fifty-six caps for Northern Ireland and later managed the
national team, before a spell in charge at Chelsea. In all he
played 337 League games for Spurs between 1954 and 1963,
prior to which he had also served Glentoran, Barnsley and
Aston Villa with great distinction.

If John White can be considered to have been the artist of
Tottenham, then Danny was the poet. He gave the side style
and verve and was a captain in every sense of the word, inspiring team-mates with performances of outstanding quality and
lifting us with words of wisdom. His contribution to the team
was as important as, on occasions more important than, that of
manager Bill Nicholson. Danny played a great game, but his
eloquence meant he was also the dressing-room tactician, and
the training ground theorist, who always put his ideas into
practice on the football field.

When Spurs played Leicester City in the 1961 FA Cup final,
the teams were presented to the Duchess of Kent. As Danny
was in the process of introducing the Spurs team to the
Duchess, she asked, 'Why do the Leicester players have their
names on the back of their tracksuits, but your players do not?'

'Well, ma'am,' Danny replied in his best Irish accent, 'we
know each other.'

Danny was more of a captain than a defender, but in saying
that I don't mean he was not a very good player – he was,
though the one person who believed that most was Danny
himself, whose play at times exuded arrogance. He oozed

confidence and that carried over into his play, where he would often bluff and double-bluff opponents. A beautiful passer of the ball, Danny was a visionary defender who never knew when he was beaten, and even if physically he didn't look up to the job, he was one of those players who, whenever an opponent came near him, appeared to be all jutting bone and elbows. Like Bobby Moore, Danny didn't possess a sledgehammer tackle, but again like Moore, his timing in the tackle enabled him to be a highly effective defender. Once in possession of the ball that brain of his ensured Danny used the ball with all the effect of the most creative of midfield players.

Danny's way with words led the *Observer* to give him his own column, which he insisted on writing himself. Though still a player at the time, he refused to compromise his views in order to conform with the wishes of the football authorities. This, needless to say, didn't make him popular with the blazer brigade, who were pre-eminent in English football at the time. Whenever someone told Danny of the wrath he had incurred among FA officials, he would reply, 'I think, therefore I'm dangerous.'

Danny was at the forefront of the fight to have the maximum wage abolished and to put an end to the contracts that tied a player to a club for life – he believed, as we all did, that such a situation was in violation of our labour rights. Danny would use his newspaper column to voice his opinion on the matter of footballers' rights, and the maximum wage in particular, questioning why such a situation should be tolerated, and often donating the fee he received for such articles to the PFA's Benevolent Fund for former players. Having read such an article of Danny's, after one international match an official of the Irish FA told Danny he was 'an out-and-out communist'.

'Now there's a thing. If you donate money to a benevolent fund for former players, you are considered kind and caring of former footballers,' said Danny. 'But if you ask why former footballers now struggle to make ends meet, and put forward suggestions that will ensure future generations of footballers will not be poor, then you're a communist!'

Just before the 1963 European Cup Winners' Cup final, Spurs manager Bill Nicholson, in warning us about Atletico Madrid, contrived to make them out to be world-beaters. Bill began systematically to go through the Atletico team, waxing lyrical about the strengths of each player, only for Danny to jump in and stop him in full flow. Danny poured cold water on the merits of the Spaniards and reminded us all of our, to his mind, superior qualities as individuals and as a team. Bill Nicholson took a back seat, and Spurs' success in that final was in no small way down to Danny and the proactive stance he took in our dressing room before the game.

Managers and coaches had to be very careful about what they said in a dressing room in front of Danny, as he would seize upon any faux pas. In 1961–2 Spurs reached a crucial stage of the season when in contention for the League Championship, the European Cup and the FA Cup.

'We've come to a crossroads', assistant manager Harry Evans told us. 'One road will take us to glory and success. The other leads to a dead end.'

'That's not a crossroads,' piped up Danny. 'It's a T-junction.'

Danny's sharp wit was legendary. Following a game against Burnley, the Clarets' skipper Jimmy Adamson was talking about his club chairman Bob Lord, who had a reputation for being somewhat bombastic, but to his credit he had built a very successful chain of butchers' shops, and had also risen to become president of the Football League.

'Success hasn't spoiled him,' said Jimmy.

'No,' replied Danny, 'he's always been insufferable.'

Danny was often controversial in what he said and wrote, and on occasions could be very cutting. Once, referring to a young player at Spurs who the press were bulling up, but in reality was not making the grade at the club, Danny said, 'He rose without trace.'

However, Danny could also be lyrical, poetic and poignant. After a Spurs victory over Arsenal, the football writer Bill Holden asked him, in light of the fact that sportsmanship was very valuable to Danny, how important it was to win games. 'Winning isn't everything,' replied Danny, 'but wanting to win is.'

To me Danny was the Oscar Wilde of Windsor Park. He would wax lyrical about football and its relation to life; football and its relation to society; football and its relation to politics; football and its relation to trouser fluff. To ask him anything about football would be to induce a reply as epic as any of Tennyson's poems, but sometimes Danny was just too high-brow for people. On one occasion, straight out of the dressing room after a game for Northern Ireland, he was confronted by a reporter, who asked for his opinion of George Best.

'George makes a greater appeal to the senses than Finney or Matthews did,' replied Danny with characteristic lyricism. 'His movements are quicker, lighter, more balletic. George offers grander surprises to the mind and the eye. He has ice in his veins, warmth in his heart, and timing and balance in his feet.'

The reporter looked up from his notebook, somewhat agitated.

'Yeah, yeah, Danny,' he said with disinterest, his pencil still poised, 'but how do you rate George as a player?'

Today Alan Hansen is known as the scourge of 'rank bad defending', and is the man who introduced the phrase 'launch it' to football's vocabulary. He was, however, anything but a practitioner of the long ball in his days as a centre back with Liverpool and Scotland, being arguably the most complete defender during the eighties. Unquestionably one of the most elegant and creative defenders in Europe, his exploits on the field redefined what the likes of Franz Beckenbauer and Gaetano Scirea had done for their clubs and countries previously. Liverpool manager Bob Paisley once described Hansen as 'the best ball-playing defender I have ever seen'. From such a manager that is praise indeed, and few would contest the view of the most successful manager Liverpool have ever had.

Having a ball player of Hansen's pedigree in defence gave Liverpool the option of retaining the ball once possession had been won in and around their penalty area, rather than having to commit to the lottery of a long-ball clearance, which was in vogue with many clubs in the eighties. He brought another dimension to that great Liverpool side. His ability to read a game and win the ball by way of interception before a tackle need be made, made him an automatic choice for a decade and more in a team that had no peer in Europe.

Hansen possessed the quality of all great players, being comfortable when on the ball and always appearing to have time. He was a top-quality central defender, but was not in the traditional mould of a colossus of scar tissue and testosterone. His build was lithe and lean, and his skills were not purely confined to defending – he loved to attack, often bringing the ball out of defence with seemingly consummate ease to create goals for his fellow team-mates and, on occasions, even himself.

In football terms, Alan Hansen was a natural, but it was not the only sport at which the young man excelled. As a teenager in Clachmannan, he represented Scotland at Under 18 level in four sports – swimming, squash, golf and volleyball – though, oddly, never football. He began his career with Partick Thistle and was only seventeen when he made his first-team debut for the Firhill club. Before long his cool and stylish performances in the heart of Thistle's defence got noticed and by the age of twenty-one both Liverpool and Newcastle United were vying for his services. A deal was agreed with Newcastle manager Joe Harvey, but the Magpies' board baulked at paying a fee of £100,000 for an 'unknown' defender. The fee, however, was no stumbling block to Liverpool. Although the manager Bob Paisley had never seen Hansen play, he acted on the recommendation of the club's Scottish scout and brought Alan to

Anfield. Little did Hansen know that in achieving his dream move to Liverpool he was part of a tax planning exercise.

At the time Liverpool had a policy of buying a player, in the words of Bob Paisley, that 'they would take a chance on for tax purposes'. The tax year ended in early May and rather than pay a large tax bill on money they had in the bank, Liverpool would sign a player who was not a big name but was someone they felt had the promise to turn into a decent player. The fee paid out reduced Liverpool's bank balance and in so doing moved them into another tax bracket, thus reducing the amount of tax they would have to pay. This policy had been in operation for some years at Liverpool and, after acquiring Hansen, in subsequent years they bought Frank McGarvey and Avi Cohen. The club became noted for signing players then putting them in the reserves for a couple of years, sup- posedly to learn the Anfield ways. This idea was, of course, really a myth, because most were, like Hansen, players the club took a chance on, and who were signed to write off tax. Bob Paisley's 'chance' signing of Hansen paid off in more ways than one. The defender quickly established himself in the first team and was the only Liverpool player to last through the club's halcyon days of the eighties, his own performances as consistently brilliant as those of the team itself. Throughout that time he developed into a refined and calculating central defender – one of the all-time greats, whose prowess was admired throughout Europe but, curiously, not always by the Scotland management. Hansen won just twenty-six caps for his country. The most plausible explanation for such a meagre haul for so wonderful a talent is that successive Scotland managers were of the mind that Hansen never reproduced his club form when playing for his country, and as a result other candidates for the position were more worthy. All I can say is if there was a better Scottish central defender around at the time of Alan Hansen, I never saw him.

Today Alan is better known as a television pundit, but what

does not often come across when he is on the TV is his tremendous sense of humour. This is also to be seen in the common perception of Hansen's team-mate, and later manager at Liverpool, Kenny Dalglish, as that of a serious, some would say, dour man. Both Hansen and Dalglish possess a wicked sense of humour and were often at the heart of fun and pranks in the Liverpool dressing room. They were also responsible for one of the greatest practical jokes ever perpetrated in football. In 1986–7 Liverpool had a forward, Alan Irvine, who they signed from Falkirk. Irvine had scored 18 goals in 116 appearances for Falkirk, and he was brought in as part of Liverpool's continued policy of wanting to take a chance on a promising young player, while at the same time reducing their tax bill. Liverpool were drawn against Luton Town in the third round of the FA Cup. The teams drew 0-0 at Kenilworth Road in January and therefore replayed at Anfield a few days later in midweek. It was a ritual at Liverpool for the players to assemble just before noon at a hotel on the outskirts of the city and have lunch, after which they would retire to their allotted rooms to sleep in the afternoon, before being woken for the short trip to Anfield.

Kenny Dalglish was player-manager at the time and late in the afternoon he instructed his staff to wake up the players. One by one they gathered in the hotel lounge until only one was missing – Alan Irvine. Kenny dispatched one of his staff to rustle up Irvine, as the rest of the players made their way to the team coach. The weather was not good, thick snow was falling and while Dalglish awaited the arrival of Irvine, he received a phone call to say the match referee had inspected the Anfield pitch, thought it unfit for play and had postponed the match. Kenny informed everyone of the situation; everyone, that is, but Alan Irvine, who was still AWOL. As the team sat on the coach, Kenny boarded the bus and told the lads he was going to have a bit of fun at the expense of 'sleepy-head'.

Eventually Alan Irvine arrived and, somewhat flustered,

took a seat at the back of the coach with Alan Hansen, Bruce Grobbelaar, Mark Lawrenson, Gary Gillespie, Ian Rush and John Wark. He had yet to play a first-team game for Liverpool, but he was in for a shock – no sooner had the team coach left the hotel than Kenny stood up and beckoned the young Scot to sit by him at the front of the bus. In all seriousness Kenny announced to Irvine that he was going to give him his debut that night against Luton. The player, flustered with excitement, told his manager he would do his best not to let anybody down.

'Dee your best, that's all I ask of you. I know you're gonna do us a good job,' Kenny told the excited Irvine.

'What role do you want me to play?' he asked. 'Will I be playing up to Rushy?'

'No, I have a special job for you to do for us tonight,' said Kenny. 'Alan has a knock. You'll be playing in central defence alongside Lawro.'

The rest of the Liverpool team watched as a flabbergasted Irvine's jaw dropped.

'Centre half? On my debut? I've never played there in my life!' said Irvine, his voice now shrill.

'I know you can play there and do us a job,' said Kenny confidently. 'You wouldn't be questioning my judgement now, would you?'

Irvine assured him that was never the case and, after thanking his boss for handing him his Liverpool debut, returned to join his team-mates who, of course, were all in on the gag. He excitedly revealed the news of his debut and the fact that he would be lining up in the Cup tie at centre half alongside Mark Lawrenson. Hansen, Lawrenson, Grobbelaar and the rest all played up to Irvine. They told him they had seen him in action in training and were of the mind that the boss was right, his best position was in central defence. The conversation eventually abated and for the rest of the journey Alan Irvine sat staring out at a snowy Merseyside, proud, excited and alone with his thoughts, while the other Liverpool lads fought to contain their laughter.

Liverpool draw their support from all parts of the country, and the announcement that the game against Luton had been postponed came too late to prevent many fans making the trip to Anfield. As the Liverpool team coach pulled up outside the players' entrance quite a number of the club's travelling support had assembled outside the stadium. The presence of so many supporters only served to add credence to Kenny's claim that Irvine was about to make his debut as a centre half that night. The team gathered in the home dressing room and Kenny Dalglish played his role to perfection. With the aid of a whiteboard, Kenny outlined his gameplan, making particular reference to the role of Alan Irvine in the centre of defence, and telling Irvine Liverpool would be playing their normal game at the back of 'one up, one round' (so that when one central defender moved forward the other would sweep across the back). The rest of the Liverpool team played their part too, asking questions of the manager and offering views on the opposition. Finally, the team talk over, Kenny told Alan Irvine to get changed, and instructed the rest of the team to go down to the foyer and distribute their complimentary tickets to family and friends.

The Liverpool players, all except for Irvine of course, simply left the dressing room and headed for home, as did Dalglish. A quarter of an hour passed and, with about half an hour to go to the scheduled kick-off, the Liverpool dressing-room attendant came to switch off the lights and lock up. As the attendant made his way along the corridor he heard the noise of a ball being kicked against a wall in the home-team dressing room. Curious as to who could be in there when everyone else had gone home, the attendant gingerly opened the door. As he did so he was taken aback to see Alan Irvine, wearing the strip of a central defender, kicking a practice ball against the wall.

'What the hell are you doing here all kitted up?' asked the perplexed dressing-room attendant.

Goals are what supporters like to see. As a former player who relished scoring, no one more than me likes to see a match containing plenty of goals. If I were to be asked which era of football I preferred between the fifties, when I began my career, and the seventies, when it all came to an end for me, I would say the fifties every time. I have said before that teams were not too worried about shipping goals as long as they scored one more than the opposition, and I don't like to see sides go a goal up then do the professional thing and kill the game. If a team is playing away from home, especially in the Champions League, and they stifle the game I often hear pundits say, 'They've done the right thing. They've silenced the home crowd'. Of course teams must try and achieve a result, but it is how some teams set about doing that which irks me. Supporters pay hard-earned money to watch their football, and call me old-fashioned but I think footballers have a duty to the fans to go out on to the park and at least try and entertain them.

I don't want to see a return to the choking, stifling tactics that beset the game in the late sixties and early seventies, when many games degenerated into a slogging battle in midfield, with defences regularly coming out on top. I am all for open, fluid and entertaining football that produces plenty of goals. That said, you might find it odd that I now say I think the art of defending in the modern game has become less of a spectacle. I love to see goals being scored, but football is about much more than goals.

In recent years the game of cricket has, to my mind, tinkered and tampered with the rules to produce a game that makes life easier for batsmen and more difficult for bowlers. This has been done because cricket's governing bodies are of the view what people want to see is runs being scored. Yet one of the fascinations of the game of cricket is the contest between bat and ball, the 'private' battle between batsman and bowler. Similarly in football, the introduction of lightweight footballs and the change in the offside law are just two aspects of the game that, to me, have been introduced for no other reason than to try and make it easier to score goals. Even though goals are what we want to see, like the contest between bat and ball in cricket there is, of course, much more to the sport than how many are scored. One of football's intrigues is the contest between attackers and defenders. I don't like to see games develop in such a way that they become like chess matches, but an area of the modern game that in my opinion needs improving is the art of defending.

The current culture of football has much to do with this art being on the wane. If you'll pardon the pun, the propensity of the modern game to think only of short-term goals has had much to do with the decline. Managers are under pressure to get results, and know they won't be at a club very long if they don't produce. Hence the quick-fix mentality runs throughout the game, and instead of working to overcome a problem, a manager will simply go out and buy a new player, or, if he hasn't money to buy, bring one in on loan.

Many managers like to rotate their squads – either through necessity, relying as they do on the loan system, or through an embarrassment of riches, as at clubs like Chelsea. We've seen with goalkeepers how rotation can unsettle players. Rotating a defence, however, deflects from its purpose. It is detrimental to understanding. One of the key elements to having a sound defence is communication between team-mates, something that is built up through training together, playing together and talking to one another. It stands to reason that should a defence be chopped and changed it will not foster under-standing. Back lines now appear to be drawn from a *South Pacific* cast list, and sometimes players seem to have been barely introduced before taking up their positions. Little wonder the prankster Karl Power was able to join a

Manchester United line-up for a photo call prior to a Champions League match, and no one, including the United players, questioned his presence. United have a more settled defence now, but during the season of Power's prank, Ferguson played Stam, Blanc, Brown, Neville, Silvestre, May and Johnsen in combinations as centre backs.

The style and appearance of today's top defenders is a far cry from how they once were. When I started out in the game there were not that many kinds of full back. One type might be short and squat, with legs like bags of concrete, and boast the build of a dance-hall bouncer. His lack of inches would be considered an advantage as it was thought a low centre of gravity allowed him to turn quickly when confronted with a tricky winger. As ridiculous as that may seem, there appeared to be a certain amount of truth in this theory. Another sort of full back would be tall, with a wizened face and a prison haircut, and as muscular as dog meat, though never muscle-bound. Both these types had to be strong enough to resist the heaviest challenge, fast enough to catch the speediest and trickiest of wingers, yet mobile enough to be always at hand when the need arose for mutual cover. Finesse was thin on the ground. Most full backs viewed the cinder track that often ran around the pitch as merely the receptacle for any winger thought to be getting above his station.

Within a couple of years of me having entered the game, these types of full back soon became a dying breed in the First Division, though they continued to prosper in the lower divisions of the Football League. The reason for their decline was, in the main, down to the influence of England manager Walter Winterbottom, whose coaching techniques gave rise to a more cultured breed of full back – players like Jimmy Armfield, Don Howe, and the emerging George Cohen and Ray Wilson. These were full backs who were more thoughtful in their approach to the game and for whom passing was more than either slipping the ball two yards to a 'schemer' or hitting a forty-yard ball on to the head of a lofty centre forward.

The centre half was always the tallest man in the team and physically the strongest. Whatever was thrown at him, he was expected to remain as unmoved as a lighthouse beset by a raging sea. In a way this was apposite because most appeared to be as tall as a lighthouse and built of similar dimensions, although for all such centre halves were highly effective, illuminating they were not. Flanking the towering centre half were the wing halves. One would normally be a creative sort of player, who used the ball intelligently and well, though this type of player could himself come in two categories. The first would have the sort of physique fortunate men are blessed with, so that whatever he chose to wear he'd always look the epitome of style. With his neatly groomed hair and film-star looks, in the way of Stan Anderson (Sunderland) and Ronnie Clayton (Blackburn Rovers), he would exude style and flair on the pitch. The other kind of cerebral, creative wing half was, in appearance, the antithesis of the film-star type. With his often balding head, gaunt facial features, thin frame and knobbly knees, he would seem old beyond his years. Far from resembling the archetypal image of a footballer, he would look more like the man from the Prudential or Pearl who called every week at your door to collect the 'insurance money'. But these cultured, intelligent wing halves could defend and they also contributed greatly to the attack with long raking passes, and a mobility that allowed them to come up from deep and score goals by arriving late in the opponents' penalty area.

In sharp contrast to the creative wing halves the other would be what we used to call a 'frightener'. When not hitting you with a bone-crusher of a tackle, the frightener would man-mark you with all the grace of a mating ostrich. His repertoire of tackles knew no bounds. As well as challenging you in the conventional way, he'd tackle with his head, neck or backside, hell-bent on winning the ball. Every part of his anatomy was utilised in a rabid quest for possession. When he had the ball, the best his manager could hope for was that he would pass to someone with the same coloured shirt. The frightener was anything but creative, and rarely would he feature among the goals. But his team needed him as the Navy used to need destroyers.

I think the most telling aspect about the game, and defences in particular, in the fifties was the formation of a team. Most still adhered to a variation of the 'WM' system. That so many goals were scored in this era wasn't down to defenders not being as good at their job as they later became – although defences were not so well organised – but the fact that with five forwards it meant that half the outfield players were devoted to attacking. This was a situation in sharp contrast to the tactics of modern gaffers like Burnley's Steve Cotterill, who is often cited as 'one of the game's up-and-coming managers'. Prior to his side's fifth-round FA Cup tie at home to Blackburn Rovers in February 2005, Cotterill gave a pre-match interview during which he announced that Burnley would be 'playing their normal game with just one man upfront'. A one-man forward line for a team at home in the FA Cup? I am not a betting man, but if I was I would have put money on that game going on to be one of stupefying boredom, and ending goalless. It was and it did.

Managers and coaches these days may spend countless hours devising systems of play in an attempt to prevent the opposition scoring a goal, and they can organise and drill defenders and defences until the cows come home, but the bottom line is that football teams are comprised of human beings and as such are subject to human frailties. We all make mistakes, and errors are going to be made on a football pitch. It is a good thing too, for if it were not for mistakes, there would be no goals to cheer. The best a manager and his side can do is to try and minimise the blunders their players make out on the pitch in the course of a game. It is commonly accepted that the higher the standard of football the fewer gaffes are made, but conversely the better the quality the more any mistakes are punished.

Today's top teams are so well organised and so well versed in technique that on occasions it is only a dreadful error on the part of a single player or a match official that will separate the sides. For some years England supporters have been riddled with angst at the way our national team has exited from major international competitions. It has got to such an extent now, it's almost become ingrained in the national psyche that we are destined to be unlucky and suffer. The goals Sol Campbell had disallowed against Argentina in the 1998 World Cup and against Portugal in Euro 2004 were harsh on England because both efforts appeared legitimate, only to be ruled out. In my opinion the respective referees made monumental errors of judgement, which serves to emphasise that some games are won and – in the case of England – lost as the result of a glaring mistake. Both those two matches were tight; there was little, if anything, to choose between the teams. England and their opponents were so well drilled, and the standard of play and technical ability so high, they could not be separated, but for an error that would result in the losers bemoaning their bad luck. That is how many games are today at the highest level. The way things have developed, there is only a fag paper's width of difference in the quality of the top teams, and they will routinely cancel one another out until the crucial moment comes when a player, or a match official, decides the issue by faltering for an instant. (David Seaman's faux pas when faced with Ronaldinho's free-kick for Brazil against England in the 2002 World Cup is another case in point.) With the margins of error being so slight, the media's saturation coverage of the game magnifies every mistake nowadays. Being a defender must be a tense business, with anxiety always under the surface, and despair and heartache, sometimes literally, only a step away.

Goals come from mistakes but in order to induce one in an opponent you have to do something with the ball that foxes him. For that to happen a team must do something creative and, more often than not, they rely on their more creative players, or as we used to call them, playmakers. There has always been, for the most part, a friendly and healthy rivalry between the playmakers, or schemers as they were once called, and those who held more workmanlike positions in the team.

At half-time during the famous 1953 FA Cup final, with Blackpool trailing 3-1 to Bolton Wanderers, after the Blackpool manager Joe Smith had said his piece, skipper and right half Harry Johnston offered a few words to his team before they took to the pitch for the second half.

'Eddie [Shimwell], Tommy [Garrett], Cyril [Robinson] and me, we will deal with the rough and tumble,' Johnston told his team-mates. 'You lot who can play, do your bit. We've got the Fancy Dan ball players with brains, who can win us this Cup. We foot-soldiers will do our bit and keep them out, so let's get out and bloody well win it.'

Harry Johnston's reference to 'Fancy Dan ball players with brains' and his self-deprecating reference to players like himself as 'foot-soldiers' for all it was said over fifty years ago, is still an attitude prevalent in dressing rooms today. Johnston wasn't being insulting to anyone; on the contrary, it was a backhanded compliment to the likes of Stan Matthews, Ernie Taylor and Jackie Mudie. Harry was as much aware of their creative gifts as he was of the limitations of his own talent, and in essence he was telling his team-mates that they had a well-balanced side, good enough to turn around a 3-1 deficit (which they did). It goes back to Just Fontaine likening a football team to a concert pianist on tour and comprising a gifted creative, an orchestrator, a string section and piano shifters.

There has always been and always will be a level of good-natured competition between the playmakers and goalscorers, who always steal the headlines, and those whose job in a team is less trumpeted, but just as essential to success. Sometimes such rivalry can induce irritation, even when it involves great players of the same family. Jack and Bobby Charlton are the most famous brothers ever to have played the game in England. Both were members of England's World Cup-winning team of 1966 and both played their part to the full. Jack was a no-nonsense centre half, a stalwart for both Leeds and England who, though very effective as a central defender, was not blessed with the thoroughbred style of his younger brother. Bobby's skills as a playmaker and his explosive and accurate shooting, particularly from long range, were the hallmark of his game, and his fine all-round ability ensured he enjoyed more headlines than Jack. Not that Jack was bothered.

Neither brother resented the other's success and while Bobby enjoyed a glamorous reputation I was never aware of any jealousy between the two of them as players. One thing that did irk Jack, though, was the tendency of people he met to talk incessantly about Bobby and Bobby's career while ignoring that of his own. Following a game between Leeds and Everton at Elland Road in the sixties, the *Sunday Mirror* football writer Sam Leitch, who also previewed games for BBC television, came into the players' lounge. Noticing big Jack having a quiet pint on his own in a corner, Sam went up to pass the time of day.

'Hello, Jack,' said Sam.

'Hello, Sam,' replied Jack.

'How's your Bobby these days?' enquired Sam.

Jack slammed his pint down on the table.

'Do you know what really gets to me about you, Sam?' said Jack tersely.

'Well, no,' replied Sam taken aback by Jack's response to his seemingly innocent enquiry.

'Every time you see me you always ask how our kid is. Which is fine. But not once do you ever ask how I am,' said Jack, peeved. 'I'm always seeing you after matches and it's always Bobby, Bobby, Bobby with you. I'm an individual in my own right, you know, not just Bobby Charlton's brother. For a change ask me how I am.'

Sam Leitch gently settled his portly frame on the seat next to Jack.

'I'm sorry, Jack,' he said sympathetically. 'I never realised. Thinking about it, you're absolutely right. It never occurred to me I was being so tactless when we met.'

'Oh, it's all right, forget it,' shrugged Jack.

'No, no. I've been thoughtless. How are you, Jack?' Sam persisted.

'I'm fine.'

An awkward silence befell the two as neither knew what to say next. Sam took a sip of his drink then put his glass down on the table.

'So you're fine, eh? That's good.' said Sam. Jack nodded. A few more awkward seconds passed as Sam thought about what he could say next.

'And how's your Bobby keeping?' asked Sam brightly.

It was understandable that people should always want to talk about Bobby Charlton as he was such a great player, in his pomp the best playmaker in world football. I owe a debt to the playmakers of football – without them, I would not have scored anywhere near the number of goals I did.

CHAPTER SEVEN

His passes were so reliable they should have arrived by registered post

In years gone by they were known as schemers. Today we refer to the highly gifted and creative midfield player as a playmaker. Like the Australian spin bowler Shane Warne, the playmaker is the connoisseur's delight. In my days as a player, schemers were usually, but not exclusively, inside forwards. These players seemed to possess more football nous, technique and skill than any other position in the team. They carried with them an air of intellectual superiority; like university students home on vacation turning out for the local works team.

For the origins of the schemer one must go back to the thirties and Herbert Chapman's Arsenal. The Gunners won the First Division Championship four times (1931 and 1933–5) and the FA Cup twice (1930 and 1936), and at the core of their success was Alex James. He was born in North Lanarkshire, a mining area of Scotland that also produced Matt Busby. This part of Scotland was renowned for yielding great footballers, some of whom went on to become great managers. South Lanarkshire produced Bill Shankly and Jock Stein! James began his career with Raith Rovers in 1922, moved to Preston North End in 1925 and was transferred to Arsenal four years later.

He began life as an orthodox inside forward but soon took up a deep-lying position in midfield, which was a unique role in football at the time. James was a supreme artist with the ball. He also possessed that rarest of gifts: being able to dictate play and inspire those about him to great heights. This ability to direct play, to set up many of Arsenal's moves, and the fact that he did so from a new deep-lying position in midfield, led the press to dub him a 'schemer'. James was that and more. To describe Alex James as simply a schemer would be to do him an injustice. He supplied the ammunition for his fellow Gunners and was widely regarded as the most astute football tactician of his era. The Arsenal of the day were a team of exceptional talent and James was their mastermind, though you would never expect it from his appearance. While his team-mates would run on to the pitch for a game, James seemed to shuffle on. He was a small, squat figure with bandy legs protruding from shorts so baggy it looked as if he was wearing a large white pillowcase around his midriff. With his toes turned in, his sleeves down but always unbuttoned at the cuff, and more often than not his socks around his ankles, one would never think this was a man who laid claim to football genius. The baggy shorts which hung well below his knees became his trademark, and at the time became as popular with cartoonists as Laurel and Hardy's bowler hats, Neville Chamberlain's umbrella and Winston Churchill's cigar.

There were many who believed Alex James' carefree appearance was natural, but others thought it part of a pose. Whatever, his slovenly appearance on the field was in sharp contrast to one of the tidiest and sharpest football brains there has ever been. Although he could be intolerant of those who did not match up to his classic artistry, he was the arch entertainer of his day – a diminutive Scottish comic, who held his audience and opponents spellbound until he delivered the killer punchline.

In 1928 James formed part of one of the smallest forward lines ever to take to a pitch, when Scotland demolished England at Wembley. The Scots cut England to ribbons that day to record a famous victory, with hat-trick hero Alec Jackson, at five-foot-seven the tallest of their five-man forward line. The newspapers dubbed that Scotland team the 'Wembley Wizards' and the young Alex James was their Harry Potter, weaving his own brand of magic to bewitch England.

James' deep-lying role of schemer was copied by most clubs in the thirties, but the problem was that most didn't possess a player of James' cerebral quality and vision who could fulfil the role effectively. There were, of course, exceptions. Raich Carter at Sunderland was, on his day, arguably a greater exponent of the role of schemer than James himself. Throughout the thirties and forties there were other super schemers, such as Jimmy Hagan (Sheffield United) and Len Shackleton (Newcastle and Sunderland), but after England's defeats at the hands of Hungary in 1953, English football, as I have previously stated, underwent a metamorphosis. In the fifties the role of the wing half was redefined and gave rise to such players as Jimmy Dickinson (Portsmouth), Archie Macauley (Arsenal), Danny Blanchflower (Spurs) and Ron Flowers (Wolves), who begat the generation of Bobby Moore and Jim Baxter. These were ostensibly defenders whose role also involved cultured creativity, based as it was on vision and exquisite passing. The era of the playmaker was getting under way.

Back in the fifties, as far as my generation was concerned, Duncan Edwards was set to become just about the greatest footballer England had ever produced. Combine the ability of Eric Cantona, and the strength and application of Roy Keane, with the distribution of Glen Hoddle and the temperament of Paul Scholes, and you are somewhere near to the sort of player Duncan Edwards was. Younger readers may well think that to be somewhat of an exaggeration, but, believe me, Duncan Edwards was that good. To say a certain player 'had everything' is usually an overblown and often unworthy description of a footballer who rose above the ordinary, but in the case of Duncan Edwards it is wholly apposite. He was born in Dudley in the West Midlands and perhaps he should have gone to Wolves or Birmingham City. However, his instinct, which was to win many a match, took him to Old Trafford, where Matt Busby had created the forerunner of all football academies. The United system would produce the 'Busby Babes'.

A phenomenal but tragically short career got off to an extraordinary start: Edwards signed for Manchester United in his pyjamas. It was early on the morning of 1 October 1952 – the day of Duncan's sixteenth birthday – when United's Bert Whalley arrived at the Edwards home with the milk. Bert had to be quick off the mark to get his boy-man because a cluster of clubs were chasing the signature of the lad who had already caused a considerable stir at schoolboy level. Whalley looked on in awe and amazement as Edwards put pen to paper for United. The young man had been playing regularly for Dudley Schools' 15-year-olds since the age of eleven. That was symptomatic of the rest of his tragically short life. As Matt Busby was later to say, 'Duncan was never really a boy. In football terms, he was a man when we signed him at 16.'

When he arrived as a sixteen-year-old at Old Trafford Duncan was already six feet tall and weighed thirteen stone. After six months at Old Trafford he was in the first team. He played in England's first-ever Under 23 international and made his full debut at senior level for the national side against Scotland in 1955. He was England's youngest-ever international when he took to the field against the Scots, and he made an immediate impression. Stan Matthews weaved his magic that day. The England centre forward, Denis Wilshaw, created a record by becoming the first England player to score four goals in an international, and Nat Lofthouse helped himself to two goals in a 7-2 victory. The headlines, however, were reserved for the debutant Edwards, whose performance had been such that Scotland's Lawrie Reilly turned to Tommy

Docherty and pointing to Edwards asked, 'Where the hell did they find him? They've built battleships on the Clyde that are smaller and less formidable.'

Duncan Edwards' ability as a player was matched by his strength and stamina. In addition to featuring in a United team that contested the League, and FA and European Cups, such was his age and ability Duncan Edwards was chosen for every representative team going. One hears managers complaining about the number of games their players have to play nowadays, but in 1956–7 Duncan Edwards – at the age of twenty-one – played an astonishing ninety-four competitive matches in the course of the season. It was the mark of the man. No one but he, with his incredible vigour and staying power, could have endured such demands on his ability during one single season.

Duncan's name is synonymous with that of the Busby Babes. For all his tender years his influence, more than that of any other player, drove United to the First Division Championship in 1956 and again the following season, when they might well have become the first side in the twentieth century to win the double, had it not been for an injury to goalkeeper Ray Wood in the Cup final. Wood had to leave the field, reducing United to ten men, and wing half Jackie Blanchflower (brother of Danny) took over in goal against Aston Villa. As Jackie was later to tell me, 'Taking over in goal in a Cup final was the moment I realised adrenalin is brown.'

In February 1958 in faraway Belgrade Duncan Edwards played his last football match. The Munich air disaster claimed his life. He hung on for fifteen days after the crash in a Munich hospital, before succumbing to injuries which, it has been said, would have proved instantly fatal to most normal people. The United assistant manager Jimmy Murphy, who had missed the trip to Belgrade because he had been fulfilling his other duty, that of manager of Wales, flew out to Munich. Having visited Matt Busby in hospital, Murphy went to see Duncan Edwards.

'What time is kick-off against Wolves, Jimmy,' Edwards asked. 'I can't afford to miss that one.'

All these years on I, and many of my generation, still miss Duncan Edwards.

In the late fifties and sixties the role of playmaker evolved – as football did too – into something altogether more sophisticated. The traditional 'WM' formation of teams was becoming as outmoded as steam trains. Football was still an overly physical game, but the players who revelled in the role of the playmaker were being positively encouraged. Footballers such as Johnny Haynes and Ivor Allchurch stamped their authority on matches. They were as smooth and invidious as panthers. Shrewd and devastating in midfield, they seamlessly linked defence to attack, often conducting play as if the other side didn't exist. The style of play of Haynes and Allchurch was to pave the way for the midfield playmakers of today.

Fulham's Johnny Haynes ensured his immortality in the English game by becoming the first £100-a-week footballer. Johnny first joined Fulham as a groundstaff boy in 1950 and turned professional two years later. His development as a player mirrored that of a changing game. When he first got into the Fulham team he was an inside forward whose primary job was to score goals. As the English game began to evolve, so too did that of Johnny Haynes. He began to play a much deeper role and became the hub around which every Fulham move turned. He could size up a situation in an instant, had complete mastery of the ball and the cunning to veil his real intentions. Johnny also had the patience to bide his time before releasing one of his trademark defence-cutting passes. I played alongside him many times for England when, in my opinion, he was in his pomp as a playmaker. As all such footballers have to be he was a very unselfish player, who kept the ball flowing constantly and brought all his team-mates into the picture.

When Johnny began to establish himself in the Fulham first

team as a teenager, the Fulham chairman Tommy Trinder was still at the height of his showbiz career as a comedian, actor and presenter on what was then fledgling television. Tommy was appearing in a show in Southsea when he received an invitation from the president of Portsmouth, Field Marshal Viscount Montgomery of Alamein, who was the man, among other landmark achievements during the Second World War, who had led the British Desert Rats to victory over Rommel in North Africa. Portsmouth had a home match on the Saturday and Viscount Montgomery, hearing that Tommy Trinder had no show that afternoon, had extended an invitation to the Fulham chairman to be his guest at Fratton Park.

After the game, Tommy was in the Portsmouth boardroom listening to the results of all the other games on the radio, keeping an ear open for the Fulham score. Finally, the radio presenter announced that Fulham had won 2-0 and that both goals had been scored by Johnny Haynes.

'That Haynes boy, he's going to be a great player,' said Tommy, glowing with pride and satisfaction. 'He has a great football brain and is an excellent passer of the ball. Mark my words, sir, Johnny Haynes will captain England one day. He's a brilliant player and only eighteen years of age.'

'Eighteen years old?' said Viscount Montgomery sternly, immediately quelling Tommy's joy and delight. 'What about his national service?'

'Well, that's the only sad thing about him,' said Tommy, thinking on his feet. 'He's a cripple.'

Johnny proved himself a sublime playmaker in the early sixties. He reached the height of his mercurial powers when captaining England during what can only be described as a phenomenal run of results. From October 1960 to May 1961, England enjoyed an unbeaten run of thirteen matches in which we scored forty-five goals. The peak came when we scored forty goals in six internationals, with the sequence of results: Northern Ireland 5-2; Luxembourg 9-0; Spain 4-2; Wales 5-1;

Scotland 9-3; and Mexico 8-0. The thirteen-match run also included a 3-2 victory over Italy in Rome. The Italians were world-famous for their *catenaccio* style of play, a sweeper system that suffocated opposing teams, and it was unheard of for Italy to concede three goals, especially at home. At the end of the game Johnny Haynes got all the England players together and led us on a lap of honour. The hundred-thousand-strong crowd whistled and booed, then suddenly stopped. At first I didn't know the reason for their abrupt silence, then I realised the supporters had been showing their disapproval of the Italian team as the players left the pitch. Once the last Italian player had disappeared down the tunnel, we continued to polite applause.

The fact that England enjoyed such an amazing sequence of results and scored so many goals was in no little part down to Johnny Haynes. In England's 9-3 victory over Scotland Johnny produced a performance that will surely ensure his place in the pantheon of football gods. Bobby Smith (Spurs) and Johnny himself each scored twice. Bobby Robson and Bryan Douglas got a goal apiece and I managed to get a hat-trick, but it was Johnny Haynes at his merciless best who was the provider. Johnny controlled the slaughter that day, pulling the Scottish defence apart with a procession of precision passes that created countless openings for his team-mates.

Johnny was also one of the first players ever to have an agent. His was Bagenal Harvey, a good old boy who negotiated for Johnny to succeed Denis Compton as the face on all the Brylcreem advertising. In many respects it was a natural progression, seeing as Harvey had also clinched the deal for Compton in the first place in the late forties. Though Bagenal acted as Johnny's agent, this was limited to what were termed 'peripheral activities'. Not at any time did Harvey ever try and represent Johnny during contract negotiations at Fulham. Not that Johnny had a need for him to do so.

Before the maximum wage was lifted in 1961, Tommy

Trinder was forever saying to Johnny, 'If I could pay you more than twenty quid a week, Johnny, I would do. This maximum wage thing is nonsense. If it were not for that, I'd pay you a hundred quid a week because your performances deserve it.'

The day the maximum wage was abolished Johnny made a beeline for Tommy Trinder's office and reminded Tom of what he had said. There was no way out for Trinder, and Johnny Haynes made headlines again, this time as Britain's first 'Hundred Pound a Week Footballer'.

I don't think it an exaggeration to say that there was a time in the early sixties when Johnny Haynes was the most famous and lauded sportsperson in Britain. Yet that cut no ice with some, even at Fulham. One day Johnny reported to the physio room at Craven Cottage for treatment on a niggling knee injury. The physio told Johnny to take a seat outside as he was already administering treatment. Haynes sat waiting for over an hour before the door finally opened and the phsyio came out . . . with a greyhound. Johnny told me, 'I may have been captain of Fulham and England, but I was left to know in no uncertain terms where I stood – second to a local greyhound when it came to treatment. Added to which there was the uncomfortable warmth of the dog on the physio's bench when I lay down.'

Fame is a capricious mistress. Johnny Haynes now runs a dry-cleaning business with his wife in Edinburgh. I often wonder how many Edinburgh householders realise that the man delivering their curtains was the architect behind the most humiliating defeat Scottish football ever suffered against England.

No chapter about playmakers would be complete without mention of Jim Baxter. As surely as Johnny Haynes was the architect of Scotland's downfall in 1961, Jim Baxter was the creative force behind the Scottish national side's victories over England at Hampden in 1962 and Wembley in 1963 and 1967. 'Slim' Jim Baxter began his career at Raith Rovers before moving to

Rangers, where he won every domestic honour in Scottish football. He was blessed with football genius, and those who saw his performance against England in 1963 will never forget it. In a game that was slowly evolving into systematisation, Jim was a highly gifted individual who was the epitome of the phrase 'let the ball do the work'. Even when a game was at its most combative and furious, the ball was always Jim's plaything. At no time was this truer than at Wembley in 1963 when, against England and in front of a huge crowd, Slim Jim produced the most audacious piece of skill I have ever seen on a football field.

Jim took time off from scoring both Scotland's goals to produce this extraordinary party piece. He found himself with the ball at his feet and in space on the left wing. As he progressed deep into the England half, Jim flicked the ball into the air with his right foot and started running, while juggling the ball in the air with his left. It was as if he was playing 'keepy-up' in his own back garden, rather than in front of a hundred thousand spectators at Wembley. The Scots in the crowd, of whom there were many that day, roared their approval. But Jim hadn't finished. He took the ball to within a few yards of the byline and let it run a little in front of him. Making a half-turn so that he was facing Gordon Banks' goal, he brought his right leg behind his left and chipped the ball across the face of goal. As Jim executed this audacious cross he clicked the first finger and thumb of each hand in a gesture of 'Ole!'. It was the first international England had played at the 'new' all-covered Wembley. Old or new, the stadium had never seen such brilliant and flamboyant impetuosity and, with the exception of the dazzling scorpion kick from a certain Colombian goalkeeper, nor would it again.

The obvious confidence Jim displayed in that game against England was in sharp contrast to the naive Jim Baxter who left Raith Rovers for Glasgow Rangers. The following is a story of Jim's naivety, and also one of how certain managers that were poorly paid used to make their money up by taking advantage of a promising, young player they were selling to a bigger club.

Jim was eighteen when he first signed for Raith Rovers. He felt out of place at his first training session when he discovered that, after him, the next youngest was a player called 'Willie' Polland, who, at twenty-six, revelled in the nickname 'Young Boy'. Raith Rovers were a Dad's Army of a team. As Jim once told me, 'The goalkeeper had so many wrinkles on his forehead he had to screw his cap on.' Raith had a veteran inside forward, 'Jock' Williamson, who, Jim also told me, with the advent of every season took out an insurance policy against collapsing and dying during a match. According to Jim, if Williamson had gone, Prudential would have gone as well.

The Raith manager, Bert Herdman, was well versed in having to run a club on a shoestring budget. In time the performances of young Slim Jim won rave notices in the Scottish press and one day he was asked to report to Bert Herdman's office. In 1959 there were three types of players' registration forms in Scotland: a white form, which was for amateur players; a green form, for professionals; and a pink form. The pink form, also for professionals, stated that if the player was sold on to another club, both he and the person who had originally signed him were entitled to a percentage of the transfer fee. Jim was a teenager who wanted nothing more than to play football and cared not a jot for paperwork and the like, so when his manager pushed a pink form across the desk and asked Jim to sign it he was only too happy to oblige.

'What is this form, boss?' asked Jim.

'What is it?' Herdman said incredulously. 'Why, laddie, it means money for you. All you got to do to get it is sign this pink form.' Jim's eyes lit up.

'Money for me, boss. How much?'

'Ten pounds!' said Herdman boastfully, throwing himself back in his chair.

At the time Jim was only earning around two pounds a week

as a part-time player at Raith. He had never seen as much as ten pounds in his life, so willingly put pen to paper. Herdman produced two crisp five-pound notes from the drawer in his desk and handed them to a delighted Jim. The next day, Jim was once again called into his manager's office. When he entered, Bert Herdman was not alone. Jim was introduced to a distinguished looking man with thin, silver hair, who Herdman informed him was Scot Symon, the manager of Rangers.

'Mr Symon is here to sign you', Herdman told Jim. 'Don't ask about wages, they'll pay you well enough. That said, you are under no pressure to go. If the press ask, tell them I didn't want you to leave Raith Rovers and sign for Rangers. Here's a pen.'

Jim signed for Rangers and went on to become a legend at Ibrox, and indeed of Scottish football.

Some months later Jim discovered, to his chagrin, the purpose of the pink form. What's more, he discovered that Herdman had made nigh on a thousand pounds out of the deal. When Rangers next played Raith, Jim was determined to confront his old manager about him signing the pink form and the issue of the money.

'This pink form ye had me signing, ' said Jim, cornering Bert Herdman after the game. 'You made nigh on a thousand pounds from me signing that form. I made ten quid!'

Bert Herdman put a fatherly arm around Jim, gazed off into the distance and smiled warmly as he swelled with pride.

'Aye, Jim, son,' said Herdman, proudly. 'We both made a killing that day, that's for sure.'

Football reflects society. The sixties promised us a better world. Likewise, England winning the World Cup, and Celtic and Manchester United the European Cups, promised a better future for British football. The masters turned pupils were once again masters. In the early and mid-sixties goals flowed. Rival supporters intermingled on the same terracing. As the football journalist Frank Butler wrote, 'English football has come a long, long way just to get to Wembley – the home of English football. Once there, to our delight we found the World Cup enveloped our game, from parks football to the First Division, with the sweet smell of success.'

But smells tend to linger rather than last. The seventies smothered society with the dark pall of cynicism and it was the same with football. As that decade got under way, George Best was disillusioned with the way the game had developed, and he wasn't the only one. I too had begun to despair. I wasn't enjoying my football any more. With a record of 491 competitive goals to my name I called it a day. I was thirty-one years of age.

I played my last Football League match for West Ham United in the First Division against Huddersfield Town. In the Huddersfield team that day was Les Chapman. He was a decent player and ended the season as Huddersfield's leading scorer, with nine goals. Need I say more?

Having initially retired in 1969, Matt Busby, who had returned to take the reins at Manchester United, announced his retirement in 1971. This time it was definite. In 1972–3 Bobby Charlton retired, as did his brother, Jack. So too did Denis Law, while in the same season tragedy contrived to remove Gordon Banks from the arena. When Matt Busby retired for a second time, he conveyed his distaste at how the game had developed. Said Matt:

The way things are going alarms me deeply. Hard men are nothing new in football. What is new and frightening about the game as we enter the seventies is that you have sides whose main assets are physical hardness and the ability to smother fluid, expansive football. They use strength and fitness in the name of professionalism to neutralise skill, and the unfortunate truth is that all too often it can be done. Of course, there are really great players who cannot be subdued all the time, but their talents are only seen in flashes

and they have to live dangerously. It's true there are still a
few teams who believe the game is about skill, talent, technique and imagination, but for any one you'll now find ten
who rely on runners and hard men.

I don't think the football of the seventies can be better summed
up than in those wise words from an intelligent man. The new
generation of playmakers – Alan Hudson, Tony Currie, Stan
Bowles and Rodney Marsh – lived dangerously, and often
found themselves marginalised. The skilled playmaker, who at
one point would take it upon himself to entertain the crowd,
had become a byword for a 'lazy' player. It was not just these
players whose professionalism was questioned. Stylish forwards with flair often found themselves playing second fiddle
to runners who could trap a ball further than they could kick it.
Leicester's Frank Worthington made only six starts for
England, looking on as, at various times, Don Revie favoured
Stuart Pearson (Manchester United), David Johnson
(Liverpool) and, somewhat bizarrely, Colin Viljoen (Ipswich
Town) and Phil Boyer (Norwich City). Arsenal's Charlie
George was another forward who displayed as much flair on the
pitch as there was flare in his trousers. George played just the
one game for England, while at Derby County, against the
Republic of Ireland in 1976. Though, saying Charlie George
had one game for England is something of a misnomer: he was
substituted after fifty-five minutes.

Football mirrors society even more closely where popular
culture is concerned. In the early seventies as David Bowie,
Stevie Wonder and 10cc battled for supremacy in the charts
with Suzi Quatro, Slade and The Sweet, Alan Hudson, Stan
Bowles and Tony Currie lived at the sharp end of an English
game populated by the likes of Arsenal's Peter Storey, Leeds'
Norman Hunter and Liverpool's Tommy Smith. Harsh reality,
with the emphasis on the former, ruled alongside cynicism,
and the Football Association was as fuddled as ever at how to

cope with this new, disturbing trend. In 1963–4, when the game was considered 'physical but fair', the FA disciplinary committee sat on three occasions. Between April and June of 1973, it convened thirty-six times. Justice wasn't only not done, it wasn't seen to be done. In 1972 Exeter City of Division Four had failed to fulfil a fixture due to a combination of injury and illness in their paper-thin squad. Despite producing bona fide medical certificates for every player deemed unfit to play, the FA fined Exeter City £5000. At a similar hearing, Leeds United received a £3000 fine suspended for two years, for having an 'appalling disciplinary record'.

The very first Charity Shield match to be played at Wembley in 1974 was also the first to be televised live. Instead of being a curtain-raiser to the season, it brought the curtain down on creative football – for some time at least. In the game Leeds United and Liverpool slugged it out, on several occasions quite literally. One of the 'bad boys' of English football, Billy Bremner, met the new 'golden boy', Kevin Keegan, and neither displayed anything like boyish charm. When the pair were sent off after yet another brawl, they removed their shirts and compounded the ignominy by throwing them in disgust across the turf as they left the pitch. Rather than being a showcase game of football, it was a travesty of a match full of sly, niggling fouls, outrageous tackles, off the ball set-to's and a major flare-up involving most of the players on the field.

Charity was nowhere to be seen in that game, and it would continue to be in short supply as football progressed through the seventies. Yet this was a decade when English clubs enjoyed unprecedented success in Europe – the era when Liverpool won two European Cups (1977 and 1978), only for that success to be emulated by Nottingham Forest (1979 and 1980). The line of success was continued by Liverpool again (1981) and Aston Villa the season after that. Of course, there were skilled players in those sides, as there were in other teams, but organisation and the ability to stop the opposition from playing their normal game were key elements in the success of English clubs in Europe. Liverpool's success in the 1977 European Cup final against Borussia Mönchengladbach apart, other wins in this competition were not victories for creative and expansive football, but triumphs of containment, the ethic of work, and runners who 'hit them on the break'. True, there were the sublime skills of Liam Brady and Kenny Dalglish to savour. Brady was never considered worthy of the Football Writers' Footballer of the Year. Dalglish was awarded that accolade in 1979, but in the two previous years the award had gone to Emlyn Hughes (1977) and Kenny Burns (1978) – players who were more effective than affected. Come the end of the seventies, the playmaker had become almost as rare in English football as had the winger in the late sixties.

In a decade in which England failed to qualify for the World Cup, the success of English clubs in Europe was in marked contrast to that of our national team. On the Continent there were Franz Beckenbauer, Michel Platini and Johann Cruyff, whose Holland were playing total football. In England the only thing 'total' we hankered after was the petrol of the same name. However, the ice began to melt with the arrival of the first overseas players. At the beginning of 1978–9 Spurs' manager Keith Burkinshaw, acting on the recommendation of Sheffield United manager Harry Haslam, brought off a sensational coup by signing the Argentine internationals Ricardo Villa and Osvaldo Ardiles. Villa was a powerful player, whose style many thought would be suited to the English game, while Ardiles was slightly built, a playmaker, and it was thought he would struggle to make an impact. On 2 September those who had doubts about the ability of the two Argentines, particularly Ardiles, to adapt to the physical, hurly-burly nature of English football had their argument strengthened when Spurs were steamrollered 7-0 by Liverpool at Anfield. Ardiles and Villa did, however, go on to make their presence known in English football. The diminutive playmaker in particular made a telling contribution to the game, and English supporters of every hue warmed to his creativity and what was a considerable array of skills. Meanwhile, Bobby Robson at Ipswich Town signed the Dutch pair, Arnold Muhren and Frans Thijssen. Muhren took the eye with his stylish play but Thijssen was every bit as important to Ipswich as their creative linchpin. He fulfilled a role that for over a decade had been the preserve of the ball-winner who hit short balls to team-mates. Thijssen was different – he linked defence to attack with great vision. His shrewd positioning in the Ipswich midfield allowed him to receive and redirect the ball to his fellow conspirators lurking upfield.

The arrival of Ardiles, Muhren and Thijssen cleared the way for the return of the playmaker. Arguably the best English playmaker of the eighties was Glen Hoddle. Curiously, when Bobby Robson acceded to the job of England manager he chose to ignore the superlative skills of Hoddle. Poor Bobby. When he left Hoddle out of the England team, the press got on his back, asking how he could ignore the most gifted and creative midfield player in England, but when he did include Hoddle, many was the press report that referred to the player as a 'luxury'. It seemed some senior football writers were still immersed in the football culture of the seventies, and were incapable of embracing the re-emergence of a talented creative in midfield.

You never stop learning in football. When I played my last-ever League game I learned something about the game – and it wasn't just that the time had come to give it up. Football is con-stantly developing and evolving, the more you know, the more you realise there is to know. In the eighties we saw a revival of the playmaker, but he was different from those of the ilk of Hudson and Currie. He had to be because the game had changed and those who influenced the course of a game were no longer the players on the pitch. The creative midfield player of the eighties was full of hustle and bustle, such as Sammy

Lee (Liverpool) and Trevor Steven (Everton). He was robust
and full of running, and made late darting runs into the opponents' penalty area. Bryan Robson (Manchester United) and
'Sid' Cowans (Aston Villa) are prime examples of the multi-
functional playmaker who graced the eighties and nineties. The
playmaker was also expected to fulfil other roles. Being the prime
creative force on the pitch was no longer enough. The hub of the
midfield in the eighties and nineties had to drop back and defend
when his team lost possession. He had to 'close down', 'squeeze'
and 'pin-out' opponents. He had to arrive in the opponents' box
in the hope of getting a goal or 'picking up the pieces' when the
opposing defence cleared the ball. There were plenty of such
midfield players in the nineties. Arguably the most outstanding
and enigmatic was Paul Gascoigne. Yet, for all the imaginative
skills of the likes of Gascoigne and Eric Cantona, the mercurial
skills of Chris Waddle from wide, and the lance-like thrusting of
David Platt, Steve McMahon and Paul Ince, their creative input
was not as great as that of the playmakers of the past.

Patrick Vieira is the archetypal playmaker of the modern game,
in that he fulfils two basic roles: those of first creating attacks
and then breaking down the attacks of opposing teams. You
would never find Glen Hoddle or Alan Hudson applying themselves fully to those two roles, although back in the early sixties
that was the role of Danny Blanchflower at Spurs. Vieira is a
more than capable player at the highest level. His aggression
and physical presence are such that I am sure he would have
felt just as much at home in the Arsenal defence as he did in the
centre of their midfield. He has the rare gift of being able to
mix power and exquisite passing, from which both Arsenal and
France have greatly benefited over the years.

Vieira honed his skills in the French Championship with
Cannes. He made his first-team debut in 1993 when he initially
played a very deep role just in front of the central defenders
that, I am sure, helped develop the defensive qualities he now

displays. During 1994–5 he was eventually given a more central role in midfield and it was in that position that his game blossomed. So much so in fact that he moved from Cannes to AC Milan. Now, I know a little about players who fail to settle at AC Milan. It is a superb club. Everything they do is first class . . . no, make that executive class. There is, however, a price to be paid for being subjected to the best of everything. Training can be very regimented and the Milan way of doing things now is not dissimilar to how it was when I was at the club in the early sixties. The players leave their homes for days on end to do their training at camps in the hills. For Italian players this is acceptable. Many Italian clubs opt to take their players away during the course of a week, but for overseas players it takes some getting used to. I didn't like it and Patrick Vieira didn't warm to it either. At Milan Vieira found himself out of sorts and out of favour. He was never given a real opportunity to show the Milan fans what he was so eminently capable of, and only played two matches for the club in Serie A. In the late summer of 1996 Arsène Wenger, before formally taking up his post as manager in September of that year, recommended that the Arsenal board take the highly gifted midfield player to Highbury. Vieira was actually Wenger's first signing. That Milan were far from cut up about losing him was down to their never having seen the best of Patrick Vieira. He had simply never been given the chance to shine.

Vieira's first season with Arsenal in 1996–7 was very much one of bedding in, as it was for Wenger himself. The player's debut appearance for the Gunners was as a substitute in Arsenal's 4-1 win over Sheffield Wednesday, and he made his full debut the following week in a 2-0 victory at Middlesbrough. This was an Arsenal side which contained Lee Dixon, Nigel Winterburn, Martin Keown, Tony Adams, Steve Bould, David Platt, Ian Wright, Paul Merson and Denis Bergkamp (who, incidentally, had been signed by Wenger's predecessor, Bruce Rioch), with bit parts being played by John

Lukic, Andy Linighan, Stephen Hughes, Scott Marshall, Paul Shaw and Steve Morrow. I mention those players because with the passing of time one is liable to forget they were instrumental in the early days of the Wenger era at Arsenal, where a very English football culture, in which a few lagers after the game was perfectly acceptable, had been omnipresent.

As it must have been difficult for Wenger to adapt and introduce his methods of management into what in essence was a hardened dressing-room culture, so too must it have been initially demanding for Vieira. The early days of Wenger were a very transient period at Arsenal in which the culture of training, match preparation and the style of play were turned on their head. The fact that Vieira dealt with this upheaval and settled in at Arsenal says much for his application and a lot about his character. In 1997–8 he was a key figure in the Gunners team that won the Premiership and FA Cup double. In November 1997 Arsenal lost 2-0 at Sheffield Wednesday and followed that with a 1-0 home defeat at the hands of Liverpool. At that stage of the season they lay fifth in the Premiership and I, like most reasoned folk, would not have given them an earthly of winning the double. Yet Wenger's side was to lose only two more matches and those when the title was already home and dry at Highbury. When the double was secured, courtesy of a 2-0 victory over Newcastle United at Wembley, Wenger and his methods were vindicated. In little over a year, though the Arsenal rearguard remained unchanged, players like Nicolas Anelka, Emmanuel Petit, Christopher Wreh, Marc Overmars and Vieira himself gave a decidedly cosmopolitan look to what had been the most traditional of English clubs.

During that, Arsenal's first double season under Wenger, Vieira was a commanding figure. His height, strength and swath of skills made him perfectly suited for the creative job in midfield, which he executed with clinical expertise. He organised the cosmopolitan talents of the Arsenal team with such skill that they eventually knitted into the smooth and highly efficient working unit that embarked upon that super run of results beginning in December 1997. Patrick Vieira was an instrumental figure again when Arsenal won the double for the third time in their history in 2001–2 and, though Thierry Henry stole the headlines with his performances and goals during Arsenal's record-breaking unbeaten season of 2003–4, the on-the-pitch mastermind behind the Gunners' historic success was Vieira. If he has any glaring fault, it is not to do with his play, but his temperament: he responds all too easily to being wound up by opponents, and this cost him and his club dear on several occasions. Vieira's penchant for reacting to robust challenges and ragging from opponents is his Achilles heel. Against Sheffield United in the FA Cup quarter-final replay at Bramall Lane in 2005 he gave every indication of being distracted when the subject of constant harrying and harassing from United's midfield. But he applied himself to the task in hand and eventually stamped his authority on the game. In that match he showed he had matured, that he was now more capable of dealing with close attention and robust play without petulant reaction. It was the mark of a player confident in his ability to create openings for his team-mates and nullify attacks from opponents, and also to deal with what Alan Shearer referred to on the night as the 'ugly but necessary' side of football. It will be interesting to see how Arsenal cope without Viera after his move to Juventus in July 2005.

Strictly speaking Eric Cantona was not a playmaker. He often led the line for Manchester United but such was his creative genius he deserves to be mentioned alongside the greatest play-maker United have ever had – Bobby Charlton. Before Cantona arrived in this country and signed for Leeds United in 1991–2 there was still a body of opinion that regarded overseas players as gilded lilies who could often be tamed by the speed of our game and British muscle. But nobody tamed Eric Cantona. Not the battery of French clubs and national team managers who failed to manage his mercurial talents to best effect; and not the opponents who could neither anticipate nor forestall his football genius. The ban he received, when a Manchester United player, for the infamous kung-fu kicking incident at Selhurst Park served simply to produce further versions of this restless enigma. Following the incident at Selhurst Park, and the lengthy ban and community-service order that followed, Cantona did what he would do with every new role he was to pursue in his later career as an actor – he reinvented himself. The Selhurst Park affair rocked him, and at the time there was talk even then of him retiring and pursuing a career as an actor. All of which was meat and drink to comics and after-dinner speakers: 'Eric Cantona is to appear in a new TV sitcom, "One Foot in the Crowd".'

The man who for many brought shame upon himself and the game in general was an exemplary trainer, a consummate professional. When Alex Ferguson responded to the Selhurst Park debacle and subsequent ban by making Cantona captain at United, it was a masterstroke of man-management. Cantona's response was to rise to the role, and arguably, having been given true responsibility for the first time in his career, he thrived on it. If people had always admired his skills and technique as a player, as captain of Manchester United he succeeded in winning our respect. The 'prima donna' image melted away as his individual world-class skills energised a United team that, though brimming with quality, had often flattered to deceive.

Even as the United captain Cantona still came in for criticism from some quarters. Several members of the media and some supporters too were not used to deep-thinking, reflective footballers who spent their spare time painting or reading plays. Asked about Diego Maradona, Cantona said, 'In the course of time it will be said that Maradona was to football what Rimbaud was to poetry and Mozart to music.' He may well be right, but it won't be said by the likes of Chris Kamara,

Mark Bright or Barry Venison. When indulging in Camus-like philosophising, referring to seagulls following trawlers for they know sardines will be there, Eric instilled in some observers, at best, wry amusement, at worst, derision. Here was a player who was a variation on the enigma. He often said the unexpected and he also contrived to produce the unexpected on the pitch. His ability to do the latter was the mark of his greatness as a footballer.

'Of all the qualities a good team must possess, the supreme essential for me is creative penetration. Eric Cantona brought the can-opener,' said Alex Ferguson in 1996. Liverpool supporters might not appreciate the fact, but it was the former Anfield boss Gerard Houllier, when manager of Paris St Germain, who played an intrinsic role in inspiring the transfer that was to transform Manchester United. In November 1992, the United chairman Martin Edwards and Alex Ferguson were discussing the club's need for a new striker. The manager felt it was a pity he had not got to hear about Cantona before the player joined Leeds United from Nîmes. Ferguson had been talking to Houllier, who had been singing the praises of Cantona, intimating he could be the missing link in the United team. United's central defence pairing of Steve Bruce and Gary Pallister had also been impressed with Cantona when United had played Leeds. 'He's a one-off, a fantastic talent. Caused us all sorts of problems,' Bruce told Ferguson.

As luck would have it, during the conversation between Edwards and Ferguson, the United chairman's telephone rang. It was Bill Fotherby, managing director of Leeds United. He wanted to know whether United were willing to sell Denis Irwin, who had started his career at Elland Road. Edwards told Fotherby that Irwin was not available for sale, but began probing the Leeds director about players the club might be willing to part with. There was talk of the Leeds striker Lee Chapman, at which point Ferguson prompted his chairman to ask about the availability of Eric Cantona. Fotherby made it

known that there was a problem with the enigmatic
Frenchman. In Leeds' Championship-winning year of 1991–2
he had made just six appearances in midfield and nine as a
substitute, unable to bolt down a regular place in the side. As
the 1992–3 campaign had begun, Cantona had started in the
Leeds' midfield but had not covered himself in glory and, in
fact, had been relegated to the bench for Leeds' previous home
match against Coventry City.

At Ferguson's prompting, Martin Edwards told Bill
Fotherby that if Leeds were willing to part with Cantona, they
would have to be quick. United had a budget to spend and
needed a striker who could play from deep, but if Cantona was
not available they would be looking elsewhere to spend their
money. There the conversation ended, but shortly afterwards
Fotherby rang back. Eric Cantona was for sale. When Martin
Edwards told Alex Ferguson the asking price, Alex rubbed his
hands with glee: Leeds United were asking for one million
pounds for Cantona.

'It's a steal,' Ferguson told his chairman, and it was. The
move was Cantona's eighth in ten years. He arrived at Old
Trafford with a reputation for dissent, broodiness and being a
disruptive influence. His career was peppered with dismissals
and there had been more yellow cards than you'd find on a
Dulux swatch. There was no grey area where he was concerned. Everything Cantona did – good or bad – was like the
man himself: larger than life.

Eric Cantona proved the catalyst to Manchester United's
revival as a successful team. Playing behind Mark Hughes, he
linked midfield and attack, conducting like the leader of an
orchestra. He scored goals, and he created them for his team-
mates. Though economical with his movement around the
pitch, his majestic skills and incisive football brain helped elevate United's football to another level and success followed
success. Premiership titles came to Old Trafford as United
went into the ascendancy in their ping-pong battle with

Arsenal for the Championship. The creative driving force behind their success was Cantona, who was to leave us with a treasure trove of golden football memories. Many believe his retirement from football was announced too early. He later admitted he sometimes felt he had hung up his boots too soon, but that his decision had been the right one. For him, but not for English football.

Eric Cantona was not a playmaker as one would define the type, and neither was Bobby Charlton when he began his career at Manchester United. Bobby, however, was to develop into the best playmaker ever to wear an England shirt. He was an exceptionally gifted athlete, as well as a truly brilliant foot-baller. I know Bob well, and I am sure he would have been a success at any game to which he applied himself, with the exception of cricket (the one sport he never took to).

I remember Bobby playing for England in his early days when he was out on the left wing. He possessed an explosive turn of pace, which prompted Johnny Haynes to say, 'This lad could race greyhounds – and win.' In those days Bobby was raw and inexperienced, but he soon stamped his authority on the game. When he did begin to blossom as a player, there was no finer sight in football. The youthful surge and acceleration were still there, but he had learned to slow opponents down. More importantly, he learned to slow himself down. On receiving the ball, he would no longer take off immediately at break-neck speed. He took his time, was more comfortable on the ball and was able to become the most cultured passer of a football in the British game.

What made Bobby Charlton a genuinely great player was his capacity at the very highest level – and by that I mean in a World Cup – to turn a game in an instant by making a pass that split wide open the most organised defence, or by scoring the kind of goal that nobody else on the pitch could. He did this time and time again: for United, when they took the European

Cup from Benfica in 1968, and notably for England, against Mexico in the 1966 World Cup finals. His goal against Mexico remains etched in the minds of all who witnessed it. Receiving a pass deep inside England's half of the field, he seemed to glide across the Wembley turf as he progressed into Mexico's half. Thirty yards from goal he pulled the trigger and let fly. The ball was still rising when it hit the back of Mexican goal-keeper Antonio Carvajal's net.

The match had been tight up to that point and, having drawn 0-0 with Uruguay, nerves were beginning to get taut and frustration was creeping into the ranks. Bobby's wonder goal put us on our way. The speed of that shot was unbe-lievable, and it's a wonder Antonio Carvajal didn't catch pneumonia from the draught the ball created as it sped past him. On the night England beat Mexico 2-0. Liverpool's Roger Hunt scored our other goal, but in the dressing room everyone was talking about Bobby's thirty-yard thunderbolt and how it had come from a run he began just outside our penalty area.

'Aye, but what you all keep forgetting is this, ' said Bobby's brother, Jack, tongue in cheek. 'I created that goal with the two-yard pass out I made to our kid that sent him on his way!'

Bobby's ability to strike the ball accurately at goal with either foot from great distance, and in almost any circumstance, was absolutely extraordinary, and one must remember we are not talking of the lightweight balls and pristine pitches of football today. Shots did not just leave his boot, they exploded from the instep, and unless the goalkeeper was poleaxed by the ball, there was no way he was going to execute a save. Bobby found his true role in the middle of midfield in time for England's assault on the World Cup in 1966. He was a great playmaker but, like all true greats of the game, he was many players rolled into one. When Bobby first came into the United team in 1955–6 he was an inside forward. Right, left, or centre, such was his ability as a footballer, it didn't seem to matter to him: he stayed around the edge of the penalty area and banged goals home. Then came the Munich air disaster, which I believe served to transform him from fledgling youngster to a seasoned professional in what was a few minutes of unimaginable horror. To his credit Bobby came back after the crash, though understandably, given what he had been through and experienced, he found playing again difficult and moved out to the left wing.

In 1965 he switched to the centre of midfield where, whether playing for United or England, he began to direct operations with aplomb. He remained the hub of England's tactical thinking for five years, before bowing out after the defeat against West Germany in Leon in 1970. Famously or, rather, infamously, with England two goals to the good, Alf Ramsey decided to substitute Bobby Charlton, replacing him with Colin Bell of Manchester City. Hindsight is a wonderful thing, it's a pity none of us have it in advance. The two great playmakers in this game, Bobby and Franz Beckenbauer, had cancelled each other out. With England seemingly comfortable two goals in the lead, Alf Ramsey, wanting to keep Bobby fresh for the semi-finals, substituted him. With Bobby out of the way, Beckenbauer came into his own, and the rest is history – from England's point of view, of the most painful kind. West Germany stormed back to win 3-2; England's hopes of retaining the World Cup were over and Alf's reputation as a shrewd international manager came under scrutiny.

Cyril Knowles once said, when asked by Spurs boss Bill Nicholson why he hadn't moved to take the ball off Bobby Charlton, 'I didn't know he had it.' Supporters of whatever hue loved to see Bobby surge past players at will, leaving them panting in his wake. If an opponent managed to get near him and tried to effect a tackle, Bobby could ride it, and the surge would gather momentum. Then, with chilling inevitability, would come the trademark piledriver shot.

It was the wide variety of skills and abilities that Bobby had at his disposal that made him such a brilliant playmaker and a difficult one to cope with. For all his speed, he never looked to have to hurry; like the Rolling Stones, he always seemed to have time on his side. Bobby Charlton was the best playmaker I ever saw, and I had the good fortune to play alongside him. These days, as a director of Manchester United, he views football from a different angle. This brings us neatly to the subject of our next chapter: the people behind the scenes.

CHAPTER EIGHT

Clubs should not give supporters what they want – They deserve much more than that

On 2 December 1962 Accrington Stanley of the Fourth Division were the subject of a winding-up petition in the Chancery Division of the High Court of Justice. The club's debts were put at £63,688 – less than the weekly wage of certain Premiership players of today. According to the High Court's 'Summary of the Statement of Affairs', Accrington Stanley had money in the bank: all of three pounds. The club's arrears, however, were crippling, and attendances had fallen to around two thousand. Accrington were forced to resign from the Football League and their record was expunged. They continued in non-League football until 1966, when debts and tiny home attendances – of around fifty – brought about the death of the old club.

Before long a group of dedicated and determined fans set about resurrecting the Accrington club, and a newly formed Stanley joined the Lancashire Combination League in 1970. It was only to be after three decades of hard work that Accrington Stanley would rise like a phoenix from the ashes. The club is now established as one of the top sides in the Conference, with high hopes of League football once again – albeit at a new ground, the Interlink Express Stadium.

Football has changed almost beyond recognition since Accrington Stanley folded in 1962, but Stanley are living proof that a football club forms an intrinsic part of the social glue and collective identity of a community. Increasingly, one has to look to the lower echelons of the Football League or non-League football for the sort of love and devotion that has been cherished on Accrington Stanley. While those who run non-League sides and teams in the lower divisions of the Football League are not in the game to make money, the same can't be said of the majority of people who run the more well-known clubs that form the higher tiers of English football.

In the early sixties when Accrington Stanley found themselves saddled with debts in excess of sixty thousand pounds, the people working behind the scenes at a football club amounted to nowhere near the number one finds today. On the football side of things there were the manager and, depending on the size of the club, around four or five personnel under his wing. These would comprise a first-team trainer-cum-coach, reserve- and youth-team managers and a chief scout. Clubs would employ any amount of scouts on a part-time or even ad hoc basis, but mainly scouting would be down to one man, as would be the management of each of a club's junior teams. This was par for the course throughout the game.

As for the national side, when I was a member of England's World Cup-winning squad of 1966, there were twenty-one other players. Manager Alf Ramsey was assisted by Leeds United's Les Cocker, who did most of the training; and Middlesbrough's Harold Shepherdson, with the official title of trainer, who though he did assist with training, also doubled up as physio and kit man. During the tournament, Alf also engaged the services of Wilf McGuinness of Manchester United to help him with the coaching. That was the extent of Alf's backroom staff – himself and three others – and it is worth noting that in addition to his duties with the senior national side, Alf also managed England Under 23s and had responsibility for the England youth team. For senior international matches other than those in the World Cup, there were just Alf, Les and Harold as the England management and backroom team. Today the England squad has as many backroom staff on the bench as we did players in 1966. Yet with a comparatively minuscule backroom staff England managed to win the World Cup.

The small set-up was no different at club level. When I was a junior player at Stamford Bridge, the Chelsea youth team was run by one man – Dickie Foss, a former Chelsea player. The youth team used to play on the Welsh Harp ground, which was situated near Staples Corner in Hendon, and more often than not when I arrived for a match I'd find Dickie sitting on a bench outside the Welsh Harp pub, enjoying a pint. 'My front office' he used to call it.

Dickie may have liked a beer, but I learned about football from him. He trained us, managed us, coached us, supervised our travel to away games, attended to our injuries during a match, put out the strips and gathered them up again at the end of a game, and we won just about every competition we entered. After I graduated to the Chelsea first team, under Dickie the youth team won the FA Youth Cup. Dickie Foss was multi-tasking before the phrase ever entered our vocabulary.

When I signed for Spurs, Bill Nicholson was manager and Harry Evans his assistant. Bill and Harry supervised our training and an ex-Spurs player, Cyril Poynton, acted as physio and kit man. Having won the double under that three-man backroom team, Spurs went on to win the FA Cup in 1961–2 and became the first British side ever to win a major European trophy when we won the European Cup Winners' Cup in 1962–3. Even though Spurs comprised, in the main, international players and I was for a time 'Britain's Most Expensive Player', I doubt whether we were treated any differently from players in the Fourth Division. Prior to one League match on a very grey and wet day, Cyril Poynton was at pains to tell us what was what.

'Listen you lot, it's pissing it down out there,' Cyril told us. 'If any of you gets injured on the far side of the pitch, I ain't running through all that rain and mud to get to ya. So if ya get injured on the far side, you gotta come over to us in the dugout. If it's a bad 'un, then you'll just 'ave to drag ya'self over, or get some mates to carry ya. OK?'

It had to be OK. Bill Nicholson, Harry Evans and Cyril had all played for Spurs in the past. Bill and Harry were stars in the fifties, whereas the career of Cyril Poynton dated back to the twenties. They had all come from the old school of hard knocks and any player who picked up an injury in the course of a game, rather than being the subject of sympathy, was, in the days before substitutes, encouraged to carry on playing. Sympathy was not just in short supply, it was non-existent. If, during a match, you turned to the bench and said to Cyril Poynton, 'I'm injured', he would offer a three-word reply. Two of which were 'I'm injured'. When your club's physio adopted such an attitude, you were left to know in no uncertain terms what was expected of you.

In those days knowledge of injuries was limited in comparison with that of today. Given the advancements in medical knowledge that is understandable, but the inability to diagnose injuries, and the desire to keep players out on the pitch when injured, often caused considerable damage to a player's body. In some cases this could be of a permanent nature. In the late fifties Wilf McGuinness was badly hurt when playing for Manchester United reserves at Stoke City. Having received attention from the United reserve-team trainer, Wilf rejoined the game with the advice to 'run it off'. In fact he had sustained a compound fracture of his left leg, but gamely Wilf returned to the fray. He endured a painful quarter of an hour, before succumbing to what was a horrendous injury. Wilf spent nigh on two years out of the game and though he did return to captain United reserves for a season, he was still troubled by his leg. He was eventually advised by doctors to give up playing football for fear of causing permanent damage. If you talk to Wilf now, he is very philosophical about that incident. 'That's the way things were back then.

People didn't know what a compound fracture was, let alone were they able to diagnose it from the side of the pitch,' he said to me.

No one can say for sure, but if Wilf's injury had been correctly diagnosed, or even recognised as being of a serious nature, and he had been taken to hospital immediately, I am sure he would have enjoyed many more years as a United player. Common sense tells us that to have played on with such a fracture of the leg must surely have added complications to what was already a very severe injury.

One of the great improvements to have taken place within the game is that the diagnosis and treatment of players' injuries are far better than in the past. Players used to be treated as commodities, to be bought and sold at will, but nowadays they are capital assets and, for all one may equally disagree with that, their new-found status within the game affords them better medical care and supervision. This can only be for the good. No one wants a return of such situations as Wilf McGuinness experienced.

Today's top clubs employ a bevy of people whose job it is to aid the fitness and diet of players. New methods are forever being developed. However, in spite of the fact that medical knowledge and the treatment of injuries have improved in leaps and bounds over the years, the presence of fitness and conditioning coaches in football today may have resulted in even more injuries to players. I take issue with those who say footballers are stronger and fitter now than they were thirty years ago. The game is quicker these days that's for sure, but that has more to do with the all-year-round pristine pitches we now see, and the lightweight footballs in use. Fitness and conditioning coaches can harp on all they like, but they will never convince me that today's top players are far fitter than those of the sixties and seventies, or even the eighties and nineties for that matter. I don't believe the average Premiership player is that much fitter than I was as a player, if at all. One only has to look at library film of George Best, Bobby Charlton and Denis Law in action for Manchester United on gluepot pitches to see that they were as fit as Paul Scholes, Wayne Rooney and Ryan Giggs. Over the years track athletes have shaved fractions of a second off previous world records, but whether new records are down to slightly better technique, preparation and so on, rather than superior all-round fitness, is open to debate. The same applies to football and footballers.

As for the claim that modern players are stronger, I refute that also. Their diet is better that's true, but are the likes of Patrick Vieira, Rio Ferdinand and John Terry stronger than, say, Roy McFarland (Derby), Ray Wilkins (Chelsea and Manchester United) or Bobby Moore? I doubt it very much. When I think of players of yesteryear like Dave Mackay, Bobby Smith, Terry Butcher and Bryan Robson, to name but four, I doubt there are any players around today whose physical and mental strength could be said to be greater.

In 1973 students at Alsager College in Cheshire conducted some research into how many First Division (Premiership-equivalent) players were unavailable to their clubs on the opening day of the 1973–4 season because of injury (either long-term or as a consequence of pre-season training or friendly matches). The students simply scanned both national and local newspapers for their information and found that twenty-nine First Division players were unavailable to their clubs – an average of 1.3 injured players per club. A litmus-test survey on the opening day of the 2004–5 Championship season indicated that of the twenty-four clubs in the divisions, ninety-eight players were deemed to be unavailable due to injury – an average of just over four injured players per club. While no statistics were available for the start of the 2004–5 Premiership season, these figures suggest that at the start of the 2004–5 campaign Championship sides had nearly four times as many players unavailable through injury than thirty years ago in the First Division. And it is worth noting that we are talking here of the opening day of the season, before a ball has been kicked in anger!

If players are meant to be fitter and stronger today, how come – in a game that is widely regarded as less physical than it was thirty years ago – players appear to suffer far more knocks these days? The answer, I believe, lies in the current training methods, and with fitness and conditioning coaching in particular. I have watched contemporary teams train and, generally speaking, the training is little different from what I did as a player. What has changed is the impact of personal training: many top players now have the benefit of a specialist fitness and conditioning coach whose job it is to individualise training. A comprehensive fitness and training programme is mapped out for each player, with a view to improving stamina, strength and speed, and avoiding injuries. The player is also offered advice on diet and good maintenance of the body.

This specific form of training is geared towards mimicking the demands placed on the body during the course of a game. All well and good. The problem, I feel, comes from players' bodies reaching optimum condition, when muscles, tissue, sinews and so on have been the subject of such intense training and conditioning that they become taut as piano wire. In the course of a match, when there is contact with another player at speed, or when the player himself overstretches, the fine-tuning of his body is knocked out of kilter. In my opinion that is why so many players today seem to suffer from injuries – as opposed to those of yesteryear – even before a new season gets under way. It would be overly simplistic and wrong of me to suggest fitness and conditioning coaches do not have a productive role to play in the modern game, but to my mind there is a downside to their influence. Statistics indicate that players suffer more niggling injuries nowadays than they did in the past. Conditioning training that results in the body reaching a peak but being suspect to the slightest knock can't be good for the player or the game.

Regarding trainers (of whatever classification) and physios of today, one thing I am happy to see them turn their back on is the cortisone injection (though one still occasionally hears of these being administered to players). Football may well be a short career, but every player knows he will sooner or later pay a price for his time in the game. It can be a dodgy knee or ankle, a problematic back, occasional aching in the neck, or a muscular problem. Years and years of tackles, twists and turning will eventually take their toll in some way or other. Today many players who plied their trade in the seventies and eighties have some sort of complaint, and the majority believe it may not be just down to wear and tear when a player.

The careers of the players of the seventies and eighties coincided with the use of what was at the time believed to be a wonder drug. Cortisone was a painkilling steroid. If a player had a muscle injury, a cortisone injection into the seat of the muscle had a startling effect: no pain. Even though they were carrying an injury, players could declare themselves fit for a match because the cortisone injection nullified any pain, stiffness or soreness. However, the injection did not cure the injury; it merely killed the pain, and there lay the problem. A player would go out and play not knowing that he could well be aggravating the injury, even doing himself permanent damage.

There are any number of players who believe the use of so many cortisone injections during their career has led to problems later in life. Former Southampton midfield player Jim Steele is a case in point. Jim was diagnosed as sterile, and claims a specialist he consulted was of the mind that his infertility was down to the number of cortisone injections he had received during his days as a player. Cortisone was not intended to treat football injuries. It became available in the fifties to reduce inflammation around the joints of people suffering from acute arthritis. The drug had no curative qualities, but it was widely used on footballers throughout the seventies and into the eighties. It has been the subject of much debate over the years and to the best of my knowledge nothing has been proved either way, although within the medical profession there appears to be wide agreement that sustained use of this steroid can result in debilitating side-effects. That cortisone injections are not widely used in football today is indicative of the mistrust many have for this steroid, and its nigh on eradication from the game is, in my opinion, a good thing.

The role of trainers has changed much over the years. Even when I was playing, training was very different from how it had been in the early to mid-fifties. That said, even Harold Shepherdson, the England trainer when we won the World Cup, had something of the 'go-for' to his role. On the occasion of England's World Cup semi-final against Portugal, Gordon Banks got into a tizzy. He was stripped and ready for action, when he noticed there was no chewing gum in Harold Shepherdson's box of tricks. The absence of chewing gum was a problem to Gordon. He didn't wear gloves and before leaving the dressing room would chew on a couple of pieces of Beechnut gum and then smear some saliva into the palms of his hands. This tacky afforded Gordon a better grip when handling the ball and also a degree of traction when palming it away or when making a diving save. Banksy also felt chewing gum helped his concentration, so when none was to be found in the dressing room, with kick-off approaching, he began to panic. Noticing Gordon was working himself into a state, Alf Ramsey asked what the problem was. Gordon told him.

'Harold, go and get some Beechnut. Now,' instructed Alf.

'Where the hell am I going to get it from?' asked Harold.

'I'm a football manager,' said Alf, 'not the bloody owner of a sweetshop.'

It was then that Jack Charlton remembered there was an off-licence at the end of Wembley Way which stayed open until quite late, and so Alf ordered Harold to run down there as quickly as possible. Harold took off his boots, donned his shoes and took off like an Olympic sprinter. Meanwhile, the buzzer rang to signal the team should make their way to the tunnel, which they did, all except for Gordon, that is.

At one end of the Wembley tunnel were two imposing wooden gates and set into one of them was a small door. With the teams on the point of taking to the pitch for a World Cup semi-final, Gordon Banks stood peering out of the open door, anxiously awaiting the return of the England trainer. Bobby Moore shouted to Alf that he should delay the referee but, as luck would have it, the band that had provided the pre-match entertainment was still in the process of leaving the pitch, and this bought Gordon another valuable minute. Banksy was standing as sentinel on that little wooden door, willing Harold Shepherdson to appear. At one point he stepped outside, where quite a number of supporters who had failed to get a ticket for the match were milling about. Heaven knows what they thought on seeing the England goalkeeper outside Wembley minutes before the kick-off of the most important game in the history of the national team.

Eventually Harold appeared, running like the clappers across the car park, one arm raised aloft, brandishing a tiny packet of Beechnut in triumph. When he reached Gordon he was so out of breath he couldn't speak, and simply thrust the Beechnut into the goalkeeper's hands, before collapsing against one of the gates. Banksy ripped open the packet, stuffed the tablets of gum into his mouth as if Beechnut needed the wrapping back, and joined the England line as they made their way up the tunnel and into the cauldron that was Wembley that night. The television footage of the teams taking to the pitch shows Gordon chomping away like mad, and the BBC commentator Kenneth Wolstenholme saying, 'And there is Gordon Banks, chewing gum and looking very relaxed'. Dear old Ken, he didn't know the half of it. For the life of me, I can't imagine Sven-Göran Eriksson despatching Tord Grip to get chewing gum for Paul Robinson minutes before an England friendly, let alone a World Cup semi-final!

During the 1966 World Cup England trained at the Bank of England training ground in Roehampton. Following training in the morning, we had lunch and then, more often than not, the squad would congregate in one of the lecture rooms, where Alf Ramsey would talk about the game ahead. That done, conversation would turn to the tournament itself and football in general. It is well known that Alf had taken elocution lessons. I can only imagine he did this to feel more comfortable in the presence of FA officials, the majority of whom were ex-public school. At one of our talk-ins, the conversation turned to football club directors. The discussion dragged on for about an hour, by which time I still hadn't made a contribution to the debate (because basically I thought if I did I would only prolong it). Finally, Alf turned to me.

'I'm surprised you haven't had anything to say on the subject, Jimmy,' said Alf. 'Would you like to give us your view on directors?'

'Not really, Alf,' I informed him. 'There's little choice in rotten apples.'

'Oh, come, come, Jimmy,' said Alf encouragingly, 'I'm certain you of all people can think of something more pertinent to say about directors than simply "There's little choice in rotten apples". We are the England football team. We speak English, the language of Shakespeare.'

'That is Shakespeare, Alf,' I told him.

I make mention of that story not to denigrate Alf, whom I had enormous respect for and still do, and not to cast aspersions upon every club director there has been either. What I said about directors in 1966 was a generalisation, for then, as now, there are good and bad directors in football. For decades club directors were, in the main, owners of local businesses who saw a position on the board of the local club as a means of increasing their prestige in the community. Some became directors for philanthropic reasons: they genuinely wanted to put money into the local club and take it forward. The Burnley chairman Bob Lord ran a chain of successful butcher's shops. Lord could be bombastic and egocentric, and was once asked by a reporter what he would have become had he not been chairman of Burnley. 'A millionaire,' replied Lord. As Danny Blanchflower once famously said of him, 'He's a self-made man who worships his creator'.

For all his faults, Bob Lord was the driving force behind Burnley in the fifties and sixties. He put his money where his mouth was and by virtue of that invested heavily in the club. Burnley enjoyed a golden period under his chairmanship, winning the Football League Championship in 1960 and finishing runners-up in the FA Cup in 1962. In 1960–61 Burnley folk had the novelty of seeing their team compete with the best in Europe in the European Cup and, what's more, they saw their team reach the quarter-finals. For a provincial town team to be rubbing shoulders with the likes of Real Madrid, Barcelona, Hamburg and Benfica was a remarkable feat, and that Burnley achieved this was in no small way down to their chairman.

Many directors, particularly those who made up the board's quota, saw their local football club as their own private social club in which to entertain fellow business people and local dignitaries. Having made what in many instances appeared to be the minimum investment in the club, this sort of director would take advantage of the free food and drink on offer in the boardroom on match days to ingratiate themselves with the people they hoped to do business with.

Some directors are autocratic, some benevolent; some, like Bob Lord, appeared to be a mixture of both. Others were incongruously obtrusive, or sensibly passive. Some were even models of restraint and common sense. Albert Booth, the chairman of Stoke City in the thirties, was one such. On arriving at the Victoria Ground one day, Booth saw two of his players smoking cigarettes while chatting to a local reporter and signing autographs for young supporters. Smoking, though popular in society at the time, was banned at the Victoria Ground where players were concerned. Despite seeing a clear breach of club rules, the Stoke City chairman didn't wade in to admonish his players as he didn't want to embarrass them in front of a local journalist and some of their young fans. Instead Albert Booth approached the players and took two cigars from the breast pocket of his suit.

'Results have been going well, lads,' said Booth. 'Here, have a cigar on me, but I'd appreciate it if you didn't smoke them here at the club.'

This was an incidence of a violation of club rules dealt with diplomatically by a benign chairman exercising common sense. Given that in the thirties directors looked upon players as little more than serfs, Booth's diplomacy and restraint must have been somewhat incongruous to the period. When a fellow Stoke City director heard of the incident of these two players smoking on club premises he asked Booth why they had not been summoned before the board and disciplined. 'No, no,' said Booth, 'it was nothing but a minor indiscretion. Let's not use a guillotine to cure dandruff.' I wish I could say most directors I have come across displayed the objectivity and good sense of old Albert Booth.

Many directors looked down on players. In 1961 when the player's union, the PFA, launched its campaign to free players from contracts that tied them to a club for life and end the maximum wage they incurred the wrath of most club directors. That some saw players as little more than mercenaries was evidenced by a conversation between a director of Chesterfield and Harold Ord, the chairman of Hartlepool United, following a game between the two clubs in the early sixties.

'What is it your chairman says about players?' asked Ord. 'He has a term for them.'

'Money-grabbing bastards,' replied the Chesterfield board member.

Such an attitude towards players was not uncommon then and I suspect it is a view still held by some directors today. Though with 'player power' being particularly strong in top-flight football, contemporary directors who hold such a view are inclined to keep their thoughts to themselves.

In the fifties and sixties teams in the lower reaches of the Football League relied heavily on financial contributions from their supporters' clubs and associations. It was not unusual for a supporters' club to raise a considerable amount of money over the course of a season, but in donating a four-figure sum to the team it often led to many an argument with the board of directors. In some cases the money raised by the supporters exceeded that of the board, and supporters took umbrage because directors had not put as much money in and, irrespective of the sums raised, fans were never granted a say in the running of the club. More often than not a board would not reveal how much it had invested in the club (as it might compare unfavourably with the amount raised by the supporters) and this led to all manner of ill feeling.

In the days when a pint cost 1s 3d (six and a half pence) and admission to matches was three shillings (thirty pence), it was amazing how much money supporters' clubs did collect from their fund-raising events. I remember once talking to Gordon Banks about his time as a player at Chesterfield. Banksy said never a week seemed to go by without the Chesterfield Supporters' Association holding a fund-raising night for the club. Players were invited to attend these fund-raisers and without exception a number of them would always put in an appearance. At one pie and pea supper Gordon once asked a supporter what he hoped the club would use the money for. 'To buy better players' was the reply. It occurred to Gordon then that he might be giving up his free time to raise money to buy a player who would do him out of a job.

When I was a teenager at Chelsea, their supporters' club held similar fund-raising nights, though not to the frequency of those at Chesterfield. I attended a few of these nights, the mark of the times being that one was a 'Gentleman's Smoker', in which players and supporters competed by playing darts, dominoes and cards with one another in a room thick with the fug of cigarette smoke. Not that Chelsea need financial donations from their supporters' club these days, but the mind boggles at the thought of Didier Drogba and Joe Cole spending an evening playing three-card brag with Chelsea supporters while puffing away on a Benson and Hedges.

Something good that can be said of the old school of director is they were invariably local to the town or city club in which they were involved. Football in the fifties, sixties and seventies was very parochial, as was the composition of the boardroom. In the main most clubs used attendance money to offset player and general-running costs. When it came to buying players, more often than not the transfer fee was paid collectively by the board, though sometimes by just one individual director.

One of the most colourful chairmen ever to have graced the game was John Cobbold, who was chairman of Ipswich Town in the late fifties and early sixties. When Cobbold appointed Alf Ramsey as manager of Ipswich in 1958, he took his new manager into the boardroom for a celebratory drink.

'This is the first and last time I will invite you into the boardroom and serve you drinks,' Cobbold told Alf. He threw the manager a key to the boardroom drinks cabinet.

'From now on, feel free to help yourself to drinks.' Knowing Alf, I doubt if he ever did.

The Cobbolds – John's brother Patrick was also on the board – were legendary hosts. The Ipswich board would drive to the local station to welcome the directors, players and officials of the opposing team, before taking to their cars and escorting their opponents' team bus from the station to

Portman Road. In all my years as a player, I never knew any
other board that did this. Back in the Portman Road board-
room, John Cobbold and his fellow Ipswich directors then took
to demonstrating their legendary hospitality. When Ipswich
Town won the First Division Championship in 1962, Frank
Wilson of the *Daily Mirror* interviewed John Cobbold.
Wilson's opening line was to say, 'Well, John, a great season for
Ipswich, which has culminated in the winning of the
Championship. I suppose this has been one long season of
wine, women and song for you and your fellow directors?'

'I can't remember us doing much singing,' replied Cobbold
in characteristic fashion. Whether Ipswich were winning cham-
pionships or battling against relegation, the attitude of John
Cobbold and his fellow directors never changed. Their
approach to football was the epitome of Danny Blanchflower's
saying, 'Winning isn't everything, but wanting to win is.'
Winning was not the be-all and end-all to John Cobbold.
Nearly two years after winning the First Division
Championship Ipswich were struggling at the foot of Division
One, and on Boxing Day 1963 the club travelled to Fulham.
They were beaten 10-1. On leaving Craven Cottage, John
Cobbold was confronted by a reporter from the *Eastern Daily
News*, who asked him to comment on the 'crisis at the club'.

'There is no crisis at the club,' Cobbold told the reporter.

'But the team are struggling against relegation and have lost
10-1 today,' said the reporter. 'You're telling me that's not a
crisis?'

'My dear boy,' replied Cobbold calmly, 'a crisis at this club
would be for the boardroom to run out of gin.'

It was not uncommon for generations of families like the
Cobbolds to be on the boards of football clubs. It may smack of
nepotism, and perhaps it was, but usually there was a gentleman's agreement that shares would pass hands for a nominal
amount, usually a pound per share. In addition to the Cobbolds
at Ipswich, the Moores family were connected with Everton for

years. As well as being the main shareholders at Everton, John and Cecil Moores owned Littlewoods pools and the mail-order catalogue and stores of the same name, and were great patrons of the arts. This was something that didn't always go down well with Blues supporters or Everton players, who wondered why the Moores brothers appeared to put more money into art than they did their football club. Towards the end of the seventies Everton were on a pre-season tour of Spain. On their day off, Everton manager Gordon Lee took the players on a sightseeing tour of an old castle, part of which had been transformed into a very chic art gallery.

'This castle was built by the Moors,' said their tour guide. The Everton winger George Telfer was unimpressed.

'Yeah, they'll spend money on the likes of this,' remarked George to his team-mates, 'but claim poverty if we ask for a rise.'

The director who joined the board of his local football club and was willing to invest, in return for the privileges afforded by boardroom membership was still largely predominant in the game until the eighties. In a decade of the Bradford, Heysel and Hillsborough tragedies, English football reached its nadir, but conversely, and somewhat perversely, given the coverage of these tragedies, television's increasing interest in football in the eighties afforded the game greater opportunity to enhance its fledgling commercial activities. To offset reduced revenue through the gate, clubs began to explore more and more ways of generating income. Matches and the teams themselves began to be sponsored, and the first sponsorship logos appeared on shirts. Supporters sponsored the kit of their favourite player, while he in turn signed lucrative deals to wear a certain brand of boot. Companies were attracted to television's burgeoning coverage of the game and saw football clubs as a cost-effective way of increasing brand awareness. When clubs began to sell replica shirts, they too enhanced their own status as a brand.

Football's blossoming commercialism and its higher profile on television attracted a new type of football director not put off by the poor image and stained character of the game in the eighties. It drew the entrepreneurial into the game. Clubs could be purchased for relatively low sums of money. Football may have been fighting for its life, but teams proved an attractive proposition to entrepreneurs with the vision to see that having reached rock bottom the only way for the game to go was up.

Clubs also boasted the most sought-after asset of all: land. The prospect of taking control of a club for a reasonably modest outlay, redeveloping or selling the existing site, while at the same time taking advantage of the money available from the Football Trust for rebuilding, proved a magnet to those with foresight. Of course, some of the moneyed men who took control did so to save the club they had supported since childhood. Jack Walker at Blackburn Rovers and Jack Hayward at Wolverhampton Wanderers were notable, though rare examples of magnates who pumped money into their respective clubs to bring about a renaissance in fortunes. It is doubtful, however, whether the same can be said of the majority of those who acquired control of clubs in the eighties and nineties.

For the new breed of 'saviour', club allegiance went by the by, as, for example, with John Hall, who had been a season-ticket holder at Sunderland for twenty-five years before taking control of Newcastle United. Entrepreneurs with little or no previous interest in football became chairmen of clubs, many of them taking control of sides hundreds of miles away from the seat of their main businesses. It did not seem to matter that such people possessed as much knowledge and passion for the clubs in question as they did for Tibetan folk songs. As far as many supporters were concerned, they didn't give a hoot if the new owner of their team had previously sworn allegiance to another club or didn't have any background in football whatsoever. The ends justified the means. If their club could redevelop, sign star players and leap on the gravy train, then past allegiances, or even a complete lack of previous involvement or interest in football, were not an issue.

The heart of the game was alien to many of this new breed of club owner. They never felt pain and frustration when their team lost because to them support of the side was not inherent. They took exception to bad results not because it ruined their week but, moreover, because it was bad for business. Managers found themselves at the whim of chairmen whose knowledge of the game could arguably be written on a piece of confetti.

Chairmen began to be referred to as club owners, and they adhered to a new principle of football management – if at first you don't succeed, you're fired. Adherence to this sort of policy led to all manner of ridiculous situations, which only served to sully the name of English football. Even well-meaning chairmen found themselves embroiled in controversy. The most telling example of this was Terry Venables' relationship with IT tycoon Alan Sugar, the then owner of Tottenham Hotspur, which turned into Whitehall farce in 1992–3. As the nineties dawned, Alan Sugar had come to Spurs' rescue when the club looked like it was going to be sold to Robert Maxwell, but on 14 May 1993 Sugar dropped a bombshell by sacking Venables, who held the post of chief executive with a remit to oversee the football side of the club. The following day, Venables was temporarily reinstated by a High Court order. In this way Spurs became a club owned by a man who had sacked his former manager-turned-chief executive, only to see him, in turn, back at his post. The Sugar–Venables affair became a magnified example of what was frequently occurring in football at the time: a power struggle between the game's new breed of entrepreneurial owners and those for whom football was vocational. To the new kind of owner, the price of club shares and the opinion of shareholders were all important; to the manager the team was the main thing. Results mattered to both, but for different reasons.

What can be said of those who entered the game with little or no previous experience of football is that they brought with them business skills, which had hitherto been sorely lacking in the game. The involvement of such people, though, had more than a whiff of the curate's egg about it. Their lack of empathy and understanding of the game, together with an ignorance of the rich history and traditions of English football, have resulted in the introduction of many policies that ride roughshod over the needs and emotions of supporters. It is no longer enough for supporters to pay admission to watch their team: they are now encouraged to sign up to the club's credit card; to buy home and car insurance in the name of the team they support; and to wear replica shirts that cost in the region of five pounds to produce and are sold for eight, sometimes ten times that amount. What's more, the majority of clubs have resolutely refused to allow these official replica shirts to be sold in supermarkets or any other outlet where the cost price may be discounted.

Club loyalty has been ruthlessly exploited in the hot pursuit of money and often to the detriment of the feelings of a club's supporters. Peter Murgatoyd is a Derby County fan who wrote to a writer friend of mine after his side had been beaten 5-0 in their previous home game. In his correspondence Mr Murgatoyd told how at Derby's next home match a tannoy announcement said, 'At the end of our last home game, you probably went away thinking about all the benefits I mentioned of Derby County Financial Services'.

As Mr Murgatoyd went on to say, 'That was the last thing we supporters were thinking about, having just seen our team beaten five-nil at home.' That tannoy message serves as a case in point of what to my way of thinking is football clubs' hell-bent desire to extract every last penny from supporters while having no empathy with their fans.

What also worries me is how the game has become peppered with people whose knowledge of football is scant and that some of them have acceded to positions of considerable authority. Rupert Lowe, for example, confesses to having watched his first-ever football match in 1996: some two years later he was chairman of a Premiership club, and within a few years Mr Lowe also held a key position at the FA (which at the time of writing, he still occupies). How someone whose experience of football and the game in general is so meagre can, in the space of two or three years, rise to a position of such power within the game's senior governing body is beyond me. This is especially baffling when you think there are former players and managers whose experience and expertise are not being utilised.

In his programme notes prior to Southampton's crucial final game of the 2004–5 season against Manchester United, Rupert Lowe, after referring to the possibility of relegation, wrote: 'It is always easy to forget the progress we have made as a club over the past decade when first-team results go badly. Our academy has continued to flourish, our community and educational activities have made progress, our shop is doing well, our match-day and non-match-day catering is the envy of other clubs and our radio station has made great progress . . .'

As Southampton fans mulled over the prospect of trips to Crewe Alexandra and Brighton, one doubts whether they would be pacified by the knowledge that their club shop was 'doing well' and their catering was reputedly the 'envy' of Chelsea and Manchester United.

Directors and chief executives are at pains to inform supporters that they are the lifeblood of the club. The reality, however, is often different. In 2004–5 a season ticket for Arsenal cost up to £1724, and there was a waiting list of nearly three years for a season ticket of any denomination. In May 2005 property developers Galliard, who are building 255 flats in London's Drayton Park as part of the regeneration scheme allied to Arsenal's move to their new Emirates Stadium in Ashburton Grove, announced that anyone purchasing a flat would receive a free Arsenal season ticket. Galliard promoted the development as an 'exciting investment opportunity', citing the rise in property value close to other redeveloped football grounds – 86 per cent at Villa Park and 51 per cent at Old Trafford. The season-ticket arrangement between Arsenal and Galliard is no doubt part and parcel of the deal struck between the two companies to redevelop Ashburton Grove. It is questionable ethics on the part of Arsenal to give away 250-plus season tickets to a property developer when loyal fans have been waiting for up to three years to purchase them.

Even in the Football League, where one would expect a greater degree of philanthropy on the part of club directors, I suspect more than a few directors are using their association with clubs to make money. They have always offered loans to clubs in return for interest, and for many years the interest return on directors' loans was low when compared with the general rate of interest. However, now that interest rates are low some directors are charging well above the base rate for loans they make to clubs. This means they receive an interest rate higher than they would if investing their money elsewhere. Again, one has to question the ethics and the motivation of such directors.

Of course, there are still directors who are loyal supporters in suits. In Scotland, Morton owe their existence to chairman Douglas Rae, vice chairman Arthur Montford and their fellow directors. Morton were on the brink of going out of business when Rae and Montford stepped in to save the club. It took more than TLC to revive the fortunes of this famous old Scottish side. That Morton are now in a relatively healthy financial state and, as a club, in the ascendancy is down to the devotion, hard work and finance provided by Douglas Rae and his board of directors, all of whom – and I say this with all due respect – can count themselves among the team's older supporters.

Morton are a rare example of a well-run club enjoying relative prosperity in Scottish football. In England Walsall, Hartlepool United and Crewe Alexandra are all examples of 'small' clubs that are well run. These three clubs continue to post profits: they never spend beyond their means and when in pursuit of a player, if the player or his agent make financial demands that are not in keeping with their respective wage structures, they would rather miss out on the player in question than pay what they cannot afford. Sadly, such simple and sensible housekeeping, as implemented by Morton, Hartlepool, Walsall and Crewe, is not to be found throughout the game. In 2005 it was reported Cardiff City were £30 million in debt. The news came as a big shock and a worry to Bluebird fans, who had expected a new era of prosperity for the club when Sam Hammam took control at Ninian Park. I should imagine Cardiff's £30 million debt is making Sam's dog go out of its mind with worry . . . that's £210 million in dog money.

Clubs are now punished by the deduction of points if they enter into administration. It seems crazy to me to penalise those who have stepped in to rescue a struggling club, together with its manager, players and supporters, for the deeds of others no longer connected to the place. Taking away points does not punish those who got the club into a financial mess, but those who are trying to pick up the pieces. The ten-point deduction imposed upon Wrexham in 2004–5 is one such example. This would have had a profound psychological effect on manager Denis Smith and his players, as they knew that irrespective of how good a start to the season they made, it would be at least four matches before they had any chance of raising themselves from the bottom of Division One. I have no allegiance to Wrexham whatsoever, but I bet I wasn't the only one keeping a close eye on their results and position in the League, hoping Denis Smith and everyone connected with the club managed to claw back that ten-point deduction and avoid relegation to Division Two. Unfortunately they didn't quite manage it.

Those who took over at clubs in the eighties have benefited in no small way from the renaissance of the game since the advent of the Premiership and the influx of millions of pounds from television, in particular Sky Television. Such people have seen the price of their shares rocket and as a consequence so has the value of the club's themselves. Some owners are now in a position whereby it is almost impossible to remove them, unless, of course, a billionaire such as Roman Abramovich appears on the scene. Aston Villa chairman Doug Ellis has been unpopular with Villa fans for some time. There have been demonstrations against his chairmanship but who, given Villa's current market value, has the financial wherewithal to buy him out and invest further millions to take the club forward? It's a tall order financially. Whatever amount of money a consortium or individual pays to take control of a club nowadays, they must have at least the same amount of money again to invest in order for the club simply to tread water, let alone progress. Hence many clubs now find themselves stuck with a majority shareholder who has, over the years, seen his personal shares rise in value to a point where in some cases it would take a hundred times the amount of money to buy him out than that he paid to acquire control of the club in the first place.

When a consortium does come along to buy out existing owners, it often finds that it has to negotiate a compromise in order to take control of the club. When an Icelandic consortium took over at Stoke City in 2000, in addition to paying a considerable amount of money to the club's two major shareholders, Peter Coates and Keith Humphreys, the group agreed to those two directors continuing on the board and being directors of the club for life. Many Stoke City supporters were exasperated to learn that the two major shareholders they had demonstrated against for so long could now never be ousted from the board of their club.

The most celebrated case of an entrepreneur taking control of a club to which he had no previous connection is Malcolm Glazer's successful acquisition of Manchester United. Throughout the early months of 2005 the spectre of the

American business tycoon loomed large over United. In May Glazer engulfed the club. Having taken his stake to 71.8 per cent, in a matter of days Glazer chipped away at other shareholders, taking his holding to 75 per cent which, in accordance with City regulations, enabled him to return United into private ownership.

Malcolm Glazer is the epitome of an entrepreneur keen to further his riches by owning a football club. That the side in question was Manchester United was somehow fitting because United have for a long time stood alone as the richest and most glamorous club in English football – they capitalised more than any other club on the renaissance of the English game, systematically exploiting every commercial avenue open to them. This even went to the point of touring the Far East to profit from the burgeoning new market of devotees, whose support of United had its roots in image and perceived lifestyle rather than any genuine love of the traditions of the club and the football played. United, more than any other club, were subjected to the rescheduling of fixtures to accommodate the needs of television: noon kick-offs may have inconvenienced supporters at home, but midday here is eight p.m. in many countries in the Far East. These kick-offs represented the perfect time to watch United matches in China or Japan. United were quick to recognise and exploit this, as was Sky. The club also cashed in on the celebrity status afforded to their top players – the image of David Beckham, for example, was ruthlessly exploited during a tour of Japan.

'That's business,' said one United fan when interviewed about the subject on BBC Radio Five Live, and so too is Glazer's acquisition of the club. Manchester United are the club that ate itself. They were ripe for takeover by a single-minded entrepreneur that didn't know Bobby Charlton from Charlton Athletic.

Glazer's intentions for the club worry many United fans. These are supporters who have always felt secure, cocooned even, in the knowledge that regardless of trophies won or lost their club would rest easy at the pinnacle of English football, a benchmark for all other sides, its image ensuring keynote status within the game, and its financial wealth affording United a security that no other club enjoyed – or so it seemed. Following the takeover by Malcolm Glazer, United supporters experienced what fans of the vast majority of clubs have endured for decades – insecurity and the anxiety of not knowing what the future may have in store. Welcome to the real world.

In 2006 it will be thirty years since English football took its first, albeit tentative, step towards the commercialisation of the game we know today. In 1976 non-League Kettering Town made national headlines. This was not for anything the team had achieved on the pitch, but was a result of the Rockingham Road club getting quite literally 'shirty' with the Football Association.

Kettering had announced a sponsorship deal with a local company, Kettering Tyres, which included the company's name appearing on the front of their players' shirts. The Football Association was totally against company logos on football shirts, and so the club and the game's governing body locked horns. Kettering adopted a stance, having taken legal advice and discovering there was nothing in FA regulations that outlawed shirt sponsorship and company logos appearing on club shirts. This was understandable given that Kettering were setting a precedent: no club had ever thought of wearing a company's logo on their shirts as part of a sponsorship deal. Little did they realise it at the time, but Kettering Town were paving the way for English football to become a multi-million-pound industry.

Kettering were so sure of their right to wear the name of a sponsor on their shirts that they threatened to take the FA to court on the matter. Eventually, a compromise of sorts was reached – the club were not allowed to wear the name of the sponsor on their shirt fronts but were given permission to display the letter T'. This nonsensical decision on the part of the FA was, however, to have a profound effect on the finances of clubs in general.

While shirt sponsorship was common on the Continent, this was the first instance of such in English football. Kettering's innovative way of raising additional finance did not, however, immediately open the floodgates. League clubs were beginning to look at new ways of raising money to offset falling attendances, but those who sought to implement Kettering's idea found themselves confronted with a seemingly insurmountable problem. Clubs had welcomed with open arms money received from the increased coverage of the game on what then was only terrestrial television. The television deal involved match highlights that were broadcast both by the BBC, on its *Match of the Day* programme, and the ITV companies, which screened highlights of regional games on a Sunday afternoon. The television companies, particularly the BBC, refused to broadcast matches that included teams with sponsors' logos on their shirts as they deemed it to be free advertising. This led to a farcical situation: teams that had negotiated sponsorship deals wore a strip bearing the name of their sponsors when not appearing on television and a traditional unbranded strip when they did.

The first League club to wear the name of a sponsor on the front of their shirts was Derby County, and by 1980 most top sides had followed suit. Strict regulations were introduced to define how large a logo could be and the actual size of the lettering. Then, in 1980, came another test case, when Brighton refused to wear shirts that did not carry their sponsor's name for a televised match against Aston Villa. At no point did they intimate they would not fulfil their fixture; the club simply wanted to adhere to the deal it had struck with its sponsors whereby the team would wear branded shirts throughout the course of the season. The FA and the Football League were presented with another dilemma that in the end was, from their point of view, fortuitously sidestepped when ITV decided to broadcast highlights of another match. Later in the season Nottingham Forest were fined seven thousand pounds for appearing in a televised game wearing sponsored shirts. Further problems arose a year later when the FA refused to sanction Coventry City's proposed change of name to Coventry Talbot as part of a £250,000 sponsorship deal the club had struck with the Midlands car company. In light of Coventry's request to change their name, the FA issued a statement, part of which read, 'Though welcoming the increasing commercialisation of English football, there is a real danger such commercial activities will have an adverse effect on the traditions of member clubs.' It was a rare thing, a little foresight on the part of the Football Association, which itself would later embrace such 'commercialisation' with open arms.

The FA did not appear to be against the commercialisation of the game per se; they were more concerned that such deals would jeopardise what, in the early eighties, were considered to be lucrative contracts with television companies. Television's efforts to curtail the showing of sponsored shirts was very much a case of King Canute and the waves. Advertising hoardings were appearing at every ground, and even strips that bore no sponsors' logo were themselves carrying logos in the form of the companies who manufactured the kits. Come 1983 television bowed to the inevitability of it all. The way was opened for football to tread the path of commercialisation, and League clubs discovered this to be paved with gold as they woke up to the fact that their identities as clubs were, just like Kettering Tyres, brands to be marketed.

This initially combustible combination of football shirts and television was inadvertently to produce a bonanza for clubs in 1993, when the newly founded Premiership was beginning to have a positive effect on attendances. Television's coverage of the League, particularly that of Sky Television, also attracted a different type of fan to football: the armchair supporter. For this new, uninitiated fan, identifying who was who on the pitch was seemingly a problem. To circumnavigate this, in 1992–3 players wore their surnames on the backs of their shirts in both the League and FA Cup finals. Although whether this was necessary for the FA Cup final is debatable, given that even armchair fans would have been familiar with the players, both Cup finals having been contested by Arsenal and Sheffield Wednesday. It was the first time the finals of the two major domestic Cup competitions had been contested by the same two teams in one season.

The Premier League was so impressed with the concept of players wearing their names on the backs of their shirts that they took up the idea in 1993–4. It is not unusual for an innovation to find a life and purpose different from that for which it was originally intended. A striking example of this kind of thing is the Sony Walkman: the original idea behind the Walkman was to enable Japanese business people to listen to tapes of company meetings while travelling to and from their places of work. The public, however, soon found other uses for the Walkman that were far removed from the original intention. It was these various uses the public put the Walkman to that led to it becoming a global bestseller for Sony. A similar good fortune was also behind the success of players' name on the backs of their shirts. A concept first introduced to enable neutral fans and the new breed of armchair supporter watching televised matches to readily identify players they were not familiar with, it was to evolve into a multi-million-pound market for football clubs.

The late eighties and early nineties had allowed fans to display support for their club, not in the traditional way of wearing a scarf, but by buying a replica shirt from the club shop. In 1993–4 supporters found that as well as buying one of their clubs' replica shirts, they could align themselves with their favourite player by having his name across their shoulder blades. In the course of a season what had been termed a 'trickle market' really took off, and the sales of replica football shirts rose by an amazing 640 per cent. They were set to continue rising. By pure accident the Premier League had opened up an entirely new commercial market in football. It proved to be a massive pot for clubs' resources (and in time it was largely to instigate the transfer of David Beckham from Manchester United to Real Madrid).

The downside to players having names on their backs was the end of the traditional numbering of shirts. With tops now bearing players' names and numbered one to eleven, the problem arose of what would happen if a manager introduced a late change to the team. The answer was to give each player his own individual squad number, rather than the traditional number associated with his position. And also the innovation of shirts displaying the name of a player and his squad number changed an aspect of football culture for evermore. Traditionalists grumbled, but their protests were smothered by the sound of club cash registers ringing. What did tradition and football culture matter when there were healthy profits to be made?

Football was by this point marketing itself big time. The new type of shirt became a brand symbol for clubs, but it was also to have another marked effect on the game. The introduction of numbers on shirts coincided with managers' thinking of their teams in terms of a squad. This notion was furthered in 1993 when more substitutes were allowed to participate in matches. The last Premiership side to field a team wearing the traditional numbers one to eleven was Charlton Athletic, who did so in their first two Premiership matches of the 1998–9 season. And so died another long-held tradition of English football. Little by little innovations were changing the culture and the face of the game – sponsorship, beginning with a non-League club associating itself with a local tyre company, and the emergence of replica shirts, which later bore the names of players, were the catalysts of what was to become a multi-million-pound cult-celebrity-led industry. To stimulate the market, teams changed the style of their strips every season. The game was changing rapidly, by design.

As clubs looked for more ways to exploit their identity and also to handle negotiations with players' representatives and image agents, it was felt 'experts' were needed. The bigger clubs recruited chief executives to deal with players' contracts and the key issues of club business. Marketing and commercial managers came in from outside the game to generate sales to supporters and the corporate sector. PR managers began to handle the media. IT graduates set up club websites to carry the club message. From being the new rock'n'roll, English football was refined and redefined, undergoing a sophistication make-over. Roy Keane's comment about Old Trafford being populated by non-football types munching on prawn sandwiches soon became passé. The professional classes who had suddenly taken to football were to be found munching on guacamole taco dips, wild-mushroom risotto cakes and sipping Nuit St George. One half-expected to hear supporters chant, 'Who ate all the *rognon de veau à la perle*?' – particularly at Norwich City, where Delia Smith had taken control. One of the marketing people's biggest selling points for the new £365 million Wembley was that it would, according to a press release, be 'a gastronomic as well as a sporting experience'. Note which benefit was given precedence. Wembley, we were told, would boast the four largest restaurants in London: the Arc, the Atrium, the Corinthian and the seemingly less classical Venue. Stephen Wheeler, formerly head chef at Harrods and tutored by Terence Conran, was to take up his position in January 2005, more than a year before the first match was due to be staged. Plenty of time to defrost the burgers and stew the onions.

The restaurants at Wembley will not be catering to the average fan of Bolton Wanderers or Sunderland. They are for the exclusive patronage of the game's new breed of corporate football connoisseur – only those with a minimum of six thousand pounds to spend will become a member of the Corinthian or Executive Gold areas of 'Club Wembley'. The ordinary supporter of Bolton or Sunderland will have to make do with what are quaintly referred to as the 'public access seats', where more modest fayre will be on offer from the myriad fast-food outlets ringing the new concourse. Even before the first match had been staged the new Wembley emerged as a symbol of what English football had become – a monument to the have and have-not culture that now besets the game.

There was a sketch in the sixties on American television's *Show of Shows* in which Mel Brooks played a man from the year 1 BC presenting himself before a Roman scribe as part of a population census.

'Occupation?' asks the scribe.

'Peripatetic Senior Executive Prophylaxis Marketing Consultant,' replies Brooks boastfully.

'What's that?' asks the scribe incredulously.

'Companies consult me. I advise them on interchangeable linear commodities, capitalised asset redemption, substantive restitution and remission of sustainable commutative sales, and speculative brokery marketing,' says Brooks proudly.

The scribe heaves a sigh and offers Brooks a world-weary look.

'I'll put you down as "Bullshitter",' says the scribe matter-of-factly.

I am often reminded of that Mel Brooks sketch when I hear some club chief executives and marketing directors talk about the game I love. It is only right and proper that clubs should want to expand their commercial activities, but in appointing so-called experts from outside the game football has paid a high price. It is now being marketed in much the same way as soap powder or loo rolls. There appears to be a culture that views supporters as there to be bled dry. It is a disturbing trend that has become entrenched within the game. For example, what passes for official club merchandise is often tacky and crass, when not downright absurd. A few years ago the Chelsea club shop had on its counters 'Gus Poyet Pot Pourri', while Leeds marketed 'David Batty Dustbusters' and Aston Villa, slinky 'Villa Lingerie'. It seems every conceivable product, from credit cards to underpants, is marketed in the name of demonstrating club loyalty. The game is in danger of becoming an asylum run by the inmates. Some may be forgiven for thinking that is already the case.

Those who are now responsible for the running and marketing of clubs have introduced an entirely new language to football. Chief executives and marketing directors seem to revel in all manner of buzzwords and phrases. Clubs advertise for vacancies in their commercial departments with the prerequisite that the successful applicant should be able to demonstrate 'blue-sky thinking' – and here we are not simply talking of opportunities to work at Manchester City or Coventry City. Just as the legal profession devised a language all of their own in order to protect the industry and ensure we outsiders who do not understand legalese will always have to call upon their services, so the new class of chief executive and marketing director in football have secured their positions by bamboozling everyone with fatuous and esoteric terms and phrases that are alien to the uninitiated. To me it smacks of the king's new clothes, if not the Mel Brooks 'Bullshitter' sketch as well . . .

CHAPTER NINE

I'll put you down as 'Bullshitter'

In 2005 a well-known club placed this advertisement in a broadsheet newspaper.

▇▇▇▇▇▇▇▇▇▇▇ **are looking to add these new posts to their non-football management team:**

DIRECTOR OF SALES

£ attractive incl. performance related bonus plus car

Responsible for the key revenue generating areas of the business, this role will be expected to review, challenge and deliver the sales and marketing strategy for the business. The successful candidate will have a proven B2B and B2C track record including the negotiation and delivery of high value contracts. Deliverables will include the attainment of new sponsorship contracts and development of the Affinity Partnership Programme.

DIRECTOR OF CORPORATE COMMUNICATIONS

£ attractive incl. performance related bonus plus car

Responsible for the corporate communications and marketing of the business,. The successful candidate is likely to have a marketing degree but with proven (min 5 years) corporate affairs or senior PR responsibility. Deliverables will include the setting and execution of the corporate communications strategy. This role will have direct responsibility for the Press Office, Marketing and Public Relations departments and the club's Football in the Community programme.

For all the roles we are looking for energy and enthusiasm to build on the hard work, commitment and results that have already been delivered by the commercial team. Experience within professional football and / or sports industries preferred, but not essential.

I rest my case.

CHAPTER TEN

Over the years he supported them through thin and thinner

The *Sentinel* newspaper once asked a Stoke City supporter, Phil Mellor, if a poor season for his club had affected his support. 'This season I haven't missed a first-team game, home or away,' said Mellor. 'I turn up for every midweek reserve-team home match, and have seen about half a dozen reserve-team away games as well. On Saturday mornings I watch the academy team. Stoke's performances this season have really got to me. I used to be a fanatic.'

Even in disillusionment, the average supporter remains loyal to his club. For the best part of the twentieth century the football club was at the hub of the local community, and though players earned more than the ordinary working person, the differential was nowhere near as great as it is today. Supporters were able to identify with players and their lifestyles. The vast majority of players lived in the town or city in which their clubs were situated and had supporters for neighbours. They met on a daily basis in the local newsagent's or barber's and, in the days when teams travelled by train, would often journey to away matches together. Professional footballers may well have been placed on a pedestal by supporters but it was at such a height that a player was able to keep his feet on the ground. By contrast, the only contact supporters have with today's top players, apart from watching them play, is seeing them on television or reading about their lifestyles in celebrity magazines.

Living in close proximity to supporters, of course, had its

drawbacks, even in the fifties. Ally McLeod is best known for being manager of Scotland in the 1978 World Cup finals in Argentina. In his playing days, however, he was a flying winger with Blackburn Rovers and a member of their FA Cup final team of 1960. Ally had two Blackburn supporters living either side of him and his family. He warmed to one of them, not least because this fan was always telling him he believed Ally to be the best winger Blackburn had ever had. One day Ally fell into conversation with his other neighbour and in the course of their chat repeated his next-door neighbour's opinion of him as a winger.

'Well, that's right, he's always saying that about you,' said neighbour number two, 'but this is the man who also believes his radio works because there are tiny people inside it.'

Like every other aspect of football, supporters have changed much over the years. When one looks at old photographs of fans at a game, the most striking thing is that they all appear to be smiling and laughing. A far cry from the photographs one sees of supporters today. Present a camera in front of a group of contemporary fans, of whatever side, and invariably what we get are snarling faces and clenched fists. If not actually conveying out-and-out aggression, supporters display devotion to their team in a way that at best is churlish and contentious, and at worst is choleric.

The way fans watch a game has changed, too. I mentioned earlier that in the fifties and early sixties rival supporters mingled happily on the terraces. Those people were no less fervent in support of their teams than fans of today, but before anything else they were supporters of football. They wanted to see their teams win, but if they didn't, as long as supporters had seen an enthralling match of football, they went home content. Football was entertainment. The players went out to try and win the games, with a view to entertaining the fans. Supporters would get animated, excited and occasionally they would feel annoyance, anger even, but only fleetingly.

Regular supporters had their own favourite spots on the terracing. More often than not this was hereditary, fathers and grandfathers having occupied the same place over decades. Football was very much community-based and a match was something of a social occasion. Supporters in their usual places would readily recognise fellow fans nearby, themselves occupying their favoured spots. Although they might not speak, they came up with nicknames for one another, such as 'Wobblygob', 'Sourface', 'The Grumbler' and 'Happyjack'. Supporters also devised their own entertainment during matches. A favourite was for one of them to write the numbers one to eleven on torn pieces of paper, which were then offered to those about them in exchange for a shilling (5p). Whoever had the piece of paper with the same number as that on the shirt of the player to score the first goal in the game would win the money. If the game was goalless, the prize money went to the supporter who had the number one, which corresponded to the goalkeeper. It was a harmless and fun pastime that would be impossible today with players wearing squad numbers.

The bedrock support of every club were working-class people who toiled on the factory floor and in the shipyards, pits and pot-banks. Added to these were those who in all probability had begun their working lives wearing overalls, but had 'got on', and now held office jobs, in some cases in positions of lower management. In keeping with their new-found status, those who had moved up seemed to gravitate from the open terraces to the stands. Even here a form of pecking order was evident. The ones who could afford a tanner more in the way of admission occupied a standing position in the paddock, while those who held positions of responsibility at work demonstrated an elevated status by occupying the seats above them in the grandstand. Many was the supporter who, having regularly watched from the terraces, when attending a reserve-team match would pay a few extra coppers for a seat just to see what a game looked like from high up in the grandstand. The 'grand' in 'grandstand' was apposite, redolent as it was of status.

Despite there being an underlying division and pecking order at matches in the past, attendance at a game was truly a shared experience. There was not the contrived atmosphere of today's corporate box, nor the assumed sophistication of the banqueting suite. Every supporter was out in the open, all the time, immersed in the Bovril, pie and cigarette smell of football. For half a crown (twelve and a half pence) the match offered conflict and art. It turned the draughtsman from the drawing office and the riveter from the shipyard into critics, happy in their judgement of the finer points of the game, and readily appreciative of a defence-splitting pass, a mazy run down a touchline, a piledriver shot, or a remarkable demonstration of reflexes from a goalkeeper. Those who were modest, moderate souls in the week suddenly turned into paradoxical partisans, loving a player one week, casting aspersions upon the same footballer's ability to play the game the next. Supporters would by turns be downcast, elated, deflated, buoyant, bitter and triumphant at the fortunes of their team, but also forever hopeful those they worshipped or maligned would create Iliads and Odysseys before their very eyes and so energise a hundred factory floors.

As a player I always took time to speak to the supporters of Chelsea or Spurs. If we were travelling on the same train to away games, as occasionally happened, there was an unwritten rule of no contact on the outward journey. However, with the match over, on the homeward leg of the journey players and supporters would happily mix in the buffet car. We talked, laughed and, above all, connected with one another. Although I understand the reasons for it, the fact that our top players today have no real contact with fans fosters a lack of understanding and mistrust.

Supporters, more than anyone else connected with football,

are at the very heart of the game. There is even an argument for saying they are its pulse. Whether a supporter in the sixties or now, it makes no difference, for the committed fan supporting their team is tantamount to a rite of passage. Each has to learn of the pain that will be inflicted in the following of their side. Committed support turns idealists into cynics and supreme optimists into those who fear the worst is but a kick of a football away. Not every supporter follows Arsenal, Chelsea or Manchester United; the family of football embraces Leyton Orient and Darlington, too. For those who support the Leytons and the Darlingtons of this world, eternal optimism is tempered by a gut feeling that their team is doomed to disappoint. Football is a cruel mistress and the ever-present shadow of flattering to deceive contains within it a harsh possibility, that of being cursed with bad luck. How many regular supporters, off the back of a good run of results for their side, have persuaded passive fans to attend the next home game (to see how useful the team really is), only for the players to produce an abject performance in front of the best crowd of the season? It normally incites the irregular supporter to say, 'It's been two years since I've been to a match and on the strength of what I've just seen, it'll be at least another two years before I come back.'

I often wonder, if the committed supporter of Rochdale or Shrewsbury Town could have their time over again would they support their chosen club? Such teams have pained their supporters too much, the balance between ecstasy and depression, historically, has always been disproportionately in favour of the latter. Yet the pull of one's roots is ever strong. To paraphrase a saying, 'You can take the boy out of Shrewsbury, but you can't take Shrewsbury out of the boy', or any other town of origin for that matter. Loyal support of Football League teams who perpetually fall short and, as such form the larger part of that competition, appears to be character-forming. In time club allegiance is aligned to championing the underdog. Such an attitude fosters eternal optimism and the very thought of rejecting one's local club would verge on self-rejection. I am sure ardent supporters of Wrexham or Kidderminster Harriers often wonder about passing on that legacy to their children but, as I say, the pull of one's roots is nigh on inescapable. Shared experience is, I believe, common to all parents, and as long as hope springs eternal the majority of seasoned supporters will gladly subject their siblings to what has played an intrinsic part in forming their own characters. Besides which, win, lose or draw, there is great comfort to be had from shuffling out of a ground, especially away from home, in the knowledge that every one of that town or city's folk believes in the worth of being there as one. Each supporter gains strength from dedication to their club and is energised by the thought that while apathy is rife elsewhere, fickleness apparent in others and club loyalty fragile among many players, they steadfastly refuse to renounce hope. They may well be aware that some of the players who wear the colours of their club are little more than mercenaries, but they know that football is forever transient and, as such, place their trust in those who are just 'passing through'. That's one hell of a commitment because, let's face it, generally speaking no one trusts anyone any more.

The football match, especially on the terraces, has always been a rich source of humour. The legendary Newcastle United centre forward Jackie Milburn was affectionately known on Tyneside as 'Wor Jackie'. Following his retirement in the late fifties Newcastle had another forward called George Hannah, and the fans assigned Hannah the nickname of 'Wor Palindrome'. It is that sort of clever, witty comment I rarely hear at football matches nowadays.

I can recall playing for Spurs at Stoke City, where they had a goalkeeper called Lawrie Leslie, a more than decent keeper. Lawrie obviously wasn't a favourite of some sections of the Stoke City fans and in this particular game was coming in for a bit of stick. At one stage in the match, Lawrie stepped forward and, arms outstretched, wafted each to either side to indicate his full backs should push out wide on the wings. 'He's bloody well swimming now!' shouted one Stoke fan.

'He's not swimming,' shouted another voice from the terrace. 'Poor blind sod's trying to feel for his posts!'

Terrace humour could be cruel, but rarely was it vindictive and at no time did it ever disgust. Supporters also appeared to respect the opposing team and their players. I once played at Roker Park against Sunderland. As the Tottenham team made our way from the changing room to the tunnel I heard a tannoy announcement: 'Ladies and gentlemen, boys and girls,' said the amplified voice, 'please give a warm Wearside welcome to our opponents today . . . Tottenham Hotspur!' We ran out to warm applause. In recent times whenever opposing teams take to the pitch, invariably they do to a chorus of booing and venomous shouting. To their credit the game's governing bodies have tried to eradicate this by making sides come on to the field together, before forming a line and shaking hands with each of their opponents. Unfortunately at international matches involving England we are still subjected to the embarrassment of so-called English fans booing continuously when our opponents' national anthem is played. The consensus of opinion is that society today is more tolerant than it was in the fifties and sixties. By and large I believe that to be true, which only serves to make booing the national anthems of other sides at England games even more bewildering.

Sterling efforts have been made in recent years by clubs, the game's governing bodies and the authorities to re-establish football as a family game. There is little doubt that English football is all the better for such efforts. In light of the millions of pounds that have been spent on upgrading grounds in recent years, one wonders what sort of health or rail service this country would now have, had those charged with modernising these services been as proactive and diligent in their allocation of budgets.

The game has come a long way since my days as a player, but as well we know, something's lost and gained in living every day. Like most players I know, I wasn't a great collector of match programmes. I have a few, but I wish I had kept more because, with the passing of time, these programmes reveal far more than they did on the day of issue. I have mentioned how football was very much a community game and this was reflected in the match programmes of the day, which now also offer an insight into the supporters of the past.

The old programmes serve as a snapshot of a game and a society that has changed fundamentally. Nowhere is this more evident than in the adverts, or the lack of them. When I began my career at Stamford Bridge, the Chelsea programme, in keeping with those at Arsenal and Spurs, did not carry a single advertisement. Amazing as it may appear now in a game where clubs explore every avenue of money-making, these three sides refused to have advertisements in their programmes. It was deemed to be an official organ of the club and the notion of such outright commercialism present in the programme would be thought to denigrate the good name of the club. How times have changed!

I have the match programme from my Chelsea debut at Spurs on the opening day of 1957–8 and it carries a report of the previous week's public trial match between Tottenham's first and reserve teams. These days we have football all year round, but back in 1957 the game took a twelve-week sabbatical. Teams might play one, perhaps two, pre-season friendlies, and the public trial match gave supporters an early opportunity to see a game of football after a three-month absence. The Spurs programme relates that a crowd of 21,600 turned up to the public trial match between the first team and the reserves. Even if the top clubs staged a public match between first team

Barry Davies, whose match commentary was always neutral. He understood how important it was not to over-elaborate and to allow space for the viewers to think for themselves. (*Action Images*)

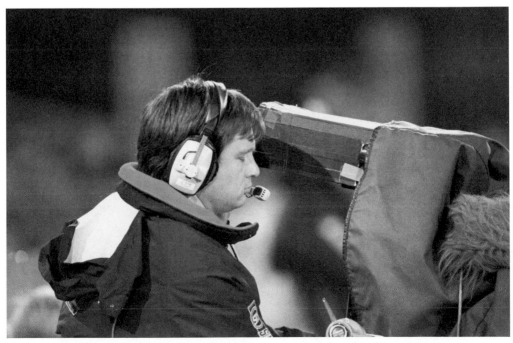

The contemporary game has a lot of plus points, but for all its frenzied pace many matches are so dull even some cameramen can't stay awake. (*Action Images*)

Concern can clearly be seen on the faces of thirsty Spurs supporters as they watch the tea ladies make their way home during a game with Manchester United in the seventies. Rarely do photographs of contemporary matches capture the crowd at a game. *(Colorsport)*

In the days before replica shirts fans displayed their support by shelling out a few bob on a scarf or a few pence on a rosette. Wembley Way prior to the 1966 World Cup final. Contrary to common belief that's not me leaving the stadium in a taxi! *(Offside)*

In the sixties it was perfectly acceptable for players to drink alcohol after a game, as managers thought a communal drink improved team spirit. Left to right: John White, Bobby Smith, me and Cliff Jones. *(Colorsport)*

Scotland's peerless football commentator Arthur Montford offers prudent advice on the economics of the game to young would-be politician Gordon Brown. Arthur is now vice-chairman of Morton. *(SMG/Empics)*

Sven-Göran Eriksson watches his 'dream team' take to the pitch. Four years into the job as England manager, Eriksson's most significant achievement has been to convince the nation that the results of England 'friendly' matches are not important. *(Action Images)*

In Sir Alf Ramsey and Bill Nicholson I was fortunate to play for two of the greatest managers in the history of English football. I would, however, love to have played for José Mourinho. José has been great for English football, even when he isn't doing anything he still attracts media attention! *(Offside)*

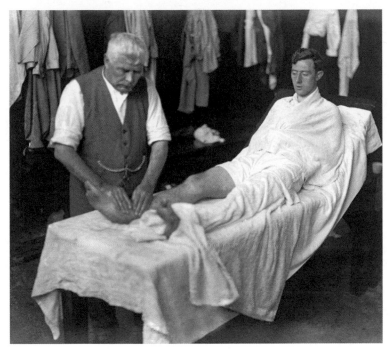

The modern game has seen the knowledge and treatment of injuries improve dramatically. A physio – looking as if he has stepped straight from the pages of D. H. Lawrence – works on a player. *(Colorsport)*

Players of today shower after a match rather than share a plunge bath. Even at top clubs like Arsenal, which had individual baths, players liked to be communal – as in this shot of Frank Stapleton, Brian Talbot and unidentified bathing companions. *(Offside)*

Supporters are the heartbeat of the game. Irrespective of the weather, many stood on their favourite spot on the terraces. *(Colorsport)*

Suitably attired shipyard workers of the twenties show their support for Newcastle United. No prizes for guessing which one was the joker in the yard. *(Colorsport)*

In the sixties and seventies English football boasted the best goalkeepers in the world. Chelsea's Peter Bonetti was known as 'The Cat', though even he would have been hard-pressed to equal the speed and agility of this performer. *(Colorsport)*

When a camera positions itself before fans today what we invariably see are clenched fists and snarling faces. In the early sixties supporters responded to a camera with smiles, laughter and whirling rattles. *(Colorsport)*

The 1960 European Cup final saw the greatest-ever performance by the greatest-ever club side. Real Madrid's 7-3 victory over Eintracht Frankfurt was to revolutionise thinking in English football. Seemingly whatever was on the dressing-room floor didn't meet with the approval of the Real players or their manager. *(Offside)*

and reserves, I can't for the life of me envisage such a game pulling a crowd of over 21,000 today.

After such a long time starved of football, any sort of match involving their team was a considerable attraction to supporters who, compared with nowadays, had little in the way of other leisure pursuits. When I travelled away with Chelsea I was introduced to my nation. The Birmingham City programme reflected the second city's industrial strength. It contains adverts for both Phillips and Hercules Bicycles; Lucas Car Lamps; Girling Brakes (under the heading, 'Football Fans' Questions Answered About How Car Brakes Work' – was that really a hot topic of conversation on the terraces?); Garringtons – 'The Largest Producers of Forgings in Europe'; Goodyear Tyres; and Standard Motor Cars. In addition to which are adverts for beer, cigarettes and – an anachronism even in 1960 – snuff. The ads in the programmes reflected the life and lifestyles of supporters, many of whom worked in the factories of the companies that advertised, and patronised the breweries and cigarette companies. Beer and fags were not only fashionable, they were cheap and affordable to supporters.

When I look back at programmes of games between Chelsea, or Spurs, and a team from the lower divisions, it only serves to emphasise further how community-based football was in those days. As opposed to the ones of big-city clubs that carried adverts for large industrial companies, the Darlington programme is chock-a-block with plugs for local pubs and shops. The Chesterfield programme has an advert for 'Joyce Mullis ALCM, AIMD (Hons), the gold-medallist soprano', offering lessons in singing and piano. It is unthinkable that a singing and piano teacher would advertise in a match programme today – apart from the cost being prohibitive, what sort of uptake would there be from supporters? The ad does, however, offer a telling insight into the supporters of the day, when it uses the selling point, 'Have your children experience what you never could'. A line in an advert in a football programme that offers a better insight into how people thought at that time than any sociology book ever could.

The ads in the match programmes mirrored football and its supporters at that time. The big multinational companies and banks had yet to realise football was a major cultural force and that they could benefit from an association with the game. When they eventually did, their interest, fuelled by television's blanket coverage of the game, signalled the end of small businesses associating themselves with their local football clubs.

The decline of these small businesses, and the large industrial companies too, such as those who patronised the Birmingham City programme, gave rise to a shifting population. You are now likely to find Darlington and Chesterfield supporters in London, Manchester and many points in between. The fragmentation of our communities has tested supporter loyalty, especially of those who support the Darlingtons and Chesterfields of this world. As the years roll by it isn't easy to maintain allegiance to a club like Darlington if most workmates around you profess to support Manchester United or Liverpool. Those who left home in search of new careers in the seventies and eighties now have children of their own, and again, if you live in Milton Keynes or Bristol, it must be a dickens of a job to encourage your children to support Darlington, or any club outside the upper echelons of the Premiership for that matter.

Football has changed and so too has the composition of the crowd. Look back at old photographs of crowd scenes and usually there are any amount of old codgers, puffing merrily on their pipes. Though the conditions in which we watch a match these days are infinitely better than forty years ago and trouble at games is rare, few elderly people now attend football. The criminals (for that is what so-called hooligans were) did their worst in the seventies and eighties. It was not only supporters who were elderly at the time that turned their backs on the game and retreated to the safety of their hearths: seemingly, a good proportion of those in their late forties and fifties did the same, hence not many elderly fans are to be seen at matches today. Of course, every club has some elderly supporters that attend every home game, the most celebrated of these being Frank Moore who, in 2005 at the age of a hundred, was still attending Barnsley games. Mr Moore has the distinction of being the longest holder of a season ticket in the history of English football, having been a regular at Oakwell since 1914.

Frank Moore is in every way an exception. The make-up of crowds these days is predominantly one of supporters under the age of sixty, the vast majority of whom appear to be under forty. This was not always so. The troubles that beset the game appear to have alienated a generation; grey power is conspicuous by its absence at matches. Other industries, such as travel, have long since recognised the buying power of the grey pound. Oddly, football clubs do little, if anything, to attract senior citizens that have been lost to the game back to football grounds. They appear to concentrate their efforts on capturing the young and those in their twenties and thirties, yet in all probability the Saga generation has more disposable income and time to attend matches. I can only assume that grey power, for whatever reason, does not register in 'B2B and B2C deliverables', and has no place in 'blue-sky thinking'!

All of this is a shame, because the combination of better facilities at grounds, the virtual eradication of the hooligan element, the establishment of the Premiership, the contribution of star players from overseas and, of course, the profile given to the game by television has resulted in a renaissance for English football. In 1985–6 attendances at Football League matches dropped to an all-time low of 16,488,577. In the subsequent six seasons attendances at matches experienced a year-on-year rise, but it was the creation of the Premiership that proved the catalyst to a resurgence in attendances. In the 2003–4 season 29,197,510 spectators attended matches in the Premiership and

Football League, with the aura of the Premiership having a knock-on effect. Attendances in the Championship (First Division as was – Second Division as used to be!) in 2003–4 were, at 8,772,780, more than double those of 1985–6 (3,551,968). It is a trend that has been followed throughout the divisions of the Football League.

Let's not forget more supporters attend Football League matches than do Premiership games. In 2003–4 a total of 13,303,136 spectators attended Premiership games, whereas the aggregate attendance at Football League matches was 15,894,374. Obviously there are more teams and consequently more games in the Football League, but the amount of coverage the national media give to the Premiership is acutely disproportionate when you think of the number of people watching Football League matches. In keeping with most national newspapers of its type, the *Daily Telegraph* has a pull-out sports section on a Saturday, and there has been more than one occasion when the only coverage given to the Football League is the printing of its fixtures for that day.

Attendances at matches are now on a par with what they were in 1968–9, though the negative football produced during that period had resulted in a gradual fall in numbers. Owing to the limits now placed on capacities at grounds and the myriad other leisure interests people have these days, we shall never get back to the forty million-plus crowds that attended games in the late forties. Nor shall football experience again the sort of figures of the fifties, when an average of 34.5 million spectators attended per season. But the steady rise in attendances is an indication that English football is in a heartening, if not entirely healthy, state.

Outside the stellar world of the Premiership there is, of course, much football to be had. The Conference is to all and intents and purposes the third division of the Football League. Conference attendances exceeded the one-million mark in 2003–4, which shows supporters have an appetite for football at that level. Crowds at clubs in the Conference North and South have also risen, and this may have as much to do with the appeal and atmosphere of matches at this level as it does the general standard of football. Nowadays most non-League teams provide supporters with decent facilities in which to watch a match. Even if the standard of football, certainly outside the Conference, is not that of the Football League and is a world away from what one sees in the Premiership, football at this level has a growing appeal to supporters. It is a hark back to when the game was community-based and fans had contact with players. Non-League football is affordable for most and the cost for a parent taking two children to a game is much less than the price of a single seat at a Premiership match and at most Championship venues, too. The fans at non-League matches can also talk to the players after the game and, as someone who played for both Barnet and Chelmsford City, my experience is that the majority of players at this level are only too happy to chat to supporters. That contact is non-existent in the Premiership and these days rare throughout the Football League as well. There is also a more convivial atmosphere at non-League grounds, even when the opponents bring a couple of coachloads of supporters.

No one goes into football at non-League level to make money. They do so for the enjoyment to be had from their involvement in the game, which is refreshing to those who support the teams. It all adds to the appeal of football at this level to a parent looking for a safe and friendly environment in which to introduce their children to football. The cheerful atmosphere which pervades non-League matches is redolent of that I experienced at grounds as a player. Sadly, higher up the scale the enjoyment factor appears to have been lost to many in the modern game.

The fact that I managed to score on my debut for every team I played for got me off to a good start with supporters. I would like to think I had a good relationship with fans at every club I represented, and some of them I got to know very well. When I was a young player at Stamford Bridge, I became friendly with a fanatical Chelsea supporter called Sam Harris. Sam managed the old Kilburn Empire picture house and any Chelsea player who turned up with his partner to see a movie wouldn't have to pay. Sam never missed a game at the Bridge, but once we had a midweek game that fell on the night Sam was due to work at the Empire. On the morning of the game Sam rang his boss, professing to be ill and conveying his apologies as he would be unable to attend work that day. Sam, of course, was as right as rain and was at the match in the evening. At half-time he was sitting in his seat reading the match pro-gramme. As he finished he was about to put the programme in his pocket when he felt a tap on his shoulder, and a voice asked, 'Could I borrow your programme for a minute, please?' Without thinking, Sam said, 'Yes', and on turning came face to face with his boss!

'I thought you were bad,' said his boss.

'I am,' said Sam.

'Then what are you doing here?' asked the boss.

'I can be here when I'm bad,' said Sam. 'When all is said and done, the Chelsea players are bloody awful, and they're here!'

The lengths some supporters will go to to watch their team never cease to amaze me. Morris Keston was a diehard Spurs fan I got to know well in my time at White Hart Lane. Spurs were due to go on a pre-season tour of Egypt, which was some-what of a problem to Morris as he was Jewish. Relations between Egypt and Israel were very volatile at the time: this was July 1967 and the Six Day War had taken place the month before. But that did not deter Morris from travelling to Egypt to cheer on Spurs. In those days, when passports detailed both the religion and occupation of the holder, Morris simply applied for a new passport and on the application form put down his religion as Church of England.

Johnny Goldstein was another avid Spurs supporter. He was known as 'Johnny the Stick' and made a decent living as a ticket tout. Johnny could get his hands on tickets for everything from the FA Cup final and the centre court at Wimbledon, to top West End shows and Buckingham Palace garden parties. He and his minder – 'One-armed Lou' – were well known around White Hart Lane, but when Spurs played away they also attended matches at Arsenal. Johnny had no liking for the Gunners whatsoever; on the contrary, he disliked them intensely. Thanks to his 'profession', Johnny would always get a seat behind the Arsenal directors and rather than watch the match would spend the whole game barracking the board, before going home happy. The Arsenal chairman Dennis Hill-Wood and his fellow directors got so fed up with the constant catcalling that Hill-Wood penned a piece in the Arsenal programme. Its basic tenet was to say that if those Arsenal supporters who barracked the board at home games could do any better, let them come forward, put some money in the club and have a go at being directors themselves. In short, 'Put up or shut up', which, of course, only encouraged Johnny and One-armed Lou to heckle the Arsenal board even more. Dear old Dennis, he had no idea the barracking he and his fellow Arsenal directors suffered at every home game came from Spurs supporters.

The tradition of playing matches on a Saturday afternoon started because it was the most convenient time for supporters. Historically, English football evolved to meet the needs of supporters. For the vast majority of people, Saturday and Sunday were days of rest after a five-day working week. Football was not allowed to take place on a Sunday for religious reasons, so that left Saturday, and moreover a Saturday afternoon as quite a number of people worked a half-shift on Saturday mornings. Up until 1969 Stoke City's home matches would kick off at 3.15 p.m. During one visit to the Victoria Ground with Spurs,

I once asked the reason for the delayed kick-off. I was told that the pottery workers, who formed the majority of the Stoke support, worked in the pot-banks on a Saturday morning on an extended shift which didn't finish until 2 p.m. The 3.15 p.m. kick-off had been introduced to allow these pottery workers to grab some lunch and a pint in the local pubs before going to the match. Many of them didn't have sufficient time to do this when games kicked off at 3 p.m. and found they missed the first ten minutes of the game. The club had decided to put the start of Stoke's home games back a quarter of an hour to suit the needs of many of their supporters.

In the days before clubs had floodlights, midweek matches took place on a Wednesday afternoon. Again this was to suit the supporters. The majority of towns and cities in England had what was called half-day closing, when shops and businesses would close for the day at 1 p.m. The scheduling of the Wednesday afternoon match was to comply with this and was introduced for the convenience of supporters.

Now the needs and convenience of supporters play no part in the organisation of fixtures. Games are played to suit the demands of television and, in the case of Cup matches, to generate maximum profits for the FA. In 2003 a survey of two thousand supporters conducted nationwide on behalf of a football magazine revealed that 94 per cent of them preferred the traditional kick-off time of 3 p.m. for matches on a Saturday. In 2004–5 not one game in the sixth round of the FA Cup took place at the traditional time on a Saturday afternoon, which meant some fans travelling to away games designated a noon kick-off were setting off at 5 a.m. In 2003–4 the FA Cup semi-final at Old Trafford between Millwall and Sunderland had kicked off at lunchtime. It was a Sunday and a day when there were no trains running from London to the north-west due to track maintenance. Why the whole of the West Coast mainline had to be closed no one knows as no adequate explanation was ever tendered. But closed it was, which meant every Millwall supporter had to travel by road. This was obviously not the fault of the FA, but the lunchtime kick-off meant many Millwall fans had a 4 a.m. start to their journey to Manchester in order for them to arrive at Old Trafford in good time for the game.

Supporters have returned to football in considerable numbers. The facilities and conditions in which fans watch games nowadays are better than at any other time in the history of the game. But rarely, if ever, are the needs of supporters taken into consideration in the organisation of games. Football's authorities pander to the wants of television and seem never to take into consideration the impact this has on supporters.

Even some of the minor but treasured aspects of the game have been crassly subjected to commercialism and the requirements of television. There was a time when the FA Cup draw induced excitement and mystery. It used to be the sole preserve of radio in those neat, heady days when Saturday was football day. The FA Cup draw on radio was incongruously both a major and a minor event, one that separated the true supporter from the passive fan. Television ignored it completely. The only visual representation of it was tangential: the following day's newspapers would habitually carry a photograph of a group of sideburned non-League players, their ears cocked to the type of wireless that subsequently fell out of fashion but has now made a comeback in the name of chic retro.

The sound of the wooden balls in the velvet bag was both comforting and exciting for supporters. The fingers of fate would silently disappear into the darkness and dust, followed by the octogenarian voice that announced the number . . . cue dear old Ted Croker, who would crack the code and reveal your team's fate. In this way the draw was enveloped in ritual and secrecy. There seemed no way, for example, of guessing which number represented which club. The consensus was that it was alphabetical, but no – Torquay United would be afforded number fifty-eight, which made all

Tottenham players and their supporters keep an ear open for fifty-nine, only for Manchester City to be revealed as the guardian of that number.

Then the draw went on television. Instead of being in a velvet bag, the balls appeared in a drum, the sort used in bingo halls. What's more, the balls were no longer wooden: they too had acquired a bingo-esque makeover. But then something else happened. The draw became puffed up with self-regard. Worst of all, the drama was diluted by us being told which number had been allocated to which team.

Now the draw is something of a cross between bingo and a tacky care-and-share morning television programme, with lights, graphics, plastic, gaudy colours and, would you believe it, an audience. Gone is the mystery of not knowing. So is the image of old men in wonderfully funereal suits in a wood-panelled room who spoke with faltering consonants and Lord Reithian vowels, and the sound of snooker balls in a pillowcase. The draw has been laid out before the unforgiving eye of the television camera. The vision of Churchillian characters has been replaced by former players, who always manage to look embarrassed (but not as embarrassed as we viewers). Are the two former pros supposed to make funny comments or not? They never appear to be sure themselves.

By its very nature the draw becomes less of a spectacle as the competition progresses because there are fewer teams involved. As for televising the draw for the semi-finals, well, it's like the worst sex imaginable: huge expectations quickly shattered when everything is over in less than a minute. The draw for the 2004–5 semi-finals is a case in point. For the first time in the history of the Cup both semi-finals were taking place at the Millennium Stadium, the same venue as the final itself. So there was not even the mild tension of wondering which teams would be playing at which neutral venue. Once Arsenal had been drawn to play Blackburn Rovers, what was the point in carrying on? But carry on they did.

'Number twenty-seven . . . Manchester United . . . will play? . . .'

'Newcastle!', chorused a nation of bemused and underwhelmed viewers.

Broadcasting the draw for the semi-finals of the FA Cup is a prime example of what many believe to be wrong with football today: the hype is too burdensome for the product. The FA Cup draw may well have been one of the lesser-spotted rituals of English football, but it is one the true supporter looked forward to with a mixture of excitement and anticipation. As seems to be the vogue these days, mystery has been stripped away from the draw. It no longer fuels our imagination because everything about it has been exposed. It is brash and vulgar like some Blackpool amusement arcade. Cheap showmanship has replaced intrigue, mystery and entertainment as every last drop of what the draw once offered supporters has been sacrificed in the name of tacky commercialism.

Due reverence has not been paid for some time to what is the world's oldest club cup competition, a point borne out by the FA's decision to stage both semi-finals of the 2004–5 FA Cup at the Millennium Stadium. (Surely a stealth policy to pave the way for future semi-finals to be staged at the new Wembley?) One of the most appealing aspects of the FA Cup was that it afforded players and supporters alike a special day out. Staging the final at a venue that only hosted matches of significance gave the final even greater importance. Getting there was the goal of every player and supporter. Now players and fans can get there twice. The FA had us believe that it took the decision to hold both 2005 semi-finals with supporters in mind. We were told more fans of the teams involved were able to see the games than if they had been staged at traditional neutral venues, such as Villa Park. Rather than for reasons of magnanimity, most supporters were of the mind that the FA made the decision to hold both semi-finals at the same venue as the final simply because it would generate more money and greater profits. It was another instance of supporters, especially those of Newcastle United, being greatly inconvenienced and incurring greater expense so that the FA's coffers could be bolstered. The decision to hold both semi-finals – and in all probability every subsequent semi – at the same venue as the final has further tarnished the traditions and history of what is the FA's own competition. The decision also flew in the face of the wishes of the vast majority of supporters and, indeed, players.

There is a lot to be said in favour of English football today. No one should ever forget the sterling efforts made to return the game to families, and to provide better conditions and facilities in which to watch football. Until the dark days of Bradford, Heysel and Hillsborough many grounds had remained little changed since the Edwardian age. What English football has achieved since 1990 is phenomenal. But, lest we forget, the clubs and the game's governing bodies have achieved these improvements because they were forced to. There was no alternative after Hillsborough. Clubs and the game's organisational bodies effected monumental changes that revolutionised the English game, but the fact remains that the changes we have seen in the game were the result of pressure to reform. As such, the much-improved conditions and facilities now afforded to supporters have more than an air of serendipity about them.

I find it worrying that the needs of supporters seem to come pretty low on the list of priorities of both clubs' and football's administrative bodies. Far too often decisions are made on a premise which involves no consideration of the feelings of supporters whatsoever. This is a great failing of the game today. Though clubs are careful to say the supporters are their lifeblood, they rarely act as if they are. Increasingly, supporters are there to be bled dry. The price of admission to matches is now seen as just one aspect of how supporters can be utilised to generate revenue. From replica shirts retailed at unrealistically inflated prices to credit cards and insurance, every avenue of commercial exploitation is now explored, and all in the name of 'loyalty to one's club'.

Chief executives, agents, commercial directors, marketing johnnies and, of course, television have changed English football beyond recognition, when in the past it was football itself, and certain games in particular, that did this.

CHAPTER ELEVEN

'Matches don't come any bigger than FA Cup quarter-finals'

Neil Warnock

There was a time when a single match could change the face of football not only in this country, but the world. In this chapter I want to offer a personal view on some games I believe had a significant role to play in what is the constant evolution of football. Here I am talking of the football itself, not of dark tragedy such as that which occurred at Hillsborough in 1989, the consequences of which were to effect monumental change of a different sort on English football.

The following is not meant to be an appraisal of great games. One supporter's great game is normally a game to forget for those who were supporting the losing team. As well we know, history books are always written by those who won. Likewise, accounts of great football matches. I have visited Germany on many occasions but have yet to see a glowing description of the 1966 World Cup final in any book. Ask any Southampton fan of a certain age for their all-time great Saints game, and the chances are you will be told of the 1976 FA Cup final when Lawrie McMenemy's side triumphed 1-0 against Manchester United. If you ask any United fan for their opinion of that match, however, unquestionably you will be told it was the dourest ninety minutes of football they have ever had the misfortune to see.

Equally, not every classic game of football is ennobled with the power to change how people thought about and played the game. The 1970 World Cup final between Brazil and Italy produced what is arguably the greatest performance from an international team. In defeating Italy 4-1 Brazil firmly planted their flag on football's aesthetic summit for all future teams to try and emulate. As Liverpool's Bob Paisley said after watching Pele and Co., 'At least we all now know what can be done in the name of football'. Yet the beautiful attacking football of Brazil in 1970 failed to inspire a legion of even pale imitators. No team in the world were capable of reproducing the samba-style soccer of Brazil, and there was no crime in that. The crime, however, lay in the fact that no team were even willing to try. Brazil themselves turned their backs on the exhilarating attacking football that had won them the World Cup and the admiration of the football world. Come the World Cup finals in Germany in 1974, a Brazil devoid of the likes of Pele and Tostao had become exponents of dour football and crude tactics.

If there is one single game that can be said to have effected a profound change upon the way football was played in this country it is England's 6-3 defeat at the hands of Hungary in 1953. It was the first time England had been beaten at home by foreign opposition but it was not so much the manner of England's defeat as the style of Hungary's victory that was to change football in this country for ever.

An indication of what might be in store was evident when the teams took to the pitch. England wore heavy white cotton shirts with buttoned collars and cuffs, long baggy shorts and thick woollen socks that resembled pipe lagging. The players were shod in ankle-length boots with bulging toe-caps, which were only to shine that day with the dubbin that had been applied to them. In their light cherry-coloured shirts with V-neck collar, white lightweight shorts that came down no further than to half-thigh height and boots cut low below the ankle the

Hungarian team cut an altogether different pose. As the teams strode across the Wembley pitch, radio commentator Raymond Glendenning said, 'Looking at the cut of the teams as they now enter the bowl that is Wembley, it is almost as if the football of the past is about to meet the football of the future'. Though Glendenning could not have known it at the time, that is exactly what happened.

At the home of English football, England found themselves to be strangers in a strange land. Playing to the old formation of two full backs, three half backs and five forwards, they found themselves chasing cherry-red spirits that flitted here and there at will across Wembley's turf. Harry Johnston was as good a centre half as there was in British football at the time. It was expected he would simply mark the opposing centre forward that would be wearing the number nine shirt. Hungary's Nandor Hidegkuti may well have been wearing number nine, but he played a deep-lying role that saw him spend almost all the game in an advanced midfield position. Johnston didn't know whether to push forward and mark Hidegkuti or stay in his accustomed role in the centre of defence. He chose the latter and Hidegkuti's running from deep into space in the England penalty area resulted in him scoring three of the Magyars' six goals.

There was a path up the middle of the English defence as wide as the Strand and down it Hungary strode in triumph. Stanley Matthews apart, the skill and technique of the Hungarians, in particular that of Ferenc Puskas, embarrassed the English players. At one point, near the byline, Puskas pulled the ball back with the sole of his boot in so doing evading England captain Billy Wright, who tackled thin air. Then with one swift and deft turn of his body, Puskas swivelled to rifle the ball past England goalkeeper Gil Merrick. Puskas' audacious drag-back was summed up beautifully and succinctly in Geoffrey Green's match report in *The Times*: 'Billy Wright rushed into the tackle like a man racing to the wrong fire.'

Such was the brilliance of Ferenc Puskas that he is to this day revered by other greats of the game. In the early eighties, George Best and Denis Law were coaching teenagers in Australia. Every youngster wanted to be in a group being taught by either George or Denis, so you can imagine the disappointment of one group of lads that were put under the charge of a portly, heavy-jowled man so overweight his stomach spilled over the top of his tracksuit bottoms. On the first morning of the coaching course, the stout coach had been the subject of a number of cruel jibes from the young Aussies placed in his charge. By lunchtime, the boys were taking no notice of their coach whatsoever.

As George and Denis walked across the playing fields to where they were to take lunch, they became aware of what was going on and detoured to join the group. The teenagers immediately flocked around George and Denis, keen to rub shoulders with two such football greats. George didn't say much. He just lined up ten footballs some twenty yards from goal, gathered the boys around him and invited their coach to address the first ball. George told the group their coach was going to strike them from there with the intention of hitting the crossbar.

'How many times do you think coach will hit the crossbar?' asked George. Various numbers were called out, but one lad who had previously had a lot to say for himself shouted 'None! He won't be able to see the balls for his belly.'

Giggles swept around the group. George then invited their coach to try his luck. The youngsters looked on slack-jawed as one after the other each ball crashed against the crossbar. When it came to the final ball, the coach flipped it up into the air, caught it on his forehead and let it rest there for a moment before flicking his head to the side and catching the ball on his left shoulder. Jerking his body, the ball fell, only for the coach to catch it on the heel of his boot. He flicked the ball up again and produced a perfect volley that had so much power behind it it left the crossbar reverberating like a tuning fork. The youngsters broke into spontaneous applause and some even cheered.

George and Denis turned away as the suitably impressed youngsters gathered around their coach wanting to know how he was able to do such a remarkable thing.

'What's ya name, mate?' asked the loud teenager.

George Best spun around and confronted the lad. 'To you son, he's MISTER Puskas!' said George in no uncertain fashion.

The football genius of Ferenc Puskas dragged English football, albeit kicking and screaming, into the modern age. Clubs began to adopt Continental methods of training and introduce tactics to their games. Training became more varied, with exercises aimed at every muscle in the body. Treatment rooms began to be filled with all manner of electrical and scientific machines to measure the reaction of lungs, heart, pulse and blood pressure of players working hard on the training field. Slowly, the endless and infinitely tedious business of lapping the perimeter track, jogging and cross country runs that had formed the basis of all training for British clubs since the twenties gave way to more sophisticated techniques.

Most importantly, the ball was used in training at every opportunity. The old belief that to starve players of the ball throughout the week in training made them more hungry for it on a Saturday afternoon was considered to be, as it is, twaddle. Against England, Hungary had played one-touch football. Puskas and his team-mates demonstrated a variety of methods of taming the ball by taking it on their chests, thighs and the outside of their boots. He had shown how to volley a ball perfectly when it arrived at hip height. Such skills were virtually unknown in the English game. As Malcolm Allison, then a player at Charlton Athletic, said, 'Denying players the use of the ball at their feet in training simply meant a good many couldn't produce polished ball skills come a Saturday afternoon'.

Before the Hungary match, the England team played a style of football that was exactly the same as in League games. Now Walter Winterbottom realised that international football demanded an entirely different approach and he set about achieving that for the national side. The tempo of England games changed when facing Continental or South American opposition. The mantra was to keep possession of the ball and not go hell for leather at the opposition and end up chasing when possession was lost. When England gave the ball away, they fell back and regrouped, content to let the opposition bring the ball forward and defend just outside their own penalty area. Energy was not to be exerted in a fruitless chase of the ball.

In the time that followed, the cloth from which English strips were made changed. Kit became lighter in weight and the cut and style gradually took on a sharp new look in keeping with that worn by Hungary. Buttons disappeared from shirts, as did collars. In the 1956 FA Cup final Manchester City deployed Don Revie in the role of a deep-lying centre forward in the mould of Hidegkuti, and they were the first team to grace a Wembley final wearing the new V-necked shirts with short sleeves and what the *Daily Sketch* described as 'skimpy shorts'. City players also wore the new low-cut type of boot that was being marketed in England while their opponents, Birmingham City, opted for a traditional kit. The difference in the kits worn by the two teams had nothing at all to do with the result, but a 3-1 victory for 'modern' Manchester City only served to emphasise that the English game should shed the past and move towards modernisation and a new future.

To fall into line with the new lighter, low-cut type of boot the fifties saw the introduction of a lighter type of ball made of synthetic leather protected by a laminate coating. Three types of ball were given official blessing. The Webber Premier boasted a 'keep-clean and waterproof surface' and was available in both orange and white. Apart from anything else, that this ball was available in white caused quite a stir. When Wolves played Hungarian side Honved in a floodlit friendly match at Molineux, the second half of the match was broadcast live on television. Wolves won and one of the many talking points was the white ball used in the game. The following day boys throughout the land were raiding their dads' sheds and painting their old leather caseballs with whitewash.

The other two types of ball to be introduced as part of the modernisation of English football were the Stuart Surridge Double Crown, whose unique selling point was that it was laceless, and the Mitre Mitrox, later superseded by the Matchplay, which claimed to have 'double the life of balls made from usual leather'. The new balls were the same weight as the old ones – the Tugite and the Thomlinson 'T' ball – but unlike their predecessors, they did not soak up water, and they kept their shape. This was good news for players: on a Christmas pudding of a pitch on a rain-soaked day the old type of football would often almost double in weight. As a player if you had headed the old kind of ball when it had become saturated with water, you knew about it I can tell you.

In winning the 2005 Champions League, Liverpool contrived to produce the greatest comeback of any European Cup final. I was delighted for the club, their supporters and in particular for their manager Rafael Benitez who among other things proved that in what is increasingly a sorry and sordid game, a quietly spoken, dignified good guy can still emerge a winner.

Liverpool deserved the plaudits for their success. Their performance and comeback in the second half of the final were remarkable, but they were second best in the first half and in extra-time. Stanley Matthews once said that to win any cup competition a team need luck: in winning the 2005 Champions League, Liverpool too were blessed with such. They were often unconvincing in the early rounds but rode their luck, and in the second leg of the semi-final against Chelsea were awarded a goal when many believed the ball had not crossed the goal line. Even when 3-0 down to AC Milan in the final, such had been Liverpool's good fortune in the competition one should have had the notion that they would somehow get back into a game which appeared to all intents and purposes beyond them.

Liverpool's sensational comeback had an air of serendipity about it given Rafael Benitez had made a monumental error in playing an out-of-form Harry Kewell. As luck would have it, Kewell sustained an injury, which forced Benitez to introduce Vladimír Šmicer. Benitez later admitted that this enforced change altered his thinking regarding Liverpool's system of play. He realised they needed to be more aggressive in midfield and in the second half he immediately introduced Dietmar Hamann for Steve Finnan. Kewell's misfortune proved Liverpool's and Benitez's good fortune.

Radio Five Live's Alan Green described Liverpool's success as 'the greatest-ever European Cup final'. This, though, is an epithet that in all probability will always be afforded to Real Madrid's 7-3 victory over Eintracht Frankfurt in 1960. For all Liverpool's 2005 success was exciting, unexpected and heroic, it is unlikely to revolutionise English football in the way that of Real Madrid did.

Real Madrid had embraced the European Cup since its inception. They supported this innovative competition, and exerted a domination of the trophy that has not been equalled to this day, winning the European Cup in successive seasons in the first five years of its existence. Real's success culminated in a glorious display of football in the final of 1959–60, when they beat Eintracht Frankfurt 7-3 at Hampden Park before a crowd of 135,000 spectators that struggled to come to terms with the type of football they were seeing. The rise of Real Madrid was down to the foresight and hard work of their President Don Santiago Bernabéu. While British clubs were bound by Ministry of Labour regulations that forbade the employment of players

from outside the United Kingdom and Ireland, Real Madrid
dipped into the resources of the football world supermarket.
They scoured Europe and South America for the players calculated to fashion them into a side of unsurpassed power. One
man Real signed from South America was to become the focal
point of their team: Argentina's Alfredo Di Stefano. Another
player to join them was the architect of England's defeat at the
hands of Hungary in 1953: Ferenc Puskas.

Real's victory over Frankfurt was the greatest-ever performance by the greatest-ever club side. The football Real produced
that night seemed to have come from another planet. In the
seven years that had elapsed since England's watershed match
against Hungary, the English game had made considerable, if
at times slow, progress. Real Madrid's display against Eintracht
Frankfurt showed everybody that they had developed football
even further, taking it to greater heights.

Even in the small matter of their strip, Real Madrid displayed a new modernity. They wore an all-white strip, the cut
of which was different from the V-neck and short sleeves now
favoured in England. The Real shirt had long sleeves with elas-
ticated cuffs and had a round collar. They looked as dazzling as
the football they produced. The style of strip worn by British
teams that was thought to be the cutting edge of football fashion suddenly appeared passé. No English team could play like
Real Madrid, but at least they could look like them, and many
clubs adopted Real's style of strip with these round collars and
long sleeves. Leeds United, under their new manager Don
Revie, even went so far as to forsake their blue and gold shirts
and adopt an all-white strip.

Bob Paisley described the type of game Real produced
against Eintracht Frankfurt as 'pure football'. A wholly apposite description. Real brought new elegance to football and in
their revolutionary all-white strip were redolent of purity. The
quality they produced at Hampden Park aroused more discussion in English football than any other match since the

Hungarians had arrived to bemuse and conquer us. The echoes of that night at Hampden roared through English football. It was to shape the future of the game in this country for many years to come and play an intrinsic role in our winning the World Cup in 1966.

It was the mark of Real's greatness as a team that even the genius of Ferenc Puskas was overshadowed by that of Alfredo Di Stefano, the conductor of this symphony of football. He wore the number nine shirt and, like Hidegkuti of Hungary in 1953, played in midfield. Di Stefano found time and space through instinctive positional sense and his speed allowed him quickly to accelerate into goalscoring positions. But Di Stefano also fulfilled a utility role in the Real team. He did it all, helping out in defence, creating from midfield and demonstrating his prowess as a goalscorer when joining the attack.

For all Di Stefano's individual football genius, he always played first and foremost for the team. Real's performance demonstrated that individual ability was far more effective when deployed collectively. The majestic talents of each player masked the fact that Real were very organised, every one of them having a specific role. The superior technique of the players, coupled with astute tactics, was the key to the greatness of Real Madrid. But Real also possessed the flair and imagination to produce something different. This enabled them to be much more exciting than other teams, much more difficult to beat, much more of a potent attacking force, much more entertaining to watch and, indeed, much better than any other team in Europe at that time.

Real's victory and the manner of it provided a great fillip to England manager Walter Winterbottom's fledgling coaching courses at Lilleshall. Many players coming to the end of their careers, and looking to stay in the game as a manager or coach, signed up to Winterbottom's coaching course after the 1960 European Cup final. They were joined by trainers and coaches already in work. Everyone wanted to further their football education and learn of similar tactics and methods of play to those deployed by Real Madrid. The subsequent influence of these 'disciples' was to spread throughout the game. Come 1965, English football had changed enormously from that we saw prior to Madrid appearing at Hampden and was unrecognisable from how it had been in 1955.

The fact that English football was so eager to learn from the success of Real enabled our game to develop apace. Having been willing pupils, British clubs learned their lessons so well they became a dominant force throughout Europe. It would be too strong to say we again became the masters, but what was certainly true was we were no longer inferior to top Continental teams. I was fortunate enough to be a member of the Spurs team that became the first British club to win a major European competition in 1963, when we beat Atletico Madrid 5-1 to win the European Cup Winners' Cup. West Ham United won the same competition in 1965. Two years later Celtic were grasping European football's holy grail, beating Inter Milan to become the first team from these shores to win the European Cup. The following season Manchester United emulated the success of Celtic. In 1968 Leeds United won the Fairs (UEFA) Cup and Newcastle United retained the same trophy for England the following season, as did Arsenal in 1969–70. That season Manchester City won the European Cup Winners' Cup, which was retained by Chelsea the following year.

To my mind England winning the World Cup in 1966 was, and still is, the greatest achievement of our national team. It was my bad luck to be injured during the tournament. Geoff Hurst took my place in the team and the rest is history, of the most glorious kind. I wish I could say that in general terms our winning the World Cup was the beginning of a new and golden period for English football, but I can't. The success of English clubs in Europe in the late sixties had, as previously explained, more to do with what had gone on in the game prior to 1966 than any effect winning the World Cup may have had. Rather than heralding a new dawn, our victory was the culmination of the renaissance and development of English football since the fifties. It was the end of an era rather than the beginning of one.

What followed our World Cup success was a period of football that was often dull and, in comparison to what had gone before, negative. In the wake of 1966 the performances of the England team (even in Mexico in 1970) were efficient without ever being entertaining. When in 1971–2 West Germany beat England 3-1 at Wembley in a European Championship quarter-final, Frank Butler, sports editor of the *News of the World*, wrote:

> West Germany not only thrashed England at Wembley but in so doing played the type of football that thoroughly entertained the 100,000 crowd. The most frustrating part of it was that the Germans produced the type of football that we in England used to be proud to lay on. Ramsey has many critics these days. When he led England to victory in the World Cup in 1966, he was hailed as a genius. The tactics introduced in 1966 were not original, yet they paid off. But in so doing they brought about a type of defensive football that has become a bore to watch every Saturday as fewer and fewer goals are scored, and tough tackling defenders and midfield players lacking in creativity and imagination become the order of the day.

Euphoria is a fleeting feeling. The 1966–7 season was only a few weeks old when it became apparent that the honeymoon was over. Instead of players joyously expressing themselves on the pitch, we found ourselves subjected to cloying tactics. There was suffocation instead of inspiration. Winning the World Cup should have been the inspiration to an era of exciting and entertaining football as English football set out to prove

it really was the best in the world. Rather than winners in a
brave new world, we had football riddled with the fear of
losing.

I retired as a player in 1971 at the age of thirty-one. A major
reason in my decision to retire at such a relatively young age
was that I had become disenchanted with how football was
being played in England. The game was suffering from a phe-
nomenon curiously unique to the British, that of adopting a
good idea and developing it to the extreme until it is eventually
flogged to death. It is easier to teach defensive football and
this, in part, accounted for the emphasis coaching often placed
on defence in this period. The only way to overcome a crowded
midfield and a well-organised defence was by a combination of
planning and improvisation – the key to the success of Real
Madrid. This was why players like Mike Summerbee
(Manchester City), Charlie Cooke (Chelsea), Willie Morgan
(Manchester United), Eddie Gray (Leeds United), Jimmy
Johnstone (Celtic), Willie Henderson (Rangers), Rodney
Marsh (QPR) and the incomparable George Best were greatly
prized by their clubs and supporters alike. But part of the
problem was that not every team possessed a gifted, imagina-
tive player with sublime skills. There was only one George
Best, and as the sixties drew to a close George was becoming
downbeat about it all.

It was post-1966, too, that we began to see the first trouble
on the terraces. There are any amount of sociological reasons
for that, I am sure. But the World Cup, albeit unwittingly,
played its part in the rise of moronic tribal rivalry. It was
during that competition that I first heard fans at Wembley
chanting. At the time it was a harmless, supportive and good-
natured chant. The sound of fans singing 'Ing-ger-land!' was
heartening to the players. When it was all over and the nation
basked in the glory of having won the Cup, some supporters
wanted to recreate a similar sort of atmosphere at their own
grounds.

Supporters singing songs at football grounds has a long history. Many clubs had one specific song supporters sang that was synonymous with them in particular – 'The Blaydon Races' at Newcastle; 'I'm Forever Blowing Bubbles' at West Ham United; 'Walk On' at Liverpool; and 'Glory, Glory Hallelujah (John Brown's Body)' at Spurs. At England matches and the FA Cup final at Wembley there would be community singing. Song sheets sponsored by the *Daily Express* were issued with the match programme and contained the lyrics of old standards and favourites such as 'I'm a Lassie From Lancashire', 'Land of Hope and Glory' and the perennial favourite hymn, 'Abide With Me'. The singing was friendly and happy, if rather twee.

Those looking to recreate the big-match atmosphere at their own grounds aped the 'Ing-ger-land' chant heard at Wembley, simply substituting the name of their team for that of England. New words, usually of a provocative nature and insulting to other clubs, were given to the old standards sung at Wembley such as 'Land of Hope and Glory'. Whereas before the singing of a club song such as 'The Blaydon Races' was indulged in by most of the crowd, those who chose to chant gravitated together to form a single body of fans. They would congregate in the centre of terracing behind one of the goals, which, to all intents and purposes, became their 'territory'.

At the same time, away support began to attend matches in increasingly large numbers, thanks partly to the new motorways making travel much easier. These fans made their presence felt and heard at games, often causing animosity among the home fans, especially the chanters behind one of the goals. I suppose the latter group felt their territory was being invaded. What had begun as good-humoured rivalry in the singing stakes soon turned into something altogether darker. This attracted the local tearaways that, on the pretence of supporting the local team, began to attend matches for reasons other than purely the football. You may be of the mind that

that is too unsophisticated a view of how the so-called hooligan element surfaced in the English game, and you would be correct in that assumption. But as a player at the time, that's how it appeared to be.

The 1966 World Cup was the first to be commercially exploited on what was then a grand scale, and the effect of this was to increase the rivalry between fans. This first venture into marketing saw scarves and hats being sold that bore the word 'England' and the crest of the FA. Once the tournament was over, scarves and woollen hats began to be manufactured for particular teams, with the club's name and badge prominent. The emergence of this type of merchandise helped set apart supporters of different clubs. Football became more tribal than ever and the provision of distinguishing gear, together with terraces that offered relative anonymity to a minority bent on venting their malevolence, blackened the heart of the game. This new rivalry between certain supporters did not change the way the game was played, but it did change how many people viewed football. Slowly, the more seasoned supporters began to drift away to the safety and peace of their homes. No doubt they still loved their teams and football in general, but the future of the game for such supporters was to be confined to television and radio.

When Celtic met Inter Milan in the European Cup final of 1967, in every sense of the word it was a clash of styles. In the mid-1960s, Inter were considered to be the most advanced team in the world. European champions in 1964 and 1965, they were the most accomplished proponents of *catenaccio*, a system of play I had encountered during my brief sojourn in Italian football with AC Milan. *Catenaccio* is Italian for 'door-bolt' or 'lock', and the system was widely adopted in Italy in the sixties. This was not just cautious football, it was defensive in the extreme – a system based on a 4-3-3, 4-4-2 or sometimes a 4-1-4-1 formation that involved a midfielder reverting to an extra defender when necessary by playing in front of a central defender and a sweeper. His job was to prevent the opposing striker (note the singular) having the ball played into his feet. The idea behind *catenaccio* was to limit, or better still to deny, opponents scoring opportunities by defending the 'scoring space' and adopting man-to-man marking. The teams who used this system, such as Inter Milan, relied on swift counter-attacks and breakaways to score goals. Once that had been achieved the object was for the team to go into its shell and defend that lead. *Catenaccio* was excruciatingly frustrating to play against and mind-numbingly boring to watch. It was, however, highly effective. The system had first been developed in the late thirties by the Austrian Karl Rappan, who was manager of Switzerland at the time. Rappan's system was called *verrou*, which also means 'bolt', and involved the use of a sweeper and a dependence on counter-attack. Switzerland adopted the system during the 1938 World Cup when the Swiss reached the quarter-finals. It also proved the undoing of England in the same year. Having just recorded a sensational 6-3 victory over Germany in Berlin, England came a cropper in Zurich, losing 2-1 to a Swiss team that comprised part-time players. I remember Stan Matthews telling me that that day England came up against a type of football he had never encountered before: 'I couldn't understand it,' said Stan. 'Switzerland were content to sit back and let us come at them. They might as well have sited the Matterhorn in their penalty area for all the impression we made. In terms of football it was dreadful, with the emphasis on "dread".'

Inter Milan's ultra-defensive style was also in sharp contrast to that of Celtic, which brimmed with the joie de vivre of attacking at every opportunity. It is an old adage of football that teams tend to reflect their managers' characters and this was very true of Inter and Celtic. Inter's Helenio Herrera revelled in his nickname of 'Il Mago', the magician. Herrera had managed Puteaux and Stade Français in France, where he had become friends with leading figures in the French entertainment and movie industries. From there he went on to manage at Atletico Madrid, Malaga, Real Valladolid, Seville and Barcelona before returning to Italy to take charge at Inter. In Italy he mixed with leading politicians and film directors such as Federico Fellini. Herrera was intelligent, articulate, well read and knowledgeable, which enabled him to be comfortable in any strata of society, especially Italian high society in which he was fêted. Character-wise he was considered by many to be self-regarding, a man so confident in his ability as a coach to achieve success that it bordered on arrogance. In short, Herrara as a coach was very good, he knew it and had no compunction in demonstrating such – a trait not dissimilar to a current Premiership manager of note.

Celtic manager Jock Stein was totally different. Stein was admired at Celtic and throughout Scotland because he was the perfect example of the Scottish working-class hero. He was the unpretentious embodiment of that older, better code of which Bill Shankly and Matt Busby were also fully paid-up members. With Jock openness, honesty, straight talking and simple homespun philosophy came first, and there was never the remotest danger that he would be contaminated by social butterflies or perceived self-importance. There was a cogency and combative quality to all he said, but without exception everything he said about football made simple sense to the genuine lover of the game.

Stein wouldn't have known Fellini from grissini, but he knew how to handle himself and his team. In keeping with Denis Bergkamp, one of Jock's players, the Celtic winger Jimmy Johnstone, had a great fear of flying, and would often be left at home when Celtic played an away tie in Europe. In 1966 Celtic drew Dynamo Kiev in the Cup Winners' Cup. Before the first leg at Parkhead, Stein told Johnstone that if he produced a 'big game' that night and Celtic won handsomely enough to make the second leg somewhat of a formality, the winger wouldn't have to fly with the team to Kiev.

Jimmy produced a scintillating display of the winger's art in the first leg, turning and twisting the Kiev full back so many times it was a wonder the Russian wasn't rushed off to hospital with spiral blood. Celtic won 3-0, which everyone connected with the club believed would be good enough to take them through to the next round. During the post-match buffet, Stein took to the floor and paid due reverence to the efforts of Celtic's opponents before beckoning their manager to say a few words. The Kiev manager took from his pocket a piece of paper and in faltering English began to read from it:

'Gen'men, laydiz, you murst bring Jornstun to Kiev. Pleez do nort dee-ny my peoples the opp-ut-toon-tee to see theez worndherful playhar. Tharnk you.'

The room erupted into rapturous applause as the Kiev manager took his place once more among his players. In the time that passed between the two legs, Jimmy Johnstone found himself on the horns of a dilemma. Jimmy had been deeply touched by what Kiev's manager had said, and dearly wanted to play in the return leg in Russia. His fear of flying, though, was a seemingly insurmountable obstacle in spite of his desire not to disappoint the people of Kiev.

A few days before Celtic were due to fly out, Jimmy asked for a meeting with Jock Stein. He explained his predicament and the pair discussed the issue. Stein fully understood Jimmy's fear of flying but told him in light of the plea from the Kiev manager there was just no way he could let down the eighty thousand people who would be attending the game in the hope of seeing Jimmy play. After some deliberation Jimmy informed Jock Stein that he felt he had a duty to the people of Kiev and, much against his better judgement, he would play in the return leg.

Fortified by several glasses of the 'water of life', Jimmy endured a not-too-harrowing flight to Kiev and after sleeping off the effects of both his 'medicinal' aid and his first trip in an aeroplane, he was raring to go when the teams took the field for the second leg. He produced another sublime performance and the 1-1 scoreline meant Celtic were comfortably through to the next round. During the post-match buffet, Jimmy fell into conversation with someone he believed to be an official of Dynamo Kiev, and at one stage asked the man what role he fulfilled at the club. The man informed Jimmy that he was not a Dynamo Kiev official, but a teacher at the local university. Somewhat perplexed, Jimmy asked his companion the reason for his presence at the games. The man explained that he taught English, and that whenever Kiev played a team from the United Kingdom or Ireland they hired him to act as their official interpreter because no one at the club spoke a word of English.

'But what about your manager, he speaks a little English,' said Jimmy. 'After the first leg he said those kindly words about me.'

'The manager does not speak a word of English,' said the interpreter. 'He was asked if he would read the words on the paper and not wanting to be discourteous to you, the host club, he complied with the request. He did not understand a word of what he was reading.'

'So who wrote that speech and asked him to read it, then?' asked Jimmy.

'Your manager, Mr Stein,' said the interpreter.

When Celtic lined up in the tunnel for the 1967 European Cup final, they looked across at the Inter players in awe. 'They were handsome, elegant and sun-tanned. They looked like film stars', Jimmy Johnstone once told me. 'I looked behind me and there was our goalkeeper Ronnie Simpson. He was pushing forty but looked even older because he had removed his false teeth, as he did for every match. I thought to myself, Eleven lads from Glasgow. What the hell are we doing here?'

It was then that the skipper Billy McNeill, not for the first time, had a moment of inspiration. He began to sing the Celtic song and was immediately joined by the rest of the team. The Celtic players sang their club song with gusto, much to the bemusement of the Inter players. The singing of their song served to lift the Celtic players and acted as a safety valve to rid them of some of the nervousness and apprehension they were feeling. No one can know for certain, but I should imagine their vociferous singing also served to unsettle the Inter players. Out on the pitch, meanwhile, Jock Stein sat on the bench that had been allocated for the great Herrera and refused to budge when asked to do so, telling the Italian coach that one dugout was just the same as the next. Another psychological blow for the 'Bhoys': no one was going to boss them about.

Even so, Inter quickly went ahead when Mazzola scored from the penalty spot after eight minutes. Having scored an early goal, they seemed set to profit from the ruthless efficiency of the *catenaccio* system. The Italians had no desire to go in search of another goal and promptly shut up shop, comfortable and content in the knowledge that the system would again do its worst and frustrate and foil their opponents. For all their gallant efforts, at half-time Celtic left the field frustrated, as many teams facing Inter before them had done.

Celtic's wingers Johnstone and Bobby Lennox had the beating of their opposing full backs, but throughout most of the first half had delivered balls into the box from wide positions that were midway between the goal line and the edge of the penalty area. As a forward myself I appreciate how difficult this made life for Celtic's front men. The key to scoring goals is to exploit space, and to do this you need the ball early, the earlier the better, in fact. By holding on to the ball and getting into an advanced position before delivery, Celtic were allowing the Inter players the time to organise themselves in and around their penalty area and, as importantly, to snatch a brief breather.

During the half-time interval Stein told his wide men to

deliver the ball early and in front of the Inter defence while it was in the process of falling back: a minor adjustment to their play that was to reap major dividends. In the second half the Celtic attacks came in waves, each foray backed by a raucous din from their travelling supporters. The Inter goalkeeper Sarti was having a very good game, but not as good as his posts and crossbar, which were playing a blinder. The woodwork denied both Bertie Auld and Tommy Gemmell, but in the sixty-third minute the noise from the Celtic fans was replaced by another sound greater in volume and deeper in tone. Jim Craig, mindful of Stein's words at half-time, cut a dashing figure on Celtic's right but, rather than heading for a point adjacent to the Italian penalty box, turned inside with the ball and hit a cross-field pass of slide-rule precision into the path of left back Gemmell, who hit a thunderous shot to Sarti's left. The ball flew into the back of the net.

For long periods Celtic continued to pen the Inter players inside their own half. It looked for a time like Inter might profit from their larceny, but in the eighty-fourth minute justice prevailed. Bobby Murdoch tried his luck from just outside the penalty area with a low crisp shot. It looked to be on target, but there was Stevie Chalmers to deflect the ball unerringly past Sarti as it cut a swathe across the turf and into the net. That night in Lisbon, Inter not only met their Waterloo but their Saratoga, Blenheim and Hastings. Celtic had beaten them to become the first British team to win the European Cup – in itself a remarkable achievement. Their victory, however, was also a triumph of imaginative and vivacious attacking football over dour, defensive play based on a fear of losing. Jock Stein, who had not entered full-time professional football until the age of twenty-seven, had outwitted Herrera as surely as his Celtic team had outplayed Inter Milan. The Lisbon Lions had roared their way into the history books, in so doing confining *catenaccio* to the same.

That year, 1967, was the season Celtic won everything

Scottish domestic football had to offer. They had also flown in the face of the trend to play defensively minded football and scored an amazing two hundred goals in competitive matches. A statistic that, over the years, has often prompted me to wonder how English football might have evolved post-1966 had it followed the example of Celtic, rather than that of Alf Ramsey's World Cup winners.

The 1970 World Cup final between Brazil and Italy was billed as 'the unstoppable force meets the immovable object'. When set against the incomparable and irresistible attacking flair of Brazil, Italy were defence-minded, but no more so than any other team in the world at that time when faced with the joyously expressive samba football of Pele and Co. The 1970 final is widely regarded as the greatest final of all time, and I wouldn't contest that notion. Brazil produced a performance that raised football to another, much vaunted level. There was a beauty to every aspect of the Brazilians' play, and on the day in question they managed not to undersell themselves, as many acclaimed teams of the past had done when confronted with the possibility of their 'finest hour'.

Such was the sublime nature and beauty of Brazil's performance against Italy, I wish I could say this game changed football and the way the game is played for the better. That it didn't perhaps had something to do with the sumptuousness and richness of the Brazilians' play. No manager or coach felt it could be equalled and that even to try would be suggestive of failure, if not pure folly.

It was in the World Cup in Spain in 1982 that Brazil were involved in a game against Italy that was to change their football and that of other nations, especially those of Europe. In essence Italy's second group game against Brazil looked as if it would be yet another contest between the unstoppable force (Brazil) and the immovable object (Italy). I was covering the World Cup along with Ian St John for ITV and the pair of us expected a dour game with Brazil constantly pouring forward in the hope of breaching a resolute Italian rearguard. How wrong we were. When the match ended, our producer asked us to sum up the match as he was handing over to the news. I thought to myself, What we have just seen is the news.

The Brazil that contested the 1982 World Cup harked back to the Brazil of old. Here at last was a Brazil team high on sophistication and imagination whose penchant to attack took the time-honoured route: a slow, methodical build-up by way of possession then, when an opening was seen, the explosive thrust of speed that left opponents struggling to adjust and cope, let alone counteract. The sight of a walking midfield was back.

In keeping with their style of play, Brazil had swaggered through the first group stage, unbeaten in their three games, and scored ten goals in the process. In the first of their two matches in the second group phase, they scored another three against a hapless Argentina, becoming so dominant that Maradona took his frustration out on anybody in a yellow shirt and was eventually dismissed for blatantly kicking Batista. The third side in the group, Italy, had also beaten Argentina, so when Italy and Brazil met, a place in the semi-finals beckoned for the winning team.

Brazil had in their ranks Socrates, Falcao, Zico, Cerezo and Junior – players who could stand comparison with those of the 1970 World Cup-winning team. They were favourites to win the tournament, whereas Italy had no one talking them up as world-beaters. Italy's manager was Enzo Bearzot who nearly a decade before had issued the clarion call for Italian football to undergo a metamorphosis. In 1973 he had famously said, 'Italian football must change. For too long we have played the game in fear. We must rejoice in the talents of our players, and play football that allows them to demonstrate their skills, their imagination, their love of scoring goals.' There had been little evidence of that earlier in the competition, but against Brazil Italy's latent talent for attacking football would come to the fore.

Spearheading the attack for Italy was striker Paolo Rossi, a player who hitherto had struggled to find form. For someone about to embark upon a golden future, Rossi had a dark past. He had only recently returned to football after a two-year ban imposed for his part in a bribery and match-fixing scam. It was claimed his involvement had been minor but the lengthy ban had cast a heavy pall over his career. The day before the game Brazil's goalkeeper Valdir Peres said his biggest fear was that Rossi might suddenly display the form and talent for scoring goals he was so obviously capable of. Peres' prime concern was about to be realised.

Twice Rossi gave Italy the lead only for Brazil to peg them back. This was a game that did more than ebb and flow, it surged from one end to the other as both teams accentuated the positives in their play. With the two sides level on points a draw was all that Brazil needed to progress to the semi-finals by virtue of a better goal difference. At 2-2 Brazil looked relaxed, but it is not in the Brazilian nature to kill off a game. They went in search of a winning goal, not least because defensive frailty was their soft underbelly.

With fifteen minutes remaining of what had been an exhilarating and spellbinding game Italy won a corner. Brazil had two opportunities to clear their lines, but a jittery defence did its worst. The ball ricocheted around in their penalty area like a pinball before a weak clearance found Italy's Marco Tardelli lurking with intent on the edge of the box. Tardelli tried his luck at goal. It wasn't a crisp, direct effort, but fortuitously it found Rossi, who turned and with a deft touch steered the ball into the net for his hat-trick.

Finding they had yet again to chase the game, with the clock against them, Brazil surged forward and Italy nearly made it four from a breakaway. In the last minute Italy's skipper, their forty-year-old goalkeeper, Dino Zoff, produced a fantastic reaction save from the head of Cerezo. Several of the Brazilians fell to their knees in frustration and despair. It was a pertinent image.

The mood and more to the point the mindset of Brazilian football changed in the wake of their exit from the 1982 World Cup. There was a general feeling that their traditional and joyous samba-style was suspect to the more methodical approach of European teams. This homespun belief was given further credence when they exited from the 1986 World Cup, beaten by a French team inspired by the incomparable Michel Platini. With the scores level at 1-1, it was a travesty that a game which had produced the sublime skill and imagination worthy of a final should be decided on penalties. France progressed, but that Brazil's joyous approach to football had yet again failed them accelerated change at home.

The exotic side of Brazilian football was diluted in the years that followed, as Brazil adopted a more European approach. The change in emphasis in how they played the game was enhanced as world football became more homogenised and increasing numbers of top-class players from South America opted to ply their trade in Europe. By the end of the eighties Brazil were playing a style of football little different from that of European sides, and this was a policy that had also been adopted by most other countries of South and Central America. When Brazil met Italy in the 1994 World Cup final in Pasadena, Los Angeles, they triumphed on penalties. In truth it was a dull, impoverished final with little to distinguish the styles of the two teams. Brazil had become 'Europeanised'. They were world champions yet again, but by virtue of a kind of football that was pragmatic rather than rapturous and exuberant.

By and large Brazilian football and its contemporary exponents still gladden the eye. No one could dispute the exceptional and individual talent of Ronaldinho, who continues to play the game with imagination and inventiveness, as David Seaman found to his cost in 2002, and Chelsea experienced in their classic encounter with Barcelona at Stamford Bridge in 2005. But the lyrical soul of Brazilian football has been conspicuous by its absence in two decades of football and in all likelihood it will never return. The way world football has developed over two decades and the trend of many of Brazil's top players to earn a living playing in Europe have long since enforced a compromise. Samba gave way to a form of line-dancing, and the origins of the metamorphosis of Brazilian football can be found in their defeat to Italy in the 1982 World Cup.

Of course there has been an upside to all this. If you happen to watch your football in Europe, that is. In recent years it has not just been the traditional destinations of Italy and Spain that have benefited from having Brazilian players grace their domestic game. Most of the top European leagues now boast Brazilian players, and the Premiership is no exception. The status of our top flight and the wages on offer have attracted Brazilian players of exceptional quality and, I should imagine, more Brazilians will find their way to these shores after the 'showcase' of the 2006 World Cup.

The one exception to this homogenisation of world football is Africa, where many teams continue to play with joyous abandon. This may well explain why, in the 1990 World Cup, so many people were appreciative of the efforts of Cameroon. As Europe dips ever deeper into the well of African football talent, one can only hope that the style of play of the likes of Nigeria, Cameroon, Mali and Senegal does not suffer a similar fate to that of Brazil and become absorbed into the standardising nature of world football. The signs, it has to be said, are not good in this respect.

To borrow from John Prescott, the idea that a single game has the capability of shifting the tectonic plates of football appears now to belong to the past. It is impossible to think that a single international defeat for England today, such as happened against Hungary in 1953, could revolutionise the way the game is played in this country. That it did then had much to do with the fact that English football had remained largely unchanged for twenty years and more. Such advances as were witnessed in the fifties were long overdue and for a good many years only enabled England to catch up. No single loss for England today could effect such major changes throughout English football simply because the game has been transformed in the past decade alone.

If Danny Blanchflower were return to this earth and see a Premiership match in action he would, I am sure, struggle to come to terms with the game he once so sublimely graced. English football is forever evolving and it continues to adapt. Such changes, however, appear not to have so much to do with the playing of the game. They are the result of the influence of the game's governing bodies, the financial wherewithal of certain individuals and the subject of the next chapter: the role of the media.

CHAPTER TWELVE

Televised football has become chewing gum for the eyes

There is little doubt that the media's mass coverage of football has re-established the game in the psyche of the nation. There isn't a day in the week when some sort of match is not broadcast on television. Over the years radio has also greatly increased its coverage of the game. More column inches are devoted to football in newspapers than ever before, and one can even receive the latest football news via a mobile phone. Then there is the Internet. The nature of this animal being what it is, the Web offers the widest spectrum, from informed comment and 'on-message' club websites, to platforms for uncouth, vindictive jibes that make radio phone-ins sound like BBC Radio 4's *The Moral Maze*.

In the 1960s after a Spurs home game, the players would mix with the press in the White Hart pub. I remember Laurie Pignon, who, if my memory serves me right, worked for the *Daily Sketch*, once asking me if the rumours of a training-ground fight between two prominent players in the team were true.

'Yeah, there was a bit of a set-to', I informed him. 'They were having a go at one another in a five-a-side. They got into a tangle, a few punches were thrown. They wrestled each other to the ground and rolled about. A few of us helped Eddie Baily separate them, and that was it.'

'So, it was nothing really?' said Laurie.

'Nah, just a training-ground dusty. It happens.'

It *did* and it *does*. That a reporter from a national newspaper didn't consider two internationals throwing punches at each other on the training ground newsworthy was the mark of the time.

In the sixties Manchester United travelled to Holland to play Tilburg Willem in the European Cup Winners' Cup. United full back Shay Brennan didn't play in that tie but travelled with the party. Shay told me that on the night before the game the press boys enjoyed a few drinks in the team hotel. More than a few as it turned out. Shay along with a couple of other United players had to help an unsteady Frank Wilson of the *Daily Mirror* upstairs to his room and put him to bed. United secured a 1-1 draw and back at their hotel manager Matt Busby allowed the players to have a few beers. Shay seemingly had a thirst to quench that night because, according to him, United's Maurice Setters and Frank Wilson ended up carrying Shay to his room.

Again, that story never made the press. Such a situation would not arise nowadays. I shudder to think of the repercussions in the press and media as a whole if a reporter had to help to his room a current Manchester United player who had had a few drinks after a European game. Players and the press operated to unwritten rules. There was a gentleman's agreement about what could and could not be written. The press may have seen minor indiscretions on the part of players, but kept them to themselves.

Occasionally players of the past would impart some information that was useful to a reporter, such as an impending transfer or imminent team change, nothing of jaw-dropping significance but useful 'insider' copy for all that. Both press and players considered it to be fair game if a reporter lambasted a player for his performance in a particular match. If some current players think they are harshly criticised, believe me, it is nothing compared with what the likes of Desmond Hackett and Frank Butler would write. When they felt you had a bad game their criticism was withering. Off the field, it was a different matter. Players and press would often confide in one another. In certain respects the press would protect the off-the-pitch interests of players and offer advice. In my time as a player with AC Milan and Tottenham Hotspur, outside of my family, numbered among my closest friends were football writers such as Ian Wooldridge, Brian Glanville, Ken Jones, Donald Saunders, Peter Lorenzo, Roy Peskett and Tony Stratton-Smith. I wonder how many Premiership players consider any of today's football writers as a close friend?

I can't say with a degree of certainty when the relationship between players and the press changed irrevocably, though I suspect it may have begun during the 1982 World Cup in Spain. Ron Greenwood was the England manager and, not wanting his players to be harassed constantly by the press, Ron arranged for a daily morning press conference in which one or two of the squad would be available for interview. Ron's morning press conference allowed the media to get their story for the day at one fell swoop, leaving the England team to train and relax for the remainder of the day. At first this worked well, until Ron was approached by a reporter from a tabloid. The red-top reporter asked Ron if some of the England players would pose for a photo shoot with some members of a local ballet school. Ron thought this might make for good PR with the locals, so readily agreed to the request. When the reporter and photographer turned up with the ballet dancers some of the senior England players smelled a rat.

The 'ballet dancers' were dressed in very short skirts and wore skimpy tops that did little to hide their ample bosoms. As Peter Shilton remarked to Ray Clemence, 'I don't know anything about ballet other than what I have seen on television, but these girls are like no ballet dancers I have ever seen.' Sensing something was up, the senior England players declined to have their photographs taken with the girls. The younger singletons, however, jumped at the opportunity. The following day photographs of England players with the girls appeared in a tabloid newspaper under the headline, 'England Players Cavort with Strippers'. Ron Greenwood was understandably livid. Although it had been only one reporter who had set up those young players, the England squad became very distrusting of all press during the tournament and thereafter.

After the 1982 World Cup the FA decided to appoint a press officer to deal with the media and act as a buffer between management, players and the press. The working relationship between players and the media that in truth had become less and less convivial throughout the seventies took on all the attributes of a 'them and us' situation, and the press were the root cause of the problem. Not, it has to be said, those who reported on football, but the 'newshound' type of journalists, who were assigned to cover big matches in the hope of finding a story that would titillate readers.

The days when players and football writers got together after a game to put the football world to rights were long gone. Players became more guarded in what they said to reporters. The situation has become more acute since clubs created their own PR departments, part of whose job it is to ensure any player interviewed stays 'on message'. Should a player express a personal view that is not in keeping with club policy or which is seen as being detrimental to the club, he is disciplined and fined. When Tim Sherwood was a Spurs player, he gave a press interview in which he said he didn't believe Tottenham were good enough to win the Premiership. No one would argue with such a statement. Except Spurs that is, who fined Sherwood a considerable amount of money for saying what most people believed, and subsequent results would prove, to be the truth.

The way the press report football has changed. There was a time when the only way one could get the results of a midweek game (let alone find out what had happened in the match) was to read about it in the newspapers the following morning.

These days' instant, blanket coverage of football on television, radio, the Internet, teletext and mobiles phones has necessitated a change in the way newspapers cover the game. Now supporters are more likely to read the message 'Sprs WN 1-0' on their mobile phones than read a classic but corny sub's headline such as 'Spurred On' in their morning paper. Of course, newspaper match reports by their very nature still relate what happens in a game, but much of the content now takes the form of an overall view of a club's situation and the consequences of the result in question, particularly if it is seen to have a bearing on the future of one individual, such as a manager. There is nothing wrong in that for rather than simply offering the reader a blow-by-blow account of what happened in the match, such a reporting style gives a sense of perspective and objectivity to readers, who already know the result and what happened in the game.

But there is another side to the way newspapers now cover the game that is, to many people, a matter of some concern. Namely, that some national newspapers' obsession with the Premiership, and the lives of its top players, has exposed certain elements of players' personal lives and, in one or two cases, even their sexual predilections. Those who help my generation of footballer pen their autobiographies trawl through countless back pages of old newspapers, but those who will help some of today's top players may find themselves looking increasingly at the front pages instead. That a number of top players have made front-page news in recent years is one of the telling differences between the modern game's elite players and those of yesteryear. Of course, there was always George Best, but George's liking for a drink and the occasional date with a Miss World now seem part of an altogether different, more innocent world.

In 2003–4 certain allegations of a very serious nature were made against players from Newcastle United and Leeds United. These were followed by similar accusations levelled against some Leicester City players while the club was on a mid-season break in La Manga, Spain. Without ever saying as much, the way some newspapers reported these stories seemed to presume the guilt of the players involved. It was almost trial by tabloid, yet in each case no player was ever prosecuted, let alone found guilty of what were very serious allegations. To the best of my knowledge the players involved in these events had been very stupid to place themselves in a situation where such claims could be aimed at them. They may well have been 'guilty' of stupidity but, as things turned out, nothing else.

When news broke of a particular Leeds United player having been interviewed by police following an allegation of rape, the *Daily Mirror* ran with a front-page headline: 'Leeds Star Held Over New "Rape"'. Not 'Alleged Rape', you will note. As far as I know no charges were ever brought against the player in question and he was certainly never found guilty of any offence. It is the sort of headline that the *Mirror* ran with which many reasoned and rational people find disconcerting and irresponsible, for in the very wording there appears to be an assumption of guilt.

In recent years football has been subjected to pithy sleaze in some national newspapers. There is now more joy in editorial offices over one football 'sinner' who leaves his wife for a younger woman than eleven just men whose heroics win the FA Cup. Imbecilic Christmas party antics at West Ham and Liverpool, the indulgence in drugs by Mark Bosnich and Adrian Mutu , the unwise liaisons of Wayne Rooney, and the irresponsible drink-driving cases of James Beattie, Seth Johnson, Rio Ferdinand and Jermaine Pennant have all been reported with some relish. Reflecting on some of the afore-mentioned, one tabloid journalist was prompted to say, 'Serious questions must now be asked of our top footballers'. Some top footballers, but not all, surely?

In 2005 the cult of the celebrity is stronger than ever. Inane comments and the mundane nuts and bolts of daily living are afforded unmerited importance in tabloid newspapers. Is the fact that Roy Keane bought a Twix at a garage when paying for his petrol of interest to anybody? When such inconsequential minutiae of life are afforded column space, little wonder the press go on a feeding frenzy when a player indulges in what is seen to be scandalous behaviour.

Equally, some of the criticism directed at managers, particularly those who have been in charge of our national team, is often more of an attempt to vandalise the reputation and feelings of the individual concerned. Constructive criticism is perfectly valid, but some of the copy that was written about Bobby Robson, Graham Taylor and Kevin Keegan, to name just three former England managers, had more than a hint of unbridled viciousness. Some of the tabloid headlines that have preceded England matches, particularly those against Germany, France and Turkey, have been enough to make one pale. Far from espousing a form of simplified zen wisdom, these were headlines that indulged in the xenophobic. With the arrival of the finals of an international tournament those who fear the extremists that follow England will heap shame upon the country would do well to remember that some elements of our national press often beat them to it.

There is one area of the press that is dying, and it is the century-old mainstay of Saturday-night entertainment for football fans – the Saturday-night football paper. In recent years up and down the country 'Buffs', 'Pinks' and 'Green 'Uns' have disappeared from the shelves of newsagents, the victims of the saturation coverage of the game by other media. In the sixties Britain boasted around eighty such Saturday-evening football papers. Now there are about twenty in existence, and some of those have moved from a Saturday night to a Sunday in the hope of enjoying a longer shelf life.

The two great problems for the local Saturday-night football paper are competition from new media and the diffusion of football across the whole weekend. For example, the Sunderland *Football Echo* is a treasured institution on Wearside and among exiled Sunderland supporters, but in recent seasons many Sunderland matches have been played on a Sunday, which removes the 'flagship' news of the match report from the front page. The advance of new technology has had some positive effects, of course: the specialist, local football papers are now often full-colour and have taken advantage of digital photography. But the competition from new media far outweighs this.

Circulation also depends on the fortunes of the local team or teams. Liverpool's *Football Echo* sells anything between twenty thousand and thirty-five thousand copies a week, depending on how Liverpool or Everton have fared. The city is traditionally a stronghold of football and the sales figures of the *Football Echo* are sadly not reflected in other areas of the country. Most currently sell only 20 to 40 per cent of the figure of twenty years ago. One paper that appears to be bucking the trend is Brighton's *Sports Argus*, which was relaunched in 1999. Sales figures have risen steadily to around seven thousand, though this might have something to do with the fact that the club has risen through the divisions in that time and currently has a ground where demand for tickets always exceeds the capacity.

It is to be hoped that most of these brightly coloured football papers will survive on the strength of fans' dedication, the power of the ritual and the still-strong sense that they, like the local club, are a vital part of a town or city's heritage and sporting culture. One of their strengths is unabashed partisanship, which invariably goes down well with supporters, though I suspect there is a greater degree of objectivity in the reporting nowadays than there used to be. In 1960–1 Chelsea beat Newcastle United 6-1 at St James' Park. As the Chelsea team waited at Newcastle Central Station to board our London train, I caught sight of the front-page headline of the *Evening Chronicle Pink* which read 'Magpies in Seven Goal Thriller'. It was that sort of blatant bias and parochialism that endeared this sort of paper to local supporters. In the sixties Sunderland games covered in the *Football Echo* were written by a reporter who used the pseudonym 'Argus'. During a visit to Roker Park, I remember a Spurs team-mate once asking me the meaning of the word. 'It's from Greek mythology', I informed him. 'It means "all-seeing, the man with a thousand eyes".'

'Aye,' piped up Sunderland's Martin Harvey, 'and every one of them red and white.'

The traditional Saturday-night football paper may be struggling to survive, but that has not stopped certain publishing companies from attempting to secure a niche in the market by producing a national football paper. The most dogged examples of this have been *Sport First* which now publishes under the name of *Football First*, *British Football Weekly* and the *Non-League Paper*. *Sport First* appeared to style itself as the 'National Sports Paper', a British equivalent of France's *L'Equipe*, Italy's *Gazzetta dello Sport* and *Bola* in Spain. At one time *Sport First* was published twice a week, on Fridays and Sundays, but soon reverted to being a Sunday only. It is now *Football First* and to the best of my knowledge is supported by just one man, Keith Young – a football-mad Everton supporter who, it is estimated, has supported his 'baby' to the tune of nigh on seven million pounds.

The rebranded *Football First* is up against *British Football Weekly*, originally a product for Australasia that enjoys UK weekly sales of around fifteen thousand. Seemingly, one problem *Football First* faces is distribution. The paper carries reports of every Saturday game in the Premiership, Football League and Conference, together with results, scorers and attendances of the leagues in the upper echelons of the non-League pyramid. A friend informs me, however, that while he has no trouble buying a copy in the North Midlands, a colleague of his in Sheffield has yet to see a copy. Now it could well be that the Sheffield chap is going to the wrong newsagent, but sales figures of less than twenty thousand suggest many people are unaware of the existence of *Football First* or, if they are, are choosing not to buy it. Which is a shame as *Football First* offers more in-depth coverage of football than any other paper (albeit a lot of its content now appears to be produced by the Press Association).

The *Non-League Paper* appears to have secured a niche in the market and its rising sales reflect the growing attendances in what is a vivacious and buoyant non-League scene in England. The fact remains, however, that we in Britain have not taken to a national football paper in the way supporters in other countries have done. One of the biggest obstacles is that national newspapers have, over the years, greatly increased their coverage of sport and football in particular. Given there is a bias towards coverage of the Premiership, the *Daily Telegraph* sports section often runs to eight broadsheet pages whereas that of the *Daily Mail*, a tabloid, runs to double that. Sixteen tabloid pages of sport is in sharp contrast to some of the leading newspapers on the Continent. In France *Le Figaro* pays lip service to sport, offering a single page of coverage. This is a policy probably implemented in light of the terrific coverage of sport offered by the specialist daily sports paper *L'Equipe*. Similarly, in Italy the national heavyweight broadsheet *Corriere della Sera* with a single page of sport appears to have given way to competition from the pink sports paper, *Gazzetta dello Sport*, which runs to twenty-four pages on a daily basis. In 1985 the *Record* was launched in Portugal as a sports weekly. It is now published daily and is Portugal's biggest-selling newspaper. The *Record* appears to have more journalists covering Benfica than the club has players. There is even a goalkeeping correspondent whose job it is to comment on the performance of both keepers in a game. And some of our top players believe they come under the microscope from the press during games.

The success of these national football papers on the Continent has not been replicated in the UK. Our national papers enjoy solid branding that supporters trust. A new weekly football paper has to contend with this and, having no strong brand image of its own, will struggle to acquire sales. The initial investment that is required to achieve a strong identity for any new newspaper is colossal and those that now exist in the UK do not appear to have such funding. With the stock of English football continuing to rise and newspaper sales continuing to fall, under pressure from new media, I doubt whether we will ever see a strong national football newspaper in this country. I should imagine, however, this will not stop major execs trying to crack what appears to be a peculiarly British conundrum – the thought of a national newspaper devoted solely to football continues to be seen not so much as 'match of the day' as a match made in heaven.

It is a curious fact that national newspapers enjoy greater kudos and status than a local daily paper yet people are more given to believe what they read in their local evening paper than they do in their national morning paper. This element of trust, together with the sense that the local paper is a vital part of a town or city's culture, has always ensured their survival and will continue to do so in the future. If a supporter wants to know who in the reserve team has a tweaked tendon, the local newspaper will unfailingly tell him. It is this close contact with the everyday happenings at the local club that will see the local paper continue to be bought. In 2003 Northcliffe Newspapers, which owns several key provincial evening papers such as the *Leicester Mercury* and Bristol's *Evening Post*, conducted a survey among local people in the towns and cities of their newspapers. The findings were striking: 72 per cent of people said they bought the local paper for its coverage of local sport, in particular football. Evidently the old tradition of buying a newspaper, taking a quick glance at the front-page headline to ensure nothing too drastic has happened, then immediately turning to the back page and reading the newspaper in reverse is as popular as ever.

The one medium which has had the biggest impact on the

game of football itself is television. Having spent a greater part of my life working as a broadcaster than I did a footballer, I had first-hand experience of the growing influence of television on the game. In the fifties television was still very much in its infancy and even for those who owned a set, there was little in the way of football to watch. Radio still ruled the roost as far as football was concerned, as it did all sport. In the fifties and sixties the only domestic football fixture to be broadcast live on television was the FA Cup final. This was considered a real treat by football fans. Coverage of the match would start at around noon and one of the most popular items was 'How they got there', a ten-minute slot that showed round by round the goals from all the games of the two finalists. It was immensely popular simply because to see any football on television, even goals from matches played some five months previously, was a rarity.

The FA Cup final and the winning of it was big news, so much so that when television's coverage of the final was over and the station switched immediately to the news, there was the final all over again. The FA Cup final was THE gem in the football calendar. It was special for players and supporters alike. For followers of lower division clubs, television's transmission of the FA Cup final represented a rare opportunity to see two top teams in action and to put a face to players whom they had only read about. Now, alas, due to television's saturation coverage of the game, in which even the most mundane fixture is hyped to the limit, the FA Cup comes across as 'just another game'.

In the early sixties some regional ITV companies negotiated deals to broadcast on a Sunday afternoon the highlights of one of the games that took place in their area on the previous day. As English football took its first tentative steps in what were to become the very muddied waters of televised football, clubs did little to accommodate the television crews. Often the camera and commentator were sited in the corner of a ground in a Portakabin-like box perched precariously on top of scaffolding beneath one of the floodlight pylons. There were no post-match interviews. No pundits or summarisers. It was all basic stuff, but the public watched it in their droves because domestic League football was until then practically non-existent on television.

In 1964–5 David Attenborough, then the Head of BBC 2, introduced *Match of the Day* to the nation. The use of the word 'nation' is somewhat inaccurate as the first match to be broadcast – Liverpool versus Arsenal – was not seen by the majority of people because most of the country could not receive BBC 2. Yet this fact proved no obstacle to the programme's popularity. The original slot given to *Match of the Day* is perhaps indicative of how BBC execs viewed football – the programme first went out at 7.45 p.m. on a Saturday evening – but within a couple of years it had switched to BBC 1 and a much later slot on a Saturday night.

The first *MOTD*s broadcast the highlights of a single game, normally from the First Division. In keeping with ITV's coverage of regional games there was no post-match interview, no summarisers and, to begin with, no slow-motion replays. It was simple, straightforward, one-dimensional television coverage of football. Though naturally a team of people worked behind the scenes to bring viewers the highlights of a single game, the programme's closing credits consisted of only two names, those of commentator Kenneth Wolstenholme and producer Alan Weekes. That those early *MOTD* credits comprised but two names was synonymous with the simplicity of the times and indeed the tenet of the programme itself.

As it gained in popularity *MOTD* gradually expanded its remit. In addition to its featured match, the programme began to show brief highlights of a second game. As the seventies dawned, the format expanded into an hour with the highlights of a third match, usually from the lower divisions. As unlikely as it will appear now, broadcasting highlights from a match in the Third or Fourth Division proved popular with viewers, as for many it was the first time they had seen the likes of Bristol Rovers or Grimsby Town in action. There was also the curiosity appeal of seeing what the grounds of these clubs looked like, and the added bonus of perhaps spotting a rising star. By now *MOTD* had the added appeal of colour and the dubious honour of having Jimmy Hill offer his comments on matches. I have known Jim since his days as a Fulham player. I like the man, he's genuine, good-natured and possesses a ready wit, though being the first pundit on national television his views didn't always meet with the approval of viewers. But that's football. It is a game of varying opinions, as the guy standing next to you at the bar would no doubt disagree.

As the BBC and ITV increased their coverage of the game both sides of the border, its commentators became household names. The likes of Ken Wolstenholme, Barry Davies, Brian Moore, Hugh Johns, Gerald Sinstadt and, north of the border, the peerless Arthur Montford exuded authority and a deep-seated knowledge of the game that they combined with the voice of reason. Their understanding of football was profound and to a man they were true lovers of the game, its history and traditions. Genuine supporters except in warmer coats.

Whether those who aspire to commentate on football today will ever achieve the professionalism and broadcast quality of those names remains to be seen. I suspect not. The old school of commentator understood the value of pausing to allow the viewer to think and make up their own minds before treating us to their assessment of a situation. They were calm and collected, had respect for the viewer and never tried to exude superiority by reverting to historical or literary references in the form of metaphor. The likes of Barry Davies, Hugh Johns and Arthur Montford remained objective, neutral and never let their emotions get the better of them. The same cannot be said of some of our contemporary match commentators – even after the most mundane incident, Five Live commentator Alan

Green still manages to sound like a man whose pants are on fire.

In 2004 Barry Davies announced his retirement from the BBC. After thirty-five years with Auntie, Davies decided to call it a day rather than be moved down the roster of BBC football commentators. I suspect it was not just demotion that prompted Davies to announce his retirement. Perhaps, like many of us, he too was not enamoured with some of the new commentators who now cover the game. Barry Davies, like the rest of his generation of commentator, was always impartial. When covering an England game, you never heard him use the words 'us' and 'we' – words that have increasingly formed part of the commentary of the latest generation of match commentator.

This new breed of commentator seems to fill every second with commentary when there is no need. Barry Davies always allowed the viewers to think for themselves, with just two or three words on his part prompting such thoughts. In Euro 96 when Gareth Southgate missed the penalty that ended England's hopes of winning the Championship, Davies' response was simply to say, 'Oh, no'. There followed from him, a few seconds of dead air. That silence emphasised the cruelty of England's plight and allowed us viewers to think the situation through and come to terms with it.

Underplaying situations was his forte and by not saying anything for a few seconds, Barry Davies demonstrated that sometimes less is more, a lesson that appears to go unheeded in match commentary nowadays. When Francis Lee returned to Manchester City with Derby County emotions were running high. As the former Maine Road favourite weaved his way past his old team-mates, Davies didn't scream and shout. 'Interesting' was his response. When Lee's corkscrew dribble then ended with him firing a shot from twenty yards into the roof of the net, there was no manic response from Davies. His reaction was to say 'Very interesting'. Like other commentators of his generation, he would never attempt to second guess the thoughts and emotions of players and managers. That happens all too often these days, and you are left thinking: How can the commentator possibly know what the manager is thinking?

What has crept into football commentary nowadays is the use of the extended metaphor. No one perpetuates this more than John Motson, who appears to work to a specific imagery for each game. When England played Wales at Old Trafford in 2004 Motson appeared to opt for that of schooling: 'The return of young master Rooney means there are now three keen goal collectors in the front row of the England class,' he informed viewers. Goal collectors? To the best of my knowledge not a term ever attributed to yours truly, or any other forward in the history of the game. Clearly it was an old public school that John was referring to, or so it seemed from the reference to 'young master Rooney'. A form of address much favoured in the Billy Bunter books by Frank Richards I read as a boy but less common, I should imagine, in the Liverpool comprehensives of the new millennium. Undaunted, John carried on: 'In the back row Ferdinand and Campbell are pals again,' he said, 'and Nicky Butt is back in the form room after a sick-note kept him out of the first two qualifiers.' At this point I was in need of a sick-note myself. Not content to afford England overblown metaphors, John then extended them to Wales:

'One of their mature students, Andy Melville, has failed in the end to make it to the pitch,' to which was later added, 'Pembridge and Speed were awarded their international diplomas a long time ago'. Given the setting was Old Trafford, John wasn't going to let the fact that Ryan Giggs considers that to be home territory escape his attention: 'I guess Ryan Giggs had to make sure he went to the right classroom to get changed today'. Come the final whistle we were left to reflect that John 'could do better'.

Having seen the pace and indeed the standard for metaphor set by John Motson, lesser lights at the BBC followed suit.

Apparently sucked into Motson's slipstream, *MOTD2* presenter Adrian Chiles also referred to Wayne Rooney as 'young master Rooney' when looking back on the previous day's goalless draw between Manchester United and Blackburn Rovers in April 2005.

'Another scholarly effort from young master Rooney, further emphasising that he is in a class of his own,' said Adrian. Proof, if ever it were needed, that imitation is the sincerest form of television.

Without doubt the coverage television has given to the game, not to mention the considerable input of money, has benefited English football. But at times I am left wondering if the finance, resources and technology are far too weighty for the product. Travelling at 7000 mph, some 25,000 miles above the planet, a satellite of such complex technology that it is beyond the ken of all but a few eggheads beams a signal to a receiver dish attached to our homes. This signal then travels down a fibre-optic cable faster than the speed of light to a deceptively simple-looking receiver that unscrambles the image and relays it to a flat-screen plasma television, which in turn paints it on to the screen, line by line, twenty thousand times a second. For the privilege of doing so Sky Television pays hundreds of millions of pounds to football. All this happens, and for what? So we can watch, not for the first time, a stupefying goalless draw involving Blackburn Rovers, or a much-hyped match during which I might drink four cups of coffee and still not manage to keep awake. One is left to think that Burnley versus Blackburn in the 2004–5 FA Cup (the former at home but, as I mentioned earlier, playing one man up front) is proof that some people will look at anything rather than each other.

It is of course true to say the Premiership also produces enthralling encounters where the level of skill and technique is of the highest order. There are no easy matches we are told, even by José Mourinho, and largely speaking that is true. Owing no little to the pristine pitches and lightness of the ball, the Premiership is fast. It is physical, of a sort, and without doubt throbbing with passion and commitment. But the skill of the past is now a rare thing. Listen to the post-match inter-views on television in which managers talk of commitment and effort, of their pleasure at how their team 'kept its shape'. Rarely, if ever, do they talk of ability. Television can only broadcast the games as they are, and increasingly what we see is something akin to a Nick Nolte action movie: all sound, fury and frenzy not exactly signifying nothing but lacking in sub-stance, coherence and panache. We live in an era of football where excitement is increasingly being mistaken for quality.

No one could deny the final day of the 2004–5 Premiership season was one of excitement and drama. However, such drama has much to do with the media, in particular television's pro-jection of the Premiership as the be-all and end-all of English football and that life outside the top flight is tantamount to football oblivion. It is indicative of the attitude that now pre-vails of the money-driven Premiership being football's nirvana, so that teams which narrowly avoid relegation consider that to be a greater achievement than winning a trophy. To maintain Premiership status has become sufficient success for clubs and their players. No one can doubt the efforts of West Bromwich Albion in avoiding the drop in 2005 were anything but laudable and worthy of praise, but as we have seen in recent years, a team that only just escapes relegation is now fêted by their supporters. They cheer the players as heroes. The players do a lap of honour and gleefully accept the plaudits. I played in a West Ham United team that barely dodged relegation and all I felt was embarrassment that the side had performed so poorly over the course of the season. The furthest thing from our minds was a lap of honour.

In the sixties and seventies neither the game's administrators nor the clubs knew if televised football, even in the form of highlights, was good or bad for the sport. The age-old adage that televising football would affect attendances was, nonetheless, still considered by some to be true. When television began major live coverage of League matches in 1983 attendances at many of these games dipped. The fall in crowds at games subject to live television was, however, mirroring what was happening throughout the game. League attendances had, with one exception, experienced a year-on-year decline since 1977, falling in the space of eight seasons from an aggregate of just over twenty-six million to eighteen million in 1983. The only season to buck the trend was 1979–80, when the aggregate attendance at Football League matches rose against that of the previous season by a nominal 83,348.

There was a total television blackout of football in 1985, but that did nothing to halt the continuing fall in attendances. In the 1984–5 season 17,849,835 spectators watched League football, but the following season that figure dropped to an all-time low of under sixteen and a half million. It was clear that live football on television was not having an adverse affect on crowds. On the contrary, football was suffering from a lack of exposure. Ratings for televised sport had even dipped alarmingly, at which point TV execs became very interested in not so much what television could offer football, but what football could offer television.

The consensus of opinion is that the creation of the Premiership and Sky Television came to the rescue when English football was at its lowest point, following Heysel, Bradford and Hillsborough. As football journalist Bryon Butler wrote, 'For football it was a minute to midnight and there was a madman at the wheel. Then along came Sky Television and the Premiership and the game steered away from disaster and headed down the road that led to a crock of gold.' There is more than an element of truth in that, but the notion that English football was on its knees until the Premiership rode into town is misleading. Having dipped to an all-time low in 1985–6, attendances at League matches experienced an annual rise in the six seasons leading up to the inception of the Premiership. In 1991–2, the last season of the Football League in its old format, aggregate attendances rose to 20,487,273 – an increase of four million from 1985–6. The trend continued with the first season of the Premiership, but only by a matter of 170,054. More significantly, attendances for the first Premiership campaign itself were down by 200,000 on the previous season, the last of the old-style First Division.

As the Premiership grew in popularity, which was in no small way down to the exposure given to it by Sky, clubs made a concerted effort to improve facilities for supporters and eradicate hooliganism. Crowds boomed. Many people under the age of forty whose previous attendance at matches had been infrequent, or even non-existent, having watched live matches on television appeared to want to be a part of what was now not only a match but an occasion. Parents of children who had become supporters of football through watching televised games did what loving parents do – they shared and encouraged this interest of their offspring by taking them to games, which it was now safe to do. What's more, they watched games from the comfort of a seat in stadiums that afforded facilities much more suited to families.

I once had a conversation with former Manchester City manager Joe Mercer, in which he expressed his concern at the impact televised football was having, and would have in the future, on the way we perceive the game.

'Every kick and incident is seen from all manner of camera angles and is discussed and analysed by studio guests. With the prospect of more football on television this will become more widespread,' said Joe. 'Nothing is being left for the supporter to make up his own mind about. Football has much to do with memories. The memory can play tricks, but supporters love to look back, think a certain player did this or that in a game, that a certain goal was scored from thirty yards. It may not have happened exactly like that, but supporters love to believe it did. Television logs everything and as such disproves the memory. It's robbing football of its romance.'

Joe had a point. The quality of the camerawork and the profusion of cameras at games today ensure no part, however small, of a game is missed. There are no longer any mysteries as to what actually occurred in a match. So invasive are television cameras that during Chelsea's Champions League tie against Bayern Munich in April 2005, one homed in on Chelsea's fitness coach seated on the bench. The sole aim was to find out if the fitness coach was receiving messages from the absent José Mourinho and subsequently passing them to assistant manager Steve Clarke.

Television has indeed laid the game bare, robbed it of its romance and nullified the conjecture that was always the source of talk for supporters around the pub table or at work. Not knowing how George Best managed to weave his way past four defenders then lob the ball over the heads of three others and into the Spurs net once galvanised pot-banks and pitheads.

One wonders sometimes why television continues with the post-match interview. The game has always purveyed the paradox of a player blessed with genius on the pitch coming across as imbecilic when asked about the game afterwards. In the past, however, players had more freedom to talk about not a match itself or what they had done in a game, but what they thought about such things and, more importantly, how they felt about it.

After Spurs' victory over Nottingham Forest in the semifinal of the FA Cup in 1967, a game in which I managed to score Spurs' first goal, I was interviewed by Kenneth Wolstenholme for BBC Television. Ken asked me three questions: 'You are not known for scoring goals from outside the penalty area, so why did you decide to shoot from twenty yards?; 'Ian Storey-Moore was causing you all manner of problems in the first half, but was far less effective in the second period. What did Bill Nicholson say to the team at half-time that brought about that change?; and, 'Alan Mullery had words with you during the second half, what did he say to you and you to him?' They were telling questions, the sort the viewer could not answer themselves.

Wolstenholme didn't simply ask, 'What did it feel like to score Spurs' first goal?', or say, 'You must be pleased that Spurs are again at Wembley . . .' These sort of questions would prompt a bland, predictable response. I remember having to think about why I opted to hit the ball on the half-volley from twenty yards when scoring Spurs' opening goal. As I did about what Bill Nich told us to do to nullify the threat of Storey-Moore, and more pertinently how we had managed to achieve that aim, and what Mullers had wanted me to do, which was to run wide to pull Forest's Terry Hennessey and Bob McKinlay out of their central defensive positions. I had to think and be objective in answering such questions. So many of today's post-match interviews are sterile and formulaic, however long they last you know that time in your life is wasted. Nothing meaningful is ever asked or said. The question once posed to Danny Blanchflower that paid homage to his sportsmanship while asking how important winning was to him induced Danny to say, 'Winning isn't everything, but wanting to win is.' Such a response now sounds quite alternative, brilliant even. It was the sort of question one never hears asked of players today, and it prompted an answer worthy of such an enquiry. When I listen to footballers being interviewed on television these days I try the brightness knob on my set, but it doesn't seem to work.

There was a time when following his retirement as a player a footballer would take over a pub. Increasingly now footballers look for work in the media. My career in television was, as I've said, longer than my career as a player. What I tried to do was entertain, fool that I may have been to suppose television was a vehicle for entertainment. I was forever careful not to try and come across as a smart-ass pundit. What I attempted to do was see the game from the perspective of the supporter. In so doing, there were times when I offered an opinion on matters that landed me in hot water. I even had writs issued against me, one in particular from a referee, who took exception to something I had said about him, which resulted in me having to pay a sum of money. That didn't deter me from offering criticism when I thought it was merited. The writs stopped coming because I learned from a lawyer how to circumnavigate legal action when speaking one's mind. The problem I encountered in my early days of commenting on football on television was that I was prone to making a personal opinion sound like a statement of fact. To get round that, I was told by the lawyer to begin any criticism with the words 'In my opinion'. That way no court in the land could convict me for having an opinion on a matter.

I don't hear many, if any, ex-pros currently working in the media use that ruse to cover themselves when criticising an aspect of the game, and this is quite simply because whenever criticism is forthcoming it is always of the mildest variety. In my opinion (see what I mean) too many ex-pros working in the media, particularly on television, don't want to go out on a limb for fear of upsetting someone and losing their job. The analysis and discussion between former players on television is too cosy. No one attempts to see a situation from the point of view of the supporter, and rarely are we offered an opinion on how match officials may have seen a situation. It's all trite and polite, the way TV execs, in my opinion, want discussion of football to be, because, let's not forget, television needs football and football needs television.

A new language has evolved among commentators and ex-players on television and radio. Ostensibly this involves the use of phrases that allude to the truth. In short, most opinions are reduced to a kind of phraseology that covers the real meaning of what people want to say:

He'll be disappointed with that – That was crap

He has great vision – Unable to play a simple ball

He's a real workhorse with a great engine – Runs around like a headless chicken for ninety minutes

He's an out-and-out striker – Too bone idle to help out in defence

He has a presence in the dressing room – Ringleader of dressing-room clique that plays evil practical jokes on quiet, unassuming team-mates

He has a great influence in the dressing room – A bully

He's still learning – At the moment he's rubbish but there is hope

Shrewd – Devious

Frank discussion – Heated argument

Very frank discussion – Punch up

There is a greater degree of urgency about their play in this half – Panicking like mad

He ran to good purpose – Did sweet FA with the ball

The referee's assistant's flag went up very late there – Only decided to give it on seeing the referee had awarded it

That was a very ambitious effort – Given up all hope of taking on and beating opposing defenders

As for relegation, I wouldn't write them off yet – Dead and buried

That's why it's such a great game – Pre-match prediction was wrong again, which shows you how much I know

It was a comfortable victory – Opposition were rubbish

Temperamental – Sulky and immature

No one is indispensable – Eminently replaceable

He's a class player – Average

He's a world-class player – Above average

Genius. Absolute genius! – Likes of Henry, Lampard or van Nistelrooy scoring a decent goal

He took it very well – Lesser light of the Premiership or Championship scoring nigh on identical goal

When television features supporters it is invariably in an exploitative way. Sky Sports' *FanZone* is an attempt to recreate a 'terrace' atmosphere that in my opinion fails miserably. Featured supporters play up to the camera and goad one another as the pendulum of the play swings from one side to the other. There is none of the humour associated with supporters, nor is there objective analysis, which most fans are more than capable of. What we see is shouting and screaming, and an abundance of 'Yeeesssss!' and 'Ahhhhhhhh!' and 'Noooh!' Predictable stuff that is unworthy of the genuine supporter of the game, and a meaningless strand in a match schedule often containing little in the way of substance.

Supporters are used as a backdrop to matches. Generally they are subjected to close camera shots purely as tokens of joy and despair, as people who are instinctively responding not to what is unfolding before them, but to the scoreline. When fans are interviewed before a match it is usually not to gain their opinions on the game, or the match in question and its possible consequences, but simply to extract from them a prediction as to the score. A wasted opportunity on the part of television, and one which reflects a lack of imagination, and indeed an absence of understanding of, and empathy for, the supporter.

By contrast, one of the most appealing aspects of television and radio's coverage of cricket is that they attempt to bring the atmosphere and surroundings of a Test ground to life, often by highlighting the insignificant and idiosyncratic. Football coverage rarely, if ever, attempts to do this. It amazes me that with up to twenty cameras following a televised football match – more for important internationals – there is never a camera situated in a position to give the viewer even a fleeting glimpse of the game from the perspective of the crowd.

Television's coverage of matches is generally dull and unimaginative, with the same format game after game: studio chat . . . usual camera angle of match . . . studio chat . . . more of the same camera work . . . studio chat . . . inane post-match

interviews in front of boards garlanded with company sponsor's logos. The cameras descend on, say, Ewood Park or
Carrow Road, but when the game is over what further have we
learned about that club? The viewer is never treated to any
pre-match behind the scenes shots in the stadium, where supporters congregate to chat, eat and drink. No shots of the club's
boardroom, trophy cabinets, dressing room, boot room, supporters' social club or banqueting suites. No interviews with
former players of the club, colourful supporters of character or
long-serving employees. Every ground and club comes across
as being like any other. There is no attempt at all to portray the
individual character of the home club, its history, culture or
traditions. In short, the very heart of the game, something Ian
St John and I were always at pains to attempt to convey during
our time working on ITV's *Saint and Greavsie* programme.

Television has been good for the game but in so doing it has
also perpetrated a radical upheaval in British football. Fixture
lists have been fragmented to accommodate the wishes of
broadcasters without any consultation of the heartbeat of the
game – its supporters. While blanket coverage is a vast
improvement on the meagre offerings of the sixties and seventies, supporters still have a right to expect better. Not in
quantity, but in quality. Television too often pays lip service to
the views of fans by way of on-screen text messages and bland
phone-ins, but it has never in my experience consulted or surveyed supporters for their opinions on how the game should be
presented on television. Other industries are careful to survey
the needs and requirements of their customers and implement
products and policies in accordance with their findings. Does
television ever do that? Do clubs ever counsel the views, opinions and, as importantly, feelings of their supporters before
putting ideas into effect?

The result is that television's massive output has produced a
new type of supporter: the consumer. Instead of attending
games, the consumer watches football on television from the

comfort of an armchair or in a pub. In essence there is nothing untoward about this, except that television gears its presentation of football towards this new breed of fan, rather than the genuine spectator whose loyalty to a chosen club is matched by a real love of the game. Attendances at matches have risen year on year in the past decade, in part thanks to the coverage of football given by television. In 2003–4 a total of 29,197,510 spectators attended matches in the Premiership and Football League, the highest figure since 1969–70. Curiously, and somewhat disturbingly, the way television now presents football, it has induced in the genuine spectators an increasing feeling of marginalisation. That of not being a part of what television has created, of not relating to what is being said and done, is a problem television executives appear not to be aware of. It may well prove to be the key factor in the future success of television's commitment to football.

CHAPTER THIRTEEN

The first Sven-Göran Eriksson knew all was not well between him and the FA was when he turned up at headquarters in Lancaster Gate and found they'd moved

At no point is the media's coverage of football more intense than when it is focused on the England team. Our national side and in particular the job of the England manager are subjected to so much scrutiny the job of England coach has been described as akin to a poisoned chalice. But I sometimes wonder just exactly who is responsible for administering the metaphorical poison – the media, the FA or the England coach himself?

When Sven-Göran Eriksson was appointed as manager of the national team many England supporters were miserable and depressed. Credit to him, Eriksson has managed to turn things around. Now those England supporters are depressed and miserable. Not all England fans may be of the opinion that Eriksson has been detrimental to a national team, whose progress now is gauged purely by qualification for major tournaments, but one increasingly feels that the majority of supporters are less than enamoured with the Swede, and I count myself among that number. It is an old saying of football that sides tend to embody their managers and I believe this to be true of Eriksson. I settle down at eight o'clock to watch an England game; an hour and a half later I check my watch and it says a quarter past eight. With notable exceptions that can be counted on one hand, England under Eriksson have been laboured, uninspiring and to date, as far as major international tournaments are concerned, unsuccessful.

When news broke of the Eriksson/Mark Palios/Faria Alam affair, I half-expected Ray Clooney to claim credit for it all. Thanks in no small way to the incompetence of the Football Association, the affair quickly moved from pants-down Whitehall farce to minor national catastrophe. Sven-Göran Eriksson responded to it in the way I expected: he adopted his trademark face of inscrutability and brazened it out. Eriksson's defence in face of revelations that he had conducted an affair with the personal assistant of FA director David Davies, Faria Alam, who was also having an affair at the same time with FA chief executive Mark Palios, was to claim that his private life was exactly that. For the vast majority of people, what they get up to behind closed doors is indeed their own business. Bill can become Betty at the weekend, so what? Anonymity for one's personal life, however, is sacrificed when someone whose job is so high profile that it is part of the national consciousness is revealed to be having an affair while reportedly still in a long-lasting relationship with another. And especially when it is also disclosed that the woman in question is herself having a rela-tionship with the England coach's boss. It must be wearing and exasperating to be constantly under the spotlight of the media, but that is one of the reasons Eriksson is reportedly paid four million pounds a year.

The post of England manager carries with it certain respon-sibilities, and among those I believe is a duty to conduct oneself in a manner befitting the role of a national team manager. That is, to act in a responsible and diplomatic manner whereby your behaviour on and off the pitch does not compromise or embar-rass the population of the nation you represent. All previous England managers had adhered to a moral code that set an example to the players under their charge: it goes with the job. If someone feels they cannot live their life by such a code, don't become England manager.

Both Terry Venables and Glen Hoddle were forced out of the England manager's job for what was reported to be conduct unbecoming. In the case of Venables, it was evidently down to a pending investigation into possible financial irregularities regarding his business affairs. To the best of my knowledge nothing untoward was discovered and Venables was certainly never charged with any offence.

Terry Venables did well as England manager. He was popular with the players, media and supporters, and how often does that happen? But seemingly he wasn't popular with the FA and subsequently vacated the position. The pressure on Venables from rumour and supposition resulted in him eventually leaving his post as England manager. Many believed this to be nothing short of disgraceful.

That Eriksson remained England manager in light of his behaviour and the damaging headlines it generated, one can only assume was down to the fact that the FA just could not afford to pay out his contract. Forgive the pun, but that is a disconcerting state of affairs, which one can date back to an approach for the services of the England coach by Chelsea. It is a widely held belief that Chelsea chief executive Peter Kenyon when in a similar role at Old Trafford almost succeeded in persuading Eriksson to take over at Manchester United following Sir Alex Ferguson's announcement that he would soon be retiring. When the press originally broke with the story of Eriksson having talks with Chelsea officials, the England coach is reported to have denied any such meetings took place, only for one newspaper subsequently to print photographs of him talking to Peter Kenyon. It was almost as if the FA then woke up to the notion that it might have a real top coach on its hands, though given the way England had performed in the previous three years one wonders just how the FA could hold such a view. Apparently the then FA chief executive Mark Palios was moved to fend off silly money with even sillier money in a quest to keep Eriksson as

England coach. Surprisingly, for someone with a Gordon Brown-esque reputation of financial prudence, Palios rewarded Eriksson with a two-year contract extension and a salary hike that ruled out any chance of the debt-ridden FA ever being able to pay it out should Eriksson's position become untenable. Once that deal was done the only way it could ever be justified would be for England to win Euro 2004. Victory in a major international tournament on foreign soil for the very first time would have convinced doubters, such as myself, that Eriksson might just be worth a salary in excess of four million.

I feel the FA would love to have a major club in Europe take Eriksson off its hands, but his track record as England manager has now made that a remote possibility. The FA is stuck with Eriksson. It can't afford to pay him off, so has to make all the right noises about him being the right man to take England forward into the 2006 World Cup. In the space of six months, the FA went from wanting to keep Eriksson so much it offered him an extension to his contract and a seven-figure pay rise, to in my opinion wanting to get rid of him so badly it would have been willing to countenance a seven-figure settlement. That the FA then executed another U-turn and intimated he had its backing and was the man to lead England to 2006 was, in my view, purely down to having no alternative but to say that as it did not have the financial means to sack him.

I firmly believe that Eriksson's contract, together with the fact he is Swedish, saved his job. If he was English, I am certain the FA would never have been as benevolent towards him in view of his affair with Alam. When Eriksson first assumed the role of national coach, he talked of the need for players to be mindful of their responsibilities as England players. A manager can't allude to a moral code of conduct for his players and not adhere to the same himself. It serves to undermine the credence of whatever else he says and, as such, his authority as well. Lest we forget, under Eriksson's management an England player failed to turn up for a drugs test and went shopping instead, albeit Rio Ferdinand was not on duty with England at the time of the incident. As a consequence the England team threatened to boycott the crucial European Championship qualifying match against Turkey. Later they refused to talk to the press after their game in Poland, in protest at the way one newspaper in particular had criticised goalkeeper David James' performance in the previous international in Austria. Eriksson took a back seat, presumably of the mind the unrest among his players in this matter was not something that came under his remit as England manager. It was a hands-off approach to management none of his predecessors would have adopted, particularly Sir Alf Ramsey.

During the 1966 World Cup the FA wanted Alf to exclude Nobby Stiles from England's quarter-final against Argentina. Some of the FA's mandarins had taken such exception to Nobby and his robust play, especially in the group game against France, they wanted him removed from the England squad altogether. The FA in its wisdom had chosen to ignore a tackle by Joseph Bonnel on me which resulted in a wound that needed fourteen stitches and put an end to my World Cup. Instead it took exception to the way Nobby had conducted himself during that specific match and in previous games. When news broke that the FA wanted to omit Nobby from the squad, all the players rallied to his defence. We had a meeting during which we talked about sending a deputation to the FA to voice our protest. Alf would have none of this.

'I am the manager,' he told skipper Bobby Moore. 'I shall deal with this matter. It is part of my job.'

Alf went head to head with the FA, which for its part was adamant its authority should not be usurped: Nobby Stiles must be dropped. Alf stood firm.

'If Stiles goes, then so do I', Alf told the FA. 'As England manager, I and I alone am responsible for the selection of the team. Should I now not have that responsibility, you must appoint another manager. It is your decision, but you must make it quick, we are playing Argentina in two days.'

Faced with that possibility the FA saw reason. It withdrew the demand that Nobby Stiles should be dropped on the grounds that the England manager was responsible not only for team selection, but for the conduct of the England players both on and off the field. As Alf told us, 'Whatever Nobby gets up to in the course of a game, the buck stops with me. A responsibility I am more than happy to undertake.'

In this particular situation Alf seized the initiative from his players, effectively putting a halt to our proposed deputation to the FA, and assumed total responsibility for the Stiles affair. Alf was unyielding in his stance over Nobby, but also diplomatic. By assuming complete accountability for Nobby's future conduct (not that he believed Nobby had done anything untoward), he offered the FA a way out of a dilemma it itself had created. Alf handled a real hot potato of a situation with aplomb in the midst of what was a hectic World Cup schedule. He was proactive and firm, and ultimately Alf further emphasised his qualities as a manager and leader of men, which only served to gain him even more respect from his players.

It is all very well for Sven-Göran Eriksson to say his private life has nothing to do with his role as England manager, but it does. How he lives his personal life is not so much the issue, but the repercussions of the way he conducted himself are. The consequences of the Alam affair sparked an ill-judged and ham-fisted cover-up by the FA. It speaks volumes of the level of incompetence of that body in this matter that how it handled the Eriksson–Alam affair eventually became 'the story'. The bungled attempt to keep the lid on Eriksson's fling proved itself a mighty repercussion of the affair, and only weakened Eriksson's claim that his private life did not in any way affect his role as England manager or English football in general.

No doubt there are many who wonder how a nation with so many problems can get so worked up about a 'private' matter among consenting adults. It is worth remembering that here we are talking of the manager of our national football side in whom we place trust. Trust to bring success to England, and to conduct oneself in such a way that does not compromise or shame our nation. There is a strong case for saying that Sven-Göran Eriksson betrayed the nation's trust. He isn't the only one, of course. Graham Kelly was sacked as the FA's chief executive for making an unauthorised loan to the Welsh FA in return for the promise of support for England's bid to stage the 2006 World Cup. Kelly felt genuine shame for instigating that situation and, credit to the man, held up his hand, admitted the folly of his ways and apologised for the shame it brought to the FA, English football and England. Glen Hoddle's position as England manager became untenable following ill-advised remarks concerning a disabled person. Hoddle's comments, offensive as they proved to be, were not a direct insult to the person concerned, rather the product of personal beliefs of a quasi-religious nature. He was made to understand how the tenet of what he had said was both insulting and demeaning to the individual concerned and though there had been no intent on his part to be that way, he subsequently offered a sincere apology. What a contrast in the reaction and behaviour of Kelly and Hoddle to controversy, to that of the current incumbents at Soho Square with their hyper-inflated salaries and stoic indifference to anyone's feelings and views but their own.

In the future, when we cast our minds back to Sven-Göran Eriksson's reign as England manager, there is a distinct possibility that should England not win the World Cup in 2006, many will reflect that his greatest achievement was an erosion of the importance of non-tournament internationals.

Years ago a friendly involving England was considered of some significance, particularly if we were up against a nation of footballing note such as Germany, Italy, Spain, France,

Brazil, Uruguay, Argentina or, unthinkable as it may appear now, Scotland. Even with the World Cup and European Championships, friendly internationals were regarded as meaningful. National pride was at stake; players considered it the pinnacle of their careers when chosen to represent their country and the result mattered. To play for England, or any country, was a sign that a player was felt to be the best in his country in his chosen position, a notion given total credence when Alf Ramsey wrested selection of the England team away from the FA's committee. In terms of recognition of talent, achievement and kudos, an appearance for one's country had no equal. Photographs in football books and magazines of those who had represented their country carried a caption that bore the player's name and that of his club, proudly followed by the words 'and England'.

The diminishing status of international friendlies can be traced back to Don Revie when early in his reign as manager he called up a hundred players to an England get-together before finally selecting his squad. In picking so many players, Revie debased international friendlies and what it meant to be called up by England. In one fell swoop everything that went with a call-up for England was severely undermined. In the minds of many seasoned internationals, it appeared that any journeyman player could now be called upon by his country.

The significance of the World Cup and the importance of the European Championship grew in accordance with television's increasing coverage of the tournaments. Throughout the sixties, seventies and into the eighties, the home nations, England in particular, did not consider elimination in the qualifiers for the European Championship to be a national disaster. The media, and football supporters in general, didn't believe the tournament to be of great merit, unlike the World Cup. It was only in the eighties when television began to broadcast every game from the finals that the European Championship took on real significance. Genuine and passive supporters wanted to watch England win, but they also wanted to see how the 'story' of the tournament ended. Other, more telling factors played a major role, too, in the growing value of the two big international competitions to the psyche of the nation. There was the commercial involvement of global companies, which, in return for sponsorship, utilised the tournament brand on their products. The World Cup and European Championship logos appeared on a vast range of goods from Coca-Cola and Mars bars, to breakfast cereal and mineral water. The projected importance of the World Cup and now the European Championship entered people's homes and touched our daily lives before a ball had been kicked in the finals, thus fuelling further the tournaments' prestige in the minds of passive supporters and even non-football-minded folk.

In the era of Sven-Göran Eriksson as England manager the two major international tournaments took on even greater significance as other international matches were treated almost with disdain. After home defeats in friendly internationals to Australia and Denmark, Eriksson intimated that the results of these matches did not matter. Former internationals such as myself, Alan Ball and Gordon Banks were aghast. We wondered how our national football team could ever have reached the point where an England manager implied to the nation that an England defeat was of no importance. An England defeat matters. It has meaning to England supporters and all who have pride in our country.

One particular skill that Sven-Göran Eriksson appears to have honed particularly well is his ability to make people believe he is right and their perception of matters is wrong. Just as he played down the significance of his affair with Faria Alam and his meetings with Chelsea officials, Eriksson underplays the seriousness of an England defeat in what is now ubiquitously referred to as a friendly international, when years ago all games involving England were prized internationals.

Eriksson has just cause to play down the relevance of internationals that are not a part of qualification for a major tournament. Up to and including England's game against Spain in November 2004, under Eriksson England had played twenty-one international friendlies since February 2001 and won only eight. If my memory serves me correctly, in those twenty-one matches Eriksson made a total of 182 substitutions, an average of 8.6 per game. In four matches he made eleven or more substitutions, and against Australia an entirely different team took to the field for the second half.

It seems the England coach made so many substitutions in order to learn something about each player, in terms of how they knitted into the team and what contribution they would make at international level. One wonders, however, what on earth he could learn about these players in the short time they were on the pitch that he didn't already know. The sheer number of substitutions used ruins the game as a spectacle. As a former player myself a soundbite of a game is not conducive to showing what you can do, while those who do start the game do so mentally not at their best because they expect to participate in only part of the match. The plethora of substitutes used in international friendlies is detrimental to the entertainment for the supporter, yet at no time has the FA ever offered reduced admission to fans to watch these games. The gross receipts for home friendly internationals from February 2001 to October 2004 are reported as being in excess of twenty-four million pounds. A nice earner from games where the result 'does not really matter'.

The fact that we have an England manager who places little significance on friendly internationals has, I am sure, contributed to the modern trend of players announcing their retirement from international football. If friendlies are not taken as seriously as other internationals by the England manager, why should playing for England in these games matter to the players? For Brian Clough there was no such thing as a friendly match. Every friendly played by Derby County or

Nottingham Forest under his management was taken seriously by Clough and his assistant Peter Taylor. Clough's
attitude to these matches was typical of most managers. Spurs
once provided the opposition in a testimonial for a player at
non-League Dunstable Town. The game was played in midweek in October and manager Bill Nicholson named more or
less the first team for the match. One substitute was allowed
in League football at the time, but in such games as testimo-
nials any amount of substitutes could be used as long as the
respective managers agreed on the number before kick-off.
Bill Nich named just the one substitute for this game, Jimmy
Robertson. Though the match was a testimonial and Spurs
won at a canter, so serious was Bill's approach he never
brought Jimmy on.

    When England lost their first international in a friendly at
home against foreign opposition in 1953, it was the catalyst to
much soul-searching and a revolution in English football
that eventually led to our World Cup success of 1966. In
downplaying the value of friendly internationals by saying
repeatedly the results are not important, sadly Eriksson has
lulled the FA and most of the nation into believing just
that.

Four years into the job Sven-Göran Eriksson has yet to prove
a success as England manager. On the plus side he took over an
England team that were in some disarray and convinced them
they could win games. The 5-1 victory in Germany will stand
the test of time as being a historic England success. With the
passing of time, however, the victory in Munich now appears
an oasis in a desert. Eriksson has the benefit of having at his
disposal the best collection of England players for over thirty
years. That an England team boasting players of the calibre of
Frank Lampard, Joe Cole, Michael Owen, Wayne Rooney,
John Terry, Ashley Cole, Rio Ferdinand, Steven Gerrard and
David Beckham labours to beat the lesser lights of European

international football bears testimony to Eriksson's shortcomings as a manager and coach.

To the credit of Eriksson, the players appeared to adapt to his new regime in a seamless fashion. It isn't easy for a new manager to effect changes with players who were loyal to the outgoing manager, but Eriksson achieved this with some comfort, which says much for his man-management and ability to communicate ideas. Although one would be hard-pushed to recognise this from his book, *Sven-Göran Eriksson on Football* (Carlton). 'The power of the mind really is incredible,' says Eriksson. 'The team with the greater self-confidence is going to win, and, of course, you have got to have a little luck.' So far, so clichéd. No clues there then to his prowess as a coach-cum-manager. Confidence is an important factor in football, but many would question Eriksson's belief that the team with the greater self-confidence will win games. For example let's not forget the Greek side that won Euro 2004, or the Wimbledon FA Cup-winning side of 1988, or any one of a myriad Cup giant-killers you care to mention.

Eriksson enjoys the support and loyalty of his players. But one wonders if the relationship between the England coach and some of his charges has become too cosy. I do ask myself about the wisdom of appointing David Beckham as England captain. He is now a seasoned, experienced pro, yet still comes across as being a boy. There is nothing wrong in that whatsoever, but it is not the essence of what many believe makes a good captain. Rugby's Martin Johnson is the epitome of a great captain. Beckham, by contrast, appears to lack authority and the ability to drive, motivate and encourage team-mates to better and greater things. Is his knowledge of the game such that he can offer instructions to team-mates? I can't help thinking Beckham was given the England captaincy more for his status as a celebrity and his popularity among team-mates than for any qualities he might possess as a captain and leader of men.

Graham Taylor is often maligned for his record as England manager, but in terms of games lost his compares favourably with that of Eriksson up to May 2005. Graham Taylor was in charge for thirty-eight matches, of which England lost seven. It is a record that, on paper, stands comparison with those of most of his predecessors, as well as that of Sven-Göran Eriksson. In reality there were few performances that delighted the eye during Taylor's reign, but the same charge can be levelled at Eriksson. Another criticism of Taylor is that in all the matches he was in charge of England he only once picked an unchanged side. Eriksson, too, has rarely opted for the same eleven in successive matches. For all England lost only seven matches under Graham Taylor, these more often than not included crucial matches. Taylor suffered a torrent of abuse after England's elimination from the finals of the 1992 European Championship; likewise, when he selected an unbalanced side that lost 2-0 to Holland in 1993 to put the kibosh on any hopes of qualifying for the 1994 World Cup in the USA. England have qualified for major tournaments under Eriksson, but in crucial games have been found wanting.

England did not qualify for the finals of a World Cup in the seventies, and non-qualification had much to do with the shortcomings of a domestic game that was entrenched in negativity. The same could be said of Graham Taylor's reign as England manager, but in his defence Taylor was often denied the service, through injury, of Paul Gascoigne when in his pomp, Alan Shearer and the enigmatic John Barnes. Eriksson, however, has had the benefit of an outstanding group of players. That he has failed consistently to induce in those players the sort of performances they are so obviously capable of producing, individually and as a team, will be forever to his detriment as a coach of supposed world renown. In saying that, I firmly believe England will win the World Cup in 2006 – a notion born of the belief that the players at Eriksson's disposal are the best England has had in a long while. We are so richly endowed with talent and, more importantly, possessed of players of world class, as opposed to international class, that England, I feel, will be successful in Germany in spite of having Sven-Göran Eriksson as coach.

CHAPTER FOURTEEN

'I think we agree, the past is over'

George Bush

I can see a time when there will be a European league dominated by a dozen or so rich and influential clubs. With the
exception of the World Cup, there will be little interest and
enthusiasm for international matches. The days of international football are numbered and it will decline just as soon
as we get a full programme of international football at club
level. Television will, in some way, play a part in all this,
helping these elite clubs become even richer.

That comment of mine was given during an interview for
Soccer Star magazine in 1963, following Spurs' victory over
Atletico Madrid in the final of the European Cup Winners'
Cup. It would appear that over forty years ago I seemed to
have a fair idea of what the future might hold for the game. If
only I could predict with such seeming certainty now. Perhaps
that statement had something to do with my age. I was in my
early twenties, and not dissimilar to the son in the joke about
the man who places an ad in the small columns of his local
newspaper that reads: 'For sale. Complete set of Encyclopaedia
Britannica. No longer needed. I have a teenage son who knows
everything.'

Football is nigh on unrecognisable from what it was in the
sixties. Occasionally, when driving around the country to speak
at sporting dinners, I reflect on the many things, often of a

minor nature, that have been lost to the game for ever as it continues its inexorable march of progress. Looking back at how football once was, I used to thrive upon the mental fortitude I had to call upon before every match, the sheer physical demands that were placed upon my body, and the taste of grit, sawdust and sweat in my mouth – and that was only the burgers. In all seriousness, just as the simple, relatively innocent game I knew as a player evolved into something more callous and calculating in the seventies which in turn became something altogether darker and more sinister in the eighties, today the state of English football compels examination if it is not to implode.

The Premiership's corporate mandarins are creating a game of greater imbalance, which makes for a very unstable structure. Championship clubs receive £750,000 each per season. Showing how great the imbalance is, it would take over twenty-five years for a Championship side to receive what a club finishing bottom in the Premiership makes in a single season. This, combined with a sense that television moguls will before long show that their love of football is not infinite, will demand another more complex renaissance to take place within the game if British football as a whole is to survive in its current form.

While evidence suggests the healthy attendances for Premiership matches are beginning to level out, those at Football League and non-League matches are continuing to rise. The success of the Conference has been helped in no small way by the introduction of two-up and two-down promotion and relegation from the Football League. An indicator of the growing success and popularity of this 'fifth' division is that in 2000 the majority of Conference clubs enjoyed a thousand-plus home attendance, which was considered a sign that the League was in a good state. Five years on, on 17 April 2005, seven of the ten Conference fixtures boasted attendances of around two thousand or more. This is a far cry from the days when clubs finishing in the bottom four of the Fourth Division had to apply for re-election to the Football League. For teams such as Gateshead United, Bradford Park Avenue, Barrow and Workington Town, once Football League status had been lost there was very little hope of it being regained. A problem compounded following demotion from the Football League by such clubs finding themselves playing in regional semi-professional leagues that also contained the reserve teams of Fourth Division clubs.

This was a trend Gateshead United had the dubious, albeit unwitting distinction of instigating when the Tyneside club lost its League status in 1960. One of the reasons Gateshead United failed in their bid for re-election was the perceived poor attendances. In their last season as a Football League club, Gateshead had an average home crowd of 4007 – by contemporary standards comparatively healthy for a lower division side. Initially Gateshead United had no alternative but to apply for membership to the North Counties League, where they found themselves playing the reserve sides of Workington Town, Darlington and Carlisle United, and local teams such as Annfield Plain, Horden Colliery Welfare and Consett. Attendances at Redheugh Park immediately halved, and continued to decline. In 1968, when members of the North Regional League, Gateshead, who only five years prior to their demotion had attracted a crowd of 20,007 for a Cup tie against Spurs, were playing in front of a couple of hundred spectators.

Today's Conference league presents ambitious and well-run non-League clubs with a real opportunity of becoming members of the Football League in a way that the old system of re-election with its 'old pals' act' rarely did. In those days clubs had to apply for re-election in competition with top non-League clubs. Votes were cast by the chairmen of the other League clubs and invariably the teams that had finished in the bottom four of Division Four were re-elected, much to the chagrin of many ambitious and financially stable non-League clubs. In the sixties sides like Crewe Alexandra, Rochdale and Hartlepool United often found themselves having to apply for re-election. It was rumoured such clubs would win votes from fellow Fourth Division teams that saw them as likely to provide points the following season (whereas a former non-League club might offer sterner opposition). A story did the rounds in the seventies that in addition to offering the prospect of away points, Rochdale received votes for the wonderful buffet they put on for opposing teams, supplied as it was by directors who owned local butcher and bakery shops. There certainly seemed to be some truth in the theory of the old pals' act in 1983–4 when Hartlepool United were re-elected to the Football League for a record fourteenth time!

The creation of the Premiership has engendered greater interest throughout the game, and the success of the competition has filtered down, but what was once perceived as a pyramid system for English football is now too top-heavy. The current imbalance of riches between the Premiership and the Championship is turning the top flight into a personal fiefdom for a select band of clubs whose number is added to from time to time by a second, much smaller tier of clubs that enjoy 'provisional' membership of the Premier League.

Wigan Athletic are a rare example of a provincial town club that has the benefit of a sugar-daddy benefactor, Dave Whelan, whose financial support has been the significant factor in the rise of the club. But Championship sides like Burnley, Stoke City and Sheffield United find themselves competing in the division at a great disadvantage to those that have recently been relegated from the Premiership. Most teams relegated from the top flight prove too good for Championship sides, due to the financial support the demoted clubs enjoy, while few teams promoted from the Championship appear capable of making a sustained go of it in the Premiership. The old idea of promotion being followed by consolidation is a pipe dream for most teams promoted from the Championship because the gap financially and playing-wise is now so vast. Clubs such as Bolton Wanderers, Birmingham City and Charlton Athletic have shown what is possible by virtue of financial prudence, but for the majority of teams the Premiership and the Championship is little more than snakes and ladders. Of course, there are other clubs, such as Leeds United and Coventry City, that have found the transition from Premiership to Championship arduous for different reasons – their plight has much to do with having racked up massive debts and a subsequent struggle to handle their financial liabilities.

By renaming the First Division (Second Division as was) the Championship, it appears the marketing johnnies are attempting to build the top tier of the Football League into what they no doubt call a 'premium brand'. They can dress up English football's 'second division' in any way they choose and give it a Fancy Dan name, but the general standard of play in that division in recent years has widely been accepted as mediocre. As one manager of a Championship team said, 'The Championship is a competitive league in that every team is as bad as each other'. Which suggests the new name, the 'Championship', is a bit of a misnomer. In advance of the commencement of 2004–5 a marketing executive for the Football League told the press, 'We think supporters will like the new name, the "Championship". The new name and its new image will attract supporters in even greater numbers to matches.' The notion that people might attend football matches primarily because a league has been given a new name and image will appear to many to be evidence on the part of football marketing executives of a total lack of empathy and understanding about why supporters attend games. What the renaming of the various divisions of the Football League has achieved is to give me as a grandfather – or anyone with small children – countless problems in trying to explain the current

structure to youngsters. You feel part of a Jackie Mason mono-
logue when trying to describe the system:

'The Championship, this used to be the First Division, but
before that it was called the Second Division, because what
is now the Premiership was known as the First Division.
So now we have the Premiership and below that the Championship. Then comes League One, which until recently was the
Second Division, but prior to that was known as the Third
Division. There is no Third Division in name now, because
after League One, which – if you follow me – used to be
the Third Division, we now have League Two that, until
recently, was the Third Division and before that the Fourth
Division.'

'So how do clubs get into the Premiership, Granddad?'

'Well, the teams who finish in the bottom three places in
the Premiership are relegated to the Championship.'

'Oh, I get it, and those three teams are replaced by the teams
who finish in the top three of the Championship?'

'No, son, not quite. The teams that finish in the top two in
the Championship are automatically promoted. The teams that
finish third, fourth, fifth and sixth then play in what we call the
play-offs. The third- and sixth-placed sides play each other
over two legs, as do the fourth and fifth. The team that win on
aggregate go through to what we call the play-off final, where
they meet the winners of the other play-off semi-final.
Whoever wins that final joins the two teams that won automatic
promotion to the Premiership.'

'I see. And that system applies to what is now Leagues One
and Two?'

'Well, yes and no. It applies to League One but not League
Two. Four clubs are relegated from League One and they
are automatically replaced by the teams that finish in the
top three of League Two. The fourth promotion place is
contested between the clubs that finish fourth, fifth, sixth
and seventh in League Two. They enter the play-offs, which

then work the same way as the play-offs in League One and the Championship.'

'Is there anything else that it is important for me to know, Granddad?'

'Yes, always remember football is a simple game.'

The culture of English football is forever changing, not always for the better. Overseas players have, in the main, made a very positive contribution to our domestic game, but at the same time, they are limiting opportunities for home-grown talent to develop adequately. Foreign players have an increasing presence in our academy and youth teams, and this is a policy that is set to alter the fabric of our game even more. While EU directives allow clubs to sign players from member countries, an increasing number of non-European players are also now plying their trade in English football. This influx that has risen in recent years with the arrival of many players from the United States.

The first American player to make an impact in English football was John Harkes with Sheffield Wednesday in 1990. In the intervening fifteen years the number of players arriving from the United States has increased year on year, though their contribution and success in our game have been questionable. Roy Wegerle (Blackburn and Coventry), Kasey Keller (Leicester and Spurs), Brad Friedel (Liverpool and Blackburn) and Paul Rachubka (Charlton) can be considered success stories. Can the same be said of US and Canadian players like Cobi Jones (Coventry), Joe-Max Moore (Everton), David Yelldell (Blackburn), Jovan Kirovski (Birmingham City), Tim Howard (Manchester United) and Claudio Reyna (Sunderland and Manchester City)?

The aforementioned were in their twenties and players boasting international experience when they came to these shores, but several English clubs have also signed youngsters from the US in the hope of them developing through the respective youth systems. Jonathan Spector and Zak Whitbread are just two of a growing number of American teenagers currently with Premiership clubs and the indications are that there will be plenty more making the trip across the pond in the future. Following their close-season (surely now a misnomer) tour of the United States in 2004, Manchester United made a concerted effort to attract fourteen-year-old Freddy Adu to Old Trafford. In 2005 there were eight US teenagers at the academies of Premiership clubs and the trend is spreading. As I say, the majority of overseas players have had a good effect on our domestic game, but there is just cause to be concerned about opportunities for, and the future development of, home-grown players.

In December 2004 UEFA President Lennart Johansson expressed his concern about the number of overseas players at clubs. 'Football must adhere to freedom of movement where labour is concerned, but we must also safeguard against developing talent not being given an opportunity to develop in its own country,' said Johansson. Five months later, UEFA announced a series of initiatives it is hoped will provide opportunity for domestic players to flourish in their own countries. All teams entering European club competitions in 2006–7 must contain at least four home-grown players, and the quota is set to rise to six in 2008–9. The quotas apply to players that are either products of a club's own youth system or academy, or that of another club within the home country.

While UEFA may be applauded for implementing a policy that ensures first-team opportunities for home-grown talent, the initiative simply does not go far enough. The directive only applies to UEFA club competitions, leaving one to wonder why UEFA stopped short of extending this policy to domestic programmes, where the real problem lies. If the policy applied to domestic football it would provide greater opportunity for home-grown players to gain invaluable first-team experience and would present a sound platform for such emerging talent to flourish. In 2005 the EU took steps to reduce the number of imports from the Far East, particularly China. The action was taken to safeguard the manufacturing industries of member countries, though many will be given to thinking a similar policy should be implemented in football.

Entrepreneurs seeking power and fortune apart, if there is one football-associated job that is sure to rankle with most, it is that of the player's agent. Players' agents have been around since the fifties. I myself had one when a Chelsea player in the late fifties, though the role of Stan Thomlin in my career was nothing like that of agents today. Stan never represented me in talks with Chelsea regarding contracts, basically because Chelsea, like every other club in the world, would never countenance such. Stan dealt with what in those days were called 'peripheral earners'. That is, where there was a few bob to be made outside the game off the back of a player's name. He arranged for me to appear as the face on some adverts for Bovril. Stan made a few bob and I did. It wasn't a fortune but any extra money a player could make in the era of the maximum wage was most welcome. One or two other players had agents that secured them similar commercial deals, but the thought of an agent negotiating a player's contract or a move to another club was anathema to clubs that, as far as players were concerned, wielded all the power.

Over the years the balance has shifted so much so that we now have a situation where the power appears to lie with the top players and their agents. This was crystallised by Harry Kewell's move from Leeds United to Liverpool in 2003. His switch from Leeds to Anfield set a new standard for transfers between Premiership clubs. It also demonstrated agent power in its most extreme form, as well as the absurdity of a transfer system that allows both player and agent to bank millions while the selling club receives a pittance of the market value of the player concerned. At the time Leeds United were over a barrel with regard to Kewell. They were a club in decline, and one in desperate need of money, but were powerless to stop one of their star players leaving and his agent negotiating a deal for himself and Kewell with Liverpool, as opposed to the club receiving a transfer fee. It was reported that Kewell's agent Bernie Mandic received two million pounds when his client moved to Liverpool, which prompted some in the game to dub Mandic 'Mr Forty Per Cent'. It was also reported that Mandic negotiated a two-million-pound Leeds pay-off with a half-million pension fund top-up, a two-million signing-on fee from Liverpool and sixty thousand pounds a week wages for the Australian international. It was reported that Kewell made, all told, £19 million from the deal and that Leeds made £2.5 million. According to Kewell he had always wanted to play for Liverpool. He said to the press when leaving Elland Road: 'Money wasn't the main factor'. He is also reported as saying, 'I think Leeds fans understand'. I think they do.

Many club chairmen complain it is players' wages that are crippling club finances and preventing them making a profit. All I can say is, a club can always say no when an agent tells them what he wants in the way of wages for his client. One man doesn't make a team, no matter how good a player he is. In 2004 Everton sold Wayne Rooney to Manchester United and, later that season, Thomas Gravesen to Real Madrid. The consensus of opinion was that Rooney and Gravesen were Everton's best players, yet having sold these two, in 2004–5 Everton enjoyed their most successful season in the Premiership since its inception.

In recent years there have been calls for more transparency regarding transfers. Supporters and media alike want to know how much money is being paid to agents, and how much money is going out of the game. To their credit Manchester United have been at pains to make public the amount of money they pay to players' agents, but many deals are still clouded in secrecy. Players still move for 'undisclosed fees', making a mockery of statements encouraging fans to support the team on the premise that it is 'their' club.

The PFA has long since expressed concern about the role of players' agents. It is a widely held view within the players' union that there are many agents whose priority it is to make money from the game rather than represent the interests and welfare of their players. The PFA has always been happy to negotiate contracts and moves at the request of a player, and in March 2005 demonstrated it was willing to make a concerted effort to build up a portfolio of player representation. The former Port Vale and Birmingham City defender Phil Sproson was appointed as the union's first-ever 'player representative'. The big difference between PFA representation and that of a licensed agent is the players' union will not take a percentage of any deal it negotiates on behalf of the player. The player may, if he so chooses, make a contribution to the union's benevolent fund, but is under no compulsion to do so. The size of any donation is entirely up to the player himself. As a former player myself I should imagine every footballer would willingly make a donation in return for PFA representation.

The PFA has been very concerned about the amount of money agents are taking out of the game when such money used to circulate between the clubs themselves. Obviously the percentages paid to agents that represent Premiership players account for the lion's share of this money, but fees paid to agents who represent Football League players have risen alarmingly in recent times. In January 2005 the chairman of the Football League, Brian Mawhinney, published figures that showed payments to agents outside the Premiership between June and December 2004 had tripled to more than five million pounds. Mawhinney, like the PFA, considered that figure excessive and called for tighter regulations to curb the role within the game of players' agents. Having been one of those players that in 1960–1 lent support to the abolition of the so-called 'slavery contract' and maximum wage, I am of the mind players' agents exercise too much influence nowadays. The game needs an effective regulatory framework to ensure a level playing field for clubs when negotiating with players. Hopefully, the PFA's quest to represent more players will result in more money staying in the game, greater transparency and the players themselves receiving good counsel and what is theirs by right when bargaining with clubs.

One sad side issue of the current situation of agent representation is that it does not result in any cracking stories of contract negotiation and transfer dealings. In the days when such things were left to players and managers, no amount of comic stories unfolded. As I said previously in the past part of the brief of a manager was to sell players he felt were surplus to requirements. In 1974 when Tommy Docherty was manager of Manchester United, he was looking to move on centre half Jim Holton. Tommy considered Jim's best days to be behind him but, of course, would never let any other manager know that. Sunderland had just sold their centre half Dave Watson to Manchester City for £275,000, and knowing they were in need of a replacement and that they had money in the bank, Tommy rang the Sunderland manager Bob Stokoe. Tommy did his best to try and persuade Stokoe to buy Jim Holton. Stokoe, however, wasn't keen so Tommy decided to lay it on thick.

'He'll do you a magnificent job,' said Tommy. 'He's great in the air, an excellent passer of the ball, a great tackler and can read a game like a book. We have to be talking good money for a player like him. A hundred thousand wouldn't buy this lad.'

'I know,' said Stokoe, 'and I'm one of them.'

Roger Hunt was a prolific goalscorer with Liverpool in the sixties. When the time came to renew his contract at Anfield, Roger went in to see manager Bill Shankly.

'I was talking to a reporter from the Liverpool *Echo*, who told me you told him Ron Yeats was on eighty pounds a week,' said Roger, angling for a pay rise.

'No, no, not true,' said Shankly. 'I was misquoted.'

'And I hear you said Ian St John is on seventy-five a week,' said Roger.

'Jesus Christ, son, Saint's on nowhere near that much. If that is what you heard I said, I've been misquoted again,' Shankly informed Roger. There was an awkward silence for a moment.

'So how much are you looking for, Roger, son?' asked Shankly. Roger told Shanks how much he wanted. Again there was an awkward silence, this time much longer than the first. Roger was feeling very uncomfortable and felt he had to maintain the conversation.

'Silence is golden, eh, boss?' said Roger, for want of anything better to say.

'Silence is not only golden, son,' said Shankly, 'it's seldom misquoted.'

Blackpool winning the FA Cup in 1953; Cassius Clay defeating Sonny Liston in 1964 to become Heavyweight Champion of the World; the British Lions winning the Test series against the All Blacks in New Zealand in 1971; an Ian Botham-inspired England defeating Australia at Headingley in 1981; Manchester United winning the European Cup in 1999; and Liverpool beating AC Milan to win the same competition in 2005. All are truly great moments in sport and all have one thing in common – surprise. It is the essential element required to keep every sport compelling. The sense that different individuals or teams have a good chance of winning trophies helps make any sport attractive to its supporters. It is the capacity to surprise that is missing from the Premiership. The lack of this crucial ingredient is the difference between the Premier League being good to watch and making for compelling viewing. Blackburn Rovers' solitary success in 1995 apart, the Premiership has been without competitive balance since its inception in 1992–3. (If on a comparatively lesser scale financially, one could be forgiven for saying that Rovers' win had similarities to that of Chelsea, given that Jack Walker's millions propelled the club to greater heights in much the same way as Abramovich's have brought about a renaissance at Stamford Bridge.)

The Premiership Management Committee and the Football Association have adopted a laissez-faire attitude to the competitive imbalance of the Premier League. It is almost as if both bodies have resigned themselves to the inevitability of it all and feel nothing can or should be done to rectify the situation. The Premiership has become almost as predictable as the Scottish Premier League, where the one-sidedness and predictability of that competition have had an adverse effect on attendances at all clubs other than Celtic and Rangers and on Scottish football in general. There is an argument for saying that the current circumstances, where three clubs have a realistic chance of winning the Premiership, are healthier than those which existed in the late seventies and eighties, when the old First Division was dominated by Liverpool. Between 1974 and 1990, Liverpool won ten titles, but Leeds United, Derby County, Nottingham Forest, Aston Villa, Arsenal and Everton (twice) were also champions in that period. That the First Division was truly more competitive can be evidenced from the fact that a number of Liverpool's Championship successes were not clear-cut. In 1976 they finished one point ahead of Queens Park Rangers and the following year a single point was all that separated the Anfield club from Manchester City. In 1980 Liverpool tied up the title only on the last day of the season, finishing two points ahead of Manchester United. Likewise, their title successes of 1984 and 1986 were by virtue of three points and two points respectively. When Liverpool secured three consecutive Championships between 1982 and 1984, a different team finished runners-up on each occasion, namely Ipswich Town, Watford and Southampton. With the notable exception of Blackburn, the Premiership title has been the domain of two clubs, until the success of Chelsea in 2005.

The very idea that a provincial club such as Nottingham Forest or Derby County could win the title appears now to be fanciful, which is to the detriment of the Premier League and English football in general.

The simple solution to the Pandora's box that the Premiership has become is a more equal distribution of wealth, not just among the top-flight clubs themselves but throughout the Football League. That a Championship side would take over twenty-five years to make what the club finishing bottom in the Premiership earns in a single season is disproportionate, unfair and to the continual disadvantage of English football. One possible solution is that the money generated from any future television deal be shared evenly among all Premiership clubs, rather than according to their final positions in the table, and that a greater sum be allocated for distribution throughout the Football League. While the Premiership is more distributive than La Liga in Spain or Serie A in Italy, citing those two competitions as proof that our top flight is balanced, as some do, puts me in mind of two wrongs making a right and it does nothing to alleviate, or even acknowledge, the gross financial disparity that is now cemented throughout English football.

The Premiership is now an 'Italian Job' – it comes across as being a self-preservation society whose best interests are not served by change. Perhaps the Football Association's reluctance to pressure Premiership clubs to agree to a fairer distribution of wealth throughout the game is borne of a fear that the top sides would rekindle the idea of forming a European Super League (which would only exacerbate the current situation of haves and have-nots). Current rules stipulate fourteen clubs must be in agreement in order for the structure and financial distribution of the Premiership to change. That an imbalance remains may be put down to many of the clubs outside the big four fearing the elite would break away with the likes of Juventus, AC and Inter Milan, Bayern Munich, Real Madrid, Barcelona, Benfica and PSV Eindhoven. If that were to occur the remaining Premiership clubs would suffer financially, as would many in the Football League, which places those Premiership clubs outside the elite four in a catch-22 situation and negates them uniting to effect change.

Many supporters, too, will prefer the current set-up to what once existed, though this is largely dependent on which team you support. For fans of Charlton Athletic, Portsmouth and Bolton Wanderers, what the Premiership offers is much more preferable to standing on windswept terracing in a half-empty ground watching your team against Bristol Rovers or Rotherham United. For them, these are days of wine and roses by virtue of the fact that their respective clubs are in the Premiership now. Supporters of clubs that once graced the old First Division, such as Burnley and Stoke City, or latter-day members of the Premiership itself like Nottingham Forest, Oldham, QPR, both Sheffield clubs, Coventry City and Swindon Town, would, in all probability, not be given to agreeing that these are truly halcyon days. Yet these may well be great times for those supporters of Portsmouth whose experience encompasses years of watching Second or Third Division football and who were not around when their club won successive Championships in 1949 and 1950. The same might be said of those Bolton fans for whom Nat Lofthouse is but a legendary name and the 1958 FA Cup final a statistic in the record books. But for a great many clubs these are trying times, where every day is a struggle to make ends meet. Trying times, too, for the supporters of clubs that know the chances of their club making it to the top flight of English football are remote compared with times gone by.

There was a time when fame was the reward for exceptional talent on the football pitch. That still happens, of course, but we now live in an age where a player of above-average ability can achieve worldwide renown by being afforded celebrity status in the media. It has been widely touted that Real Madrid bought David Beckham more for his commercial potential than his abilities as a player. It is debatable whether that was truly the reason, but there is little doubt Beckham's status as a celebrity figure offers any club he plays for vast opportunities to exploit commercial revenue. It is impossible to compare Beckham as a player to, say, Stanley Matthews. Football today is far different from how it was when Stan Matthews weaved his own kind of magic up and down a thousand muddy touch-lines. Indeed, such was the longevity of the career of a man blessed with football genius, when Stan retired in 1965 the game was far removed from that in which he began his career at Stoke City in 1930. To place the length of his career into perspective, when Stan first joined Stoke City it was the year of the first-ever World Cup, Arsenal became the first southern club to win the League Championship and Dixie Dean was the most prolific goalscorer in British football. When, at the age of fifty, Stan played his final League match in the equivalent of the Premiership, it was the time of George Best and Rodney Marsh.

I was lucky enough to be asked to play in Stan's testimonial at Stoke City in 1965. It was fitting his home-town club awarded Stan a testimonial for even during his triumphant days at Blackpool his heart was still in the Potteries. Indeed, Blackpool had in the end treated him shabbily. Stan spent fourteen years at Bloomfield Road in which time his presence on the field helped Blackpool to enjoy what is still the most successful period in their history. They were the fifties equivalent of today's Manchester United. Everywhere the Seasiders played, the home club enjoyed its biggest crowd of the season. In an era when the away club enjoyed a percentage of the match receipts, Blackpool benefited enormously. With Stan Mortensen, Jackie Mudie, Ernie Taylor, Allan Brown, Harry Johnston and Bill 'The Original Champagne' Perry in their ranks, the Blackpool side was star-studded. But the player all supporters came to see was the legendary Matthews.

Throughout the fifties Blackpool played many lucrative friendlies. The fee they received for such matches was considerable and was always agreed on the condition that Stan Matthews would play. Players were never paid for friendlies: the clubs coined in the money, and Blackpool played more friendlies than most. Stan spent every summer living and coaching in South African townships, as he once told me, 'to put something back into a game that had given me so much'. On several occasions he was flown back to play for Blackpool in a money-spinning friendly, with the club using his name to negotiate a hefty fee. No one can put a figure on the money Stan helped earn for Blackpool in his appearances at those friendly matches. Suffice it to say over the years it must have come to nigh on six figures, a considerable sum of money in the fifties. Yet when the time came for Stan to leave Bloomfield Road after fourteen years, the Blackpool board did not think it fit to award him a testimonial.

When Stan had joined the club in 1947, Blackpool had in the region of seven hundred season ticket holders. When he left in 1961, that figure was nearly twelve thousand, and his performances and status throughout the football world were a significant factor in that rise. On learning that the club was asking Stoke City for a fee of £3500 for his services, and aware that his home-town club was strapped for cash, Stan approached the Blackpool board. He respectfully asked, in view of his service at the club and that he was not to be awarded a testimonial, if the directors would kindly waive the fee. His request fell on deaf ears, and it prompted a response from one director, Mr Marshall, which induced in Stan a rare emotion, that of anger.

'Waive the fee?' said Mr Marshall. 'You forget that this club and this board made you.'

'You made ME?' said Stan, totally flabbergasted. 'As a small boy I was getting up at six in the morning to train and practise my skills and I continue to do so to this day. Self-appraisal is no guarantee of merit, Mr Marshall, that I know, but my presence in the team helped Blackpool become, for a number of years, successful and the biggest draw on the road. So don't you sit there and tell me YOU made ME!'

The players who came to Stoke for Stan's testimonial left a capacity crowd slack-jawed: from the old school, Ferenc Puskas, Lev Yashin, Alfredo Di Stefano, Johnny Haynes, John Charles and Raymond Kopa; from the new, Eusebio, Francisco Gento, Uwe Seeler, Jim Baxter, Bobby Charlton, Bobby Moore and Denis Law. On the big day the letters and telegrams from well-wishers filled over forty mail bags. There were so many Stan couldn't store them in the house and had to stack them in rows on his patio. They came from our own royal family, from presidents and kings throughout the world, from millionaire owners of global companies and from the poor of Africa. Letters arrived from players he had played with and against and from football writers from almost every country on the planet. One telegram read, 'Best wishes on your retirement, Stan. From Frank and the rest of the Hollywood gang'.

As for the match itself the result was as inconsequential as the sense of occasion was great. At the end we players formed a circle in the centre of the pitch and accompanied by forty thousand spectators sang 'Auld Lang Syne' with gusto. Even hardened football writers, of which there were 187 from around the world, had never seen a night of such emotion at a football ground. After the game a pal of Stan's, Huston Spratt, who worked for the Stoke *Sentinel* as a photographer, came into the dressing room and asked him if he would pose for one last photograph. Stan complied with the request of course. When the photograph had been taken, the pair chatted away. At one point Huston Spratt told Stan that one of the reasons he admired him so much was for the way Stan understood and related to supporters.

'The labourer in the pot-bank, the worker at the coalface, the guy who sells me my newspaper on the corner of the street, I am one of their kind,' said Stan. 'I know what they are all about and where they are coming from. They relate to me and I relate to them because I feel as they do about football. Like them I experience the fleeting moments of joy, those rare moments of ecstasy, I feel the irritation, annoyance and occasional pain and like them I have spent my life living in constant hope.'

In saying such, Stan spoke of the heart of the game. For all his worldwide fame, supporters related to Stan Matthews in a way it is impossible for today's supporters to relate to David Beckham or Wayne Rooney. The sublime performances of Stan Matthews on a football pitch were more than simply a genius of a player giving full vent to his artistry. His displays spoke directly to his public in a way that no player does today. For many he captured the inner spiritual need of what it is to be human. As he scribbled football history with his pin-toed feet, Stan Matthews offered to supporters a sense of liberation, sprinkling harsh working-class lives with stardust, creating their memories while at all times conducting himself in such a way that he remained as one with supporters. He played football as an expression of his love of the game and that is the difference between Stan Matthews and the *galacticos* of today. Forty years on, our loss is that we no longer live in an age when a player like Stanley Matthews can become famous throughout the world, and we understand why.

I remain, as I always have been, optimistic for the future of the game in this country, though it could do with more than a little help. Team sports continue to decline and successive governments have done little to try and rectify that situation. I find it mind-boggling that while so much concern is expressed about the fitness and health of young people today the efforts of government to provide the facilities and circumstances for them to play sport have been woeful. Governments appear to have had no real strategy for the development of sport and, as such, football in this country. Where football is concerned, the initiative appears to lie with clubs and individuals. In 2002 the government did issue an initiative so that local grass-roots football clubs taking a greater role in their local community and running more teams comprising youngsters from their area would receive financial assistance. There were some notable successes, but by and large this initiative has failed to fulfil its purpose and for one basic reason. As well-meaning as the idea was it had a fatal flaw: amateur teams that play in local leagues are invariably run by one person, or at the most, two. The role of manager, trainer, secretary, treasurer, kit man, provider and assembler of nets, you name it, comes down to the enthusiasm of one or two individuals, who simply do not have the time, or inclination, to organise and administer the running of other teams under the banner of their club. The government initiative to encourage local grass-root clubs to form teams for youngsters was doomed from the start, and this was basically down to a lack of understanding about how such clubs function. The parks team in the local league is then a 'one-man band', and the failure to recognise this must surely have wasted a considerable sum of money setting up and administering this well-intentioned but flawed idea of central government.

The sale of many pitches owned by schools and local councils for housing has played its part in the decline of grass-roots football. Likewise, in an age when expectations have risen, poor facilities like those of some local council-owned parks where changing rooms have no electricity or running water in 2005 are nothing short of disgraceful. The grass-roots game has also suffered as result of the current trend for convenience fitness. People prefer to attend leisure clubs at a time to suit their lifestyles, whereas junior football is mainly confined to a Saturday afternoon or Sunday morning. Young people today have a great choice of other leisure pursuits and the lure of 'playing' football on computer games has also had its effect. Between 1998 and 2003, the value of the UK video games market expanded from £770 million to £1.3 billion, with sports-related titles accounting for just shy of three hundred million of those sales. The market for computer games with a sporting theme continues to grow at an annual rate of more than 7 per cent. Virtual sport has been taken up by young people in a big way and it is alarming to think it is the only type of sport with which tens of thousands of young people are now involved. A case of video killed the sporting star?

The decline of traditional industries has also had a marked effect on the number of young people playing football in this country. In the fifties and sixties in particular it was not uncommon for League clubs to sign a promising youngster from a works team. Works sides were prolific throughout the country, so much so that in many towns and cities a particular league would be made up solely of teams from shipyard companies or collieries. Following the decline of most of our traditional industries, these leagues are no more and few actual works teams now exist.

One area of football that seems to be thriving is the five-a-side game. This kind of 'informal' football has proved so popular it has become big business. One company, Goals Soccer Centres, which owns a chain of five-a-side centres, floated on the Stock Exchange in 2004. Five-a-side is a great way of keeping fit, though it is doubtful whether it serves to encourage young people to take up the eleven-a-side game. The conditions in which five-a-side is played are not conducive to regular football, but the wooden flooring, the lightweight 'hairy' lemon ball and the restricted area in which games take place, whereby the player with the ball is constantly under challenge, are good for the development or practice of skills and technique. Five-a-side fulfils its function of fun and helping its participants maintain a level of fitness, but one should imagine it plays a very minor role in getting young people to play organised eleven-a-side football.

It is cause for concern that England now has the lowest

number of people playing eleven-a-side football since records began. The trend is for them to turn their backs on team sports such as football in increasing numbers. A radical overhaul of sport at school and positive, proactive policy and financial support from central government are required to check the decline and encourage more young people to participate in sport.

However, even when initiatives are introduced to encourage youngsters to play football sometimes the very culture of these schemes proves a handicap to young people entering open-age football. I have often presented trophies to children who play in leagues for the under-12 to under-15 age groups. On more than one occasion when handing out medals I have asked which trophy the team has won, only to be informed the prizes are for finishing fifth or sixth in the league. This sends out the wrong message to youngsters. It is not simply a case of rewarding failure, for football at that age should be about fun and enjoyment. Of course young people want to win trophies, but in order to instil the right attitude and values in young footballers surely rewards of a tangible nature like medals should only be awarded to teams that win or are runners-up in competitions. Having been used to winning medals in a team that has not actually won a trophy, the expectations of many youngsters will be quickly dashed when they are of an age to compete in more strenuous competition.

Across the country there are numerous Sunday leagues for young children that encourage the participation of parents and the teams often comprise youngsters from a particular estate or community in the town or city. In theory this is a fine idea and no doubt there are many examples of where this form of football works extremely well. What has regularly happened, however, is the best young players have gravitated towards one or two particular sides rather than playing for the teams in their neighbourhoods. This creates an imbalance, with one or two teams becoming virtually unbeatable and defeating weaker teams by cricket scores. It serves to have a double negative effect on the development and enthusiasm of young players. Many of those who are beaten week-in week-out become disillusioned with football and take up other interests. The best players that formed the all-conquering teams get used to winning every game, often by large scores. When these players move on to open-age football many also quickly become disillusioned, finding football is not the easy game their limited experience suggested. Having been used to sauntering through games, open-age football comes as something of a shock to the system. What's more, the ease with which the better young players have been winning matches means many were never extended in a match situation. Having suddenly to 'work hard' at their individual and team game, many find it difficult to call upon the mental and physical attributes required in open-age football and they too become lost to the game.

It is disheartening to know that even when young people are afforded the opportunity, organisation and facilities to play football, a culture exits in some quarters that will prove a drain on their enthusiasm for and long-term involvement in the game. This, nonetheless, should not be seen as a barrier to further funding and facilities for youngsters of both sexes to have the opportunity to play organised football. Since Labour assumed power in 1997, the Treasury's net profit from sport has doubled to £5 billion, £2.7 billion without monies received from betting tax. Yet the money the government invests in sport is only a fraction of the Treasury's net profit, some £600 million. Labour's record of investing in sport is poor, but in the interests of fairness, it was no better under a Conservative government. Successive governments have paid little more than lip service to the administrations of sport in this country. To borrow from the strapline in adverts for a well-known supermarket, 'every little counts', and nowhere more so than where small football clubs and money are concerned.

The Labour government often says it is doing everything in its power to help and promote sport throughout the United

Kingdom, yet the reality is somewhat different. The government's decision in 2005 to introduce a huge rise in the cost of bar licences for amateur clubs will have a considerable effect on many small football clubs. What amounts to little more than another stealth tax will force them to pay between £310 and £730 for a licence to sell alcohol on club premises. Previously the cost was in the region of £30 over three years. This vastly inflated new rate for a licence will hit small amateur clubs in particular and could well result in many folding. The government appears not to distinguish between commercial drinking venues and not-for-profit amateur sports clubs, which brings into question their supposed support for sport at grass-roots level. Community sports clubs and amateur football sides who play in local junior leagues are the bedrock of sport in this country and fulfil an important function in local communities. Rather than penalising these clubs and hampering their financial existence, the government should be doing its very best to nurture their well-being. Scrapping the new price hike in bar licences for non-profit making amateur clubs would be a start. The government line is that sports clubs which come under the 2003 Licensing Act will have to pay the higher price for a licence or choose not to hold social events with alcohol or sell a few tins to players after matches. Either way, such legislation deprives non-profit-making clubs of a valuable source of income used to meet general running costs, such as seeding and whitewash for pitches or payment to a match referee. Pardon the pun, but for all such costs may appear small beer, to an amateur football club they are a necessary expense that must be met. In order to be affected by this new ruling a club must have at least twenty-five members, but most places run at least two teams so will therefore be subjected to this new and unjust rise in the cost of a bar licence. To me this suggests that the government's quest to clamp down on binge drinking and related anti-social behaviour has also penalised the small sporting clubs that, as well as doing much good in local communities, afford many youngsters an opportunity to play football and, indeed, a variety of sports.

Football is still the nation's most popular sport, but if the game is to flourish and develop in the future it will require real and substantial funding in keeping with countries like France, where government spend on sport is eight times higher than in the UK. Politicians may 'talk a good game' and encourage people to exercise and adopt healthier lifestyles by participating in sporting activities, but realistic funding for sport appears to rank pretty low in the priorities of any government in this country. Likewise, the position of minister of sport, a ministerial appointment that in comparison with other cabinet posts appears to be afforded all the reverence and seriousness of a General Studies A-level when compared with one in the sciences.

I began this book by recalling something Danny Blanchflower said, in which he referred to what he called the 'heart of the game'. As I have attempted to detail, the heart of the game is formed of many things, but innermost is a genuine love of football and an understanding of what it does to the individual. No doubt there are a number of opinions in this book that will not meet with the approval of some, but one of the edifying and compelling attractions of football is that it is, indeed, a game of differing opinions. Blind acceptance has no role to play in football. It is a sport that compels examination without which there would be no progress, no development, colour or drama – the very essence of the game. For all we may watch the same match, if anything football is subjective. A particular game may induce irritation in some, excitement in others. I consider myself to be a laid-back guy, I do not get overly excited when watching football today, but then I never felt overt excitement coursing through my body when I scored a goal for Chelsea, Milan or Spurs. In those days I was quite convinced I could go on playing the game for ever. What football did for me then and still does is to evoke an instantaneous emotional rapport of the most personal nature. There is an alerting of the senses, a change of mood, the feeling of having been transported to the best of all possible worlds. In this I know I am not alone. All genuine lovers of football experience the richness of what it is to dwell within the heart of the game.

Index